D1594613

THE GROWTH OF THE
MEDIEVAL ICELANDIC SAGAS
(1180–1280)

ALSO BY THEODORE M. ANDERSSON

The Legend of Brynhild (1985)
with Kari Ellen Gade, *Morkinskinna: The Earliest Icelandic Chronicle of the Norwegian Kings (1030–1157)* (2000)
The Saga of Olaf Tryggvason by Oddr Snorrason (2003)

THE GROWTH OF THE
MEDIEVAL ICELANDIC SAGAS
(1180–1280)

Theodore M. Andersson

CORNELL UNIVERSITY PRESS

ITHACA AND LONDON

Copyright © 2006 by Cornell University

All rights reserved. Except for brief quotations in a review, this
book, or parts thereof, must not be reproduced in any form without
permission in writing from the publisher. For information, address
Cornell University Press, Sage House, 512 East State Street, Ithaca,
New York 14850.

First published 2006 by Cornell University Press

Printed in the United States of America

Library of Congress Cataloging-in-Publication Data

Andersson, Theodore Murdock.
The growth of the medieval Icelandic sagas, 1180–1280 /
by Theodore M. Andersson.
p. cm.
Includes bibliographical references.
ISBN-13: 978-0-8014-4408-1 (cloth : alk. paper)
ISBN-10: 0-8014-4408-X (cloth : alk. paper)
1. Sagas—History and criticism.   I. Title.
PT7181.A52 2005
839.6'309—dc22
2005025054

Cornell University Press strives to use environmentally responsible
suppliers and materials to the fullest extent possible in the publishing
of its books. Such materials include vegetable-based, low-VOC inks
and acid-free papers that are recycled, totally chlorine-free, or partly
composed of nonwood fibers. For further information, visit our
website at www.cornellpress.cornell.edu.

Cloth printing   10   9   8   7   6   5   4   3   2   1

CONTENTS

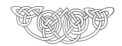

A NOTE ON ORTHOGRAPHY

Because this book is intended to be accessible to the nonspecialist reader, I have for the most part Latinized the special Icelandic consonant characters "Þ (þ)" and "ð," rendering them as "th" and "d." Following a widespread convention, I have also simplified pronunciation by dropping the nominative "r" ending following a consonant. Thus the proper name Hǫskuldr appears as Hǫskuld, Oddr as Odd. I have done this even where the final "r" has been assimilated to a preceding nasal or liquid: thus Egil for Egill, Gunnar for Gunnarr, and Kolbein for Kolbeinn.

The only deviations from this system occur in references to Icelandic scholars, the titles of Icelandic sagas, the names of Icelandic publishers, and a few technical terms such as *þáttr* 'short prose narrative' (plur. *þættir*); in these cases I use the correct Icelandic form. In a few place names, where a final component is almost identical to the English equivalent, I have used the English form of the component. Thus Hlýrskógsheiðr appears as Hlýrskógsheath and Laxárdalr appears as Laxárdale.

I have, however, retained the special Icelandic vowels "æ," "ø," "œ," and "ǫ" to preserve some of the flavor of the original. The character "æ" may be pronounced like the vowel in English "bad." The characters "ø" and "œ" may be approximated with the French "œu" as in *œuf* or *œuvre*. The character "ǫ" may be pronounced like the vowel in English "ought." Icelandic "y" and "ý" may be treated as short and long variants of French "u." I have also retained the acute accents, which are used in Old Icelandic to mark long vowels and are no impediment to pronunciation.

vii

ABBREVIATIONS

ÅNOH *Aarbøger for nordisk oldkyndighed og historie*

ANF *Arkiv för nordisk filologi*

ÍF Íslenzk fornrit. Reykjavik: Hið Íslenzka Fornritafélag

Introductory Essays *Introductory Essays on Egils saga and Njáls saga.* Ed. John Hines and Desmond Slay. [London] Viking Society for Northern Research, 1992.

JEGP *Journal of English and Germanic Philology*

MHN *Monumenta Historica Norvegiae: Latinske kildeskrifter til Norges historie i middelalderen.* Ed. Gustav Storm. 1880. Rpt. Oslo: Aas & Wahl, 1973.

MM *Maal og minne*

NVAOS Skrifter utgitt av Det Norske Videnskaps-Akademi i Oslo

ONIL *Old Norse-Icelandic Literature: A Critical Guide.* Ed. Carol J. Clover and John Lindow. Islandica 45. Ithaca: Cornell University Press, 1985; rpt. Toronto: Toronto University Press, 2005.

Sagas *Sagas of the Icelanders: A Book of Essays.* Ed. John Tucker. New York: Garland, 1989.

SBVS *Saga-Book of the Viking Society*

SI *Scripta Islandica*

Sjötíu ritgerðir *Sjötíu ritgerðir helgaðar Jakobi Benediktssyni 20. júlí 1977.* Ed. Einar G. Pétursson and Jónas Kristjánsson. 2 vols. Reykjavik: Stofnun Árna Magnússonar, 1977.

Skj *Den-norsk-islandske skjaldedigtning.* Vols. IA–IIA, *Tekst efter håndskrifterne;* vols. IB–IIB, *Rettet tekst.* Ed. Finnur Jónsson. Copenhagen: Gyldendal, 1908–15; rpt. Copenhagen: Rosenkilde & Bagger, 1967–73.

SS *Scandinavian Studies*

STUAGNL Samfund til Udgivelse af Gammel Nordisk Litteratur

Studien zum Altgermanischen *Studien zum Altgermanischen. Festschrift für Heinrich Beck.* Ed. Heiko Uecker: Berlin and New York: de Gruyter, 1994.

Studien zur Isländersaga *Studien zur Isländersaga. Festschrift für Rolf Heller.* Ed. Heinrich Beck and Else Ebel. Berlin and New York: de Gruyter, 2000.

Th Theodoricus Monachus. *Historia de Antiquitate Regum Norwagiensium; An Account of the Ancient History of the Norwegian Kings.* Trans. and ann. David and Ian McDougall; intro. Peter Foote. Viking Society for Northern Research, Text Series 11. London: University College London; Viking Society for Northern Research, 1998.

ZDA *Zeitschrift für deutsches Altertum und deutsche Literatur*

THE GROWTH OF THE
MEDIEVAL ICELANDIC SAGAS
(1180–1280)

Introduction

The Prehistory of the Sagas

This work sets out to clarify how the book-length sagas of medieval Iceland evolved in literary terms from circa 1180 to circa 1280. This approach is a departure from previous practice to the extent that the sagas, in particular those about early Iceland, have seemed to defy chronological treatment.[1] The dating indices are normally not clear enough to allow for the establishment of a firm chronology. As a result, surveys of the sagas often organize them in rough groupings or regionally rather than chronologically. The regional principle was, for example, enshrined in the important series of editions titled Íslenzk fornrit. In this text series the order of publication moves clockwise around Iceland, beginning with *Egils saga* in the West, circling to the North and East, and coming to a provisional resting place with *Njáls saga* in the South.

My book seeks to overcome the chronological impasse, to whatever extent is possible, by concentrating on the sagas with a relatively secure date. Not surprisingly, these are often the longer ones, with more scope for textual comparison and more indications of relative date. I begin with the earliest full-length sagas from the period 1180 to perhaps 1200: Odd Snorrason's *Saga of Olaf Tryggvason* and *The Legendary Saga of Saint Olaf,* the latter being a redaction of a so-called *Oldest Saga*

[1] Vésteinn Ólason (1998, 21) writes as follows: "The uncertainties of dating make it a hazardous venture to speculate about any kind of development during the thirteenth century." See also Böðvar Guðmundsson et al. 1993, 80. This caveat may be taken as the point of departure for my book. On the paralyzing critical difficulties raised by uncertain datings, see Würth 1999, 200–206.

1

of Saint Olaf, extant only in six fragments. There follows a discussion in Chapter 3 of the first sagas about Iceland. These texts are difficult to date, but I argue that they are early. I then pass on to *The Saga of King Magnús and King Harald*—which, with *Ljósvetninga saga,* I estimate to have been written around 1220—and two of the most famous and frequently read of the book-length sagas: *Egils saga,* dated between 1220 and 1240, and *Laxdœla saga,* dated between 1240 and 1260. *Laxdœla saga* appears to have inspired historical sagas on a larger scale, and two of these are dealt with in Chapter 8. At roughly the same time, or perhaps a little later, appears a group of chiseled smaller sagas that are characterized by a strong thematic emphasis, especially on the role of chieftains: *Hœnsa-Þóris saga, Bandamanna saga,* and *Hrafnkels saga.* This thematic focus culminates in *Njáls saga,* which consensus places around 1280.

There should be no illusion, however, about the certainty of the dates given here. Odd's *Saga of Olaf Tryggvason* was very probably composed in Latin between 1180 and 1200, but the Latin text is lost, and we do not know when the extant Icelandic translation was made. *The Oldest Saga of Saint Olaf* is now dated around 1200, but most of it is lost, and we must use a later redaction known as *The Legendary Saga.* When exactly that redaction came into being is quite uncertain, though it is surely older than the more elegant *Heimskringla* redaction, usually dated circa 1225. There are also real doubts about the relative dating of Odd's saga and *The Oldest Saga,* although I hope to have shown in a recent paper (Andersson 2004a) that Odd must have written first. *The Saga of King Magnús and King Harald* (in the compendium known as *Morkinskinna*) is quite likely to have been written no later than circa 1220, but a dating of *Ljósvetninga saga* is controversial; I place it around 1220, but others have dated it as late as 1260. The approximate dating of the remaining sagas is a matter more of consensus than of certainty.

I nonetheless posit a chronology because it allows for a more decisive approach to the development of saga writing in the thirteenth century. I argue that this development entails two important trajectories: on the one hand, a transition from a quasi-folkloristic gathering of tradition to an increasingly focused literary composition culminating in *Njáls saga;* on the other hand, a transition from a somewhat scattered biographical form in the Olaf sagas and the earliest sagas about Icelanders to a form in which the narrative is controlled by an ever more dominant authorial point of view. That is to say, the sagas evolve from a recording of available tradition to a literature of ideas during the century under study; at the same time, the analysis of character progresses from a somewhat nebulous hagiographical model in the Olaf sagas to a well-defined political or ideological concept in *The Saga of King Magnús and King Harald*, *Egils saga*, and *Ljósvetninga saga*, to a legendarily tinged historical idealization in *Laxdœla saga*, and finally to a pervasive critique of the older narrative conventions and institutional values in *Njáls saga*.

The dating and ordering of the written sagas are difficult enough, but more difficult still is any attempt to imagine their oral prehistory. All scholars agree that there was such a prehistory: that is, that the sagas were told in some form before they were written down. Just what that form may have been, however, is a matter of perennial debate. Hypotheses have pendulated from the extreme view that the sagas were orally performed in more or less the same shape as the written form that we now have to the skeptical view that the saga writers composed their works like novelists, using only scraps of oral tradition.[2] The belief that the sagas are fundamentally oral compositions was popular in the nineteenth century and persisted as late as Andreas Heusler's final statement in 1941.[3] But Heusler's supposition had already been overtaken by the theory that the sagas are largely thirteenth-century literary fictions, a view promoted chiefly by Icelandic scholars from the 1930s down to the 1950s and by the German scholar Walter Baetke in 1956.[4]

The problem is an old one, at least two centuries old, but in the last quarter of the twentieth century it no longer excited the same interest that had animated opposing viewpoints in the previous seventy-five years. Indicative of the decline in interest was the simultaneous appearance in 1976 of two books, one by Óskar Halldórsson on *Hrafnkels saga* and one by Rolf Heller on *Laxdœla saga*. These two scholars took diametrically opposed positions, the first on the traditionalist side of the debate and the second on the inventionist side, but they did not succeed in reigniting the discussion. In an influential paper ten years

---

[2] The debate has been reviewed in Scovazzi 1960; Andersson 1964; Mundal 1977 and 1990; and most recently in Danielsson 2002a, esp. 231–77.

[3] Heusler 1941, 200–239.

[4] The most important cumulative exposition of the inventionist view may be found in the introductions to the Íslenzk fornrit editions, vols. 2–12 (1933–56). Baetke (1956) was even more adamantly inventionist.

later, Carol J. Clover (1986) mediated between the extremes by arguing that the oral precursors of the written sagas were predominantly episodic and that the long sagas were a literary innovation; the content of a long saga may have been familiar to the audience in outline (the "immanent saga"), but in performance it is likely to have been told in smaller denominations. Clover's argument did not call forth a response until a paper of my own in 2002, which offered reasons for believing that there may have been long stories as well as shorter ones in the oral tradition.

It was therefore against the backdrop of declining interest in the oral tradition that in 2002 three new books, one by Gísli Sigurðsson and two by Tommy Danielsson, suddenly revived the problem and reinvigorated the debate.[5] These three books are broadly conceived, clearly formulated, and, in my opinion, convincing. Gísli Sigurðsson studies the sagas of the Icelandic East Fjords and concludes that they are not literarily connected but, rather, overlap because they are based on a knowledge of similar traditions: where the texts roughly coincide, it is not because one author borrowed from another but because the authors had a common fund of oral traditions inherited from the Saga Age (ca. 930–1030). Danielsson provides the most comprehensive saga study to date, focusing on the most famous East Fjord saga, *Hrafnkels saga*. He concludes that it is probably not an imaginative fiction, as Sigurður Nordal argued in a widely read monograph from 1940, but a literary recasting of an orally transmitted story about a Saga Age dispute. In a second volume he focuses on the oral transmissions in the sagas about Norwegian kings. Thus both scholars reach entirely reconcilable conclusions that reemphasize the oral components in the sagas.

Despite this convergence, both scholars are quite guarded in what they say about the form of the oral traditions. Gísli Sigurðsson, though he believes in the existence of commonly known oral traditions and accepts Clover's concept of an "immanent saga"—that is, a general narrative outline familiar to many people but not "performed" until a version was set down in writing—nonetheless insists that very little can be known about the antecedent traditions, since they were completely transmuted when they passed into written form.[6] Tommy

[5] I have reviewed these important books in Andersson 2004b, 505–27.
[6] Gísli Sigurðsson 2002, 39, 51, 325–27.

Danielsson is similarly cautious. He believes that only the short sagas are likely to have some resemblance to the oral prototypes from which they sprang and that the longer ones, such as *Laxdœla saga* and *Njáls saga,* are strictly literary creations. He argues in addition that oral traditions and written sagas interacted mutually. Thus no written saga is a simple transcription of oral tradition; each is conditioned not only by the oral record but by earlier written sagas as well. Indeed, it is quite imaginable that a growing body of written sagas could in turn have influenced the formulation of oral stories.[7]

The convergence between Gísli Sigurðsson and Tommy Danielsson is therefore not only a reaffirmation of the oral tradition but also a pessimistic assessment of our ability to draw conclusions about the nature of the traditions that preceded the written texts. That is, in the process of becoming written literature the oral tradition underwent such a transformation in gradual increments over a long period of time that the resulting texts no longer bear any useful resemblance to the antecedent tradition. They therefore permit no hypothetical reconstruction of what the oral substratum may have looked like.

This laudable caution involves a curious contradiction. On the one hand, the three new studies have greatly strengthened the hypothesis that there were full oral traditions underlying the sagas. On the other hand, they argue that these traditions are so elusive that it is pointless to speculate about them.[8] Thus, just as the oral traditions are reinforced and seem to become more palpable, they in fact become less identifiable. The operative metaphor in Tommy Danielsson's first book is *det muntliga havet* (the open sea of orality), implying formlessness and flux.[9] Therefore, we can no longer equate the oral stories with the written sagas in any way, nor do we know anything about the dimensions of the oral stories, whether they were short, long, or intermediate.

The available evidence is reviewed below, but first I turn to the indications that there was in fact a tradition of oral storytelling in medieval Iceland. The relevant anecdotes have been surveyed frequently, but they are crucial to the argument and will bear a further round of scrutiny. Aside from the well-known storytelling at the wedding at

---

[7] Danielsson 2002a, 304.

[8] The word "elusive" figures in the subtitle of Danielsson 2002a: "Fallet med den undflyende traditionen" (the case of the elusive tradition).

[9] This phrase is the title of the final section in Danielsson 2002b (385–95), but it underlies both his 2002 books generally. See in particular 2002a, 303.

Reykjahólar in 1119,[10] a passage that would seem to guarantee the reciting of *fornaldarsögur* (legendary sagas), the most famous incident of storytelling is recorded in one of the *þættir* (semiindependent tales) in *The Saga of King Magnús and King Harald* (the subject of Chapter 4).[11] According to this episode, a young Icelander comes to King Harald's court in Norway and asks to be received. The king inquires whether he has any accomplishments, and the young man replies that he can tell stories. He is therefore welcomed and entertains the court with his stories until Christmas draws near. Then he becomes downcast, and the king surmises that he has run out of stories just as they are needed most for the holidays. The Icelander confirms the truth of the king's intuition, noting that he has only one story left but that he is afraid to tell it because it is the tale of Harald's own foreign adventures. The king has no objection to hearing his own deeds recited, but he advises the Icelander to hold the tale in reserve for the upcoming holiday season. He also undertakes to make the story last for the whole duration of the holidays.

The conclusion of the matter is worth reproducing in full:

Thus it came about that the Icelander told the story. He began on Christmas and carried on for a while, but soon the king asked him to stop. The retainers began to drink and comment that it was a temerity for the Icelander to tell this story and to wonder how the king would react. Some thought that he told the story well, but others were less impressed.

The holidays advanced. The king paid close attention to the timing and with his forethought contrived that the story was concluded as the holidays came to an end. On the thirteenth day, when the story had been finished earlier in the day, the king said: "Aren't you curious to know, Icelander," he asked, "what I think of the story?"

"I am afraid to ask, sire," he said.

The king said: "I am very pleased with it. It is perfectly faithful to the actual events. Who taught you the story?"

He replied: "It was my custom back in Iceland to go to the assembly meeting every summer, and every summer I learned something of the story from Halldór Snorrason."[12]

---

[10] The Reykjahólar episode was reviewed most recently in Danielsson 2002a, 233–35.

[11] The episode is translated from *Morkinskinna* by Andersson and Gade, 222–23. See also Heusler 1941, 204–5; H. M. Heinrichs 1975 and 1976; Danielsson 2002a, 231–33.

[12] *Morkinskinna*, trans. Andersson and Gade, 223.

It must be understood that Halldór Snorrason, the son of one of Iceland's most famous and powerful chieftains, was King Harald's closest lieutenant during the time of his foreign adventures. He would have known the story as well as Harald knew it himself. Halldór may in fact have been the chief conduit of information about King Harald back to Iceland.[13]

Much has been made of the storytelling Icelander because he offers a key to how saga narrative was transmitted. His account suggests that noteworthy experiences could be transmuted quite rapidly into narrative form. The form was not haphazard but was designed to be entertaining for a larger audience; the Icelander gains admission to the court because he is a *skilled* narrator. He also has an extensive repertory and is able to entertain the court for a considerable period of time.

It appears that in the case of history, in recent memory, much importance was attached to accuracy, at least in the first instance. Older stories could presumably no longer be tested for accuracy, but the ambition to be historical may well have persisted.[14] There was in some sense a built-in contradiction in the storytelling tradition: stories were judged at least partially on the basis of historical accuracy but were required to be entertaining as well. The sagas as we have them certainly fulfill the second requirement, and we can surmise that entertainment value came to overshadow historicity as the stories were passed down from generation to generation. It is quite uncertain how much history survived in the process, but it seems clear that the thirteenth-century Icelanders thought they were in possession of a historical tradition.

That conviction would have been reinforced in good measure by the skaldic stanzas of poets who had lived at the time of the saga events. *The Saga of King Magnús and King Harald* includes no fewer than 153 whole or partial stanzas, which would have been understood as nodes of history. There has been some debate as to whether these stanzas were transmitted as part of a prose narrative or whether the prose in which they are embedded is merely a speculation extrapolated from the verse, but it seems unlikely that so much verse could have been transmitted with no explanatory context. Reciters of the verse must have been able to answer questions about the events to which the verse

---

[13] There is a special *þáttr* about Halldór in *Morkinskinna* (ibid., 187–94). See also Jan de Vries 1930.

[14] Liestøl provides a full discussion of the problem of historicity, esp. in his last three chapters (1930, 181–254). See also Meulengracht Sørensen 1994.

refs.[15] The fullest illustration of the interdependence of prose and verse is found in *Egils saga.*

Although the researches of Gísli Sigurðsson and Tommy Danielsson make it plausible that there were extensive saga traditions in the thirteenth century, there are limitations to what we can read out of the tale of the storytelling Icelander at King Harald's court. His subject matter pertains to contemporary history, not to the bygone days revived both in the kings' sagas and in the sagas about early Icelanders. To be sure, the Icelander at Harald's court has a whole repertory of stories, some of which could have been about ancient historical lore, but we cannot be certain. In the extensive prose literature passed down from thirteenth-century Iceland there is not a single episode visualizing a storyteller who reproduces the deeds or adventures of past kings or of Icelanders who lived in the Saga Age.

It is nonetheless difficult to believe that these matters were excluded from the storytelling repertories, since they came to dominate the written literature of the thirteenth century. An episode from *Njáls saga* shows that Saga Age events could at least be imagined as the stuff of storytelling. The episode occurs near the end of the saga when Flosi Thórdarson and his companions have been exiled from Iceland for their part in the burning of Njál and his household. They come to Mainland (largest of the Orkney Islands), where they are entertained by a certain King Sigtrygg and two jarls. Their hosts are curious about the news from Iceland, in particular the burning of Njál and his family: "Gunnar Lambason was charged to tell the story and he was seated on a chair."[16] It happens to be Christmas Day, and at that very moment Njál's avenger Kári Sǫlmundarson and his companions arrive at the hall and listen to the story as they stand outside:

> King Sigtrygg asked: "How did Skarphedin [Njál's son] hold up during the burning?" "Well enough at first," said Gunnar, "but he ended in tears." He gave a very biased version of the whole story and told a lot of lies.

That is too much for Kári, who rushes in, recites a stanza, and lops off Gunnar's head.

---

[15] See the summary discussion in Frank 1985, 176–77; and Danielsson 2002b, 234.

[16] ÍF 12:442–44. The translations are mine, but the full context can be read in *Njáls saga,* trans. Magnus Magnusson and Hermann Pálsson, 343; or trans. Robert Cook, 297–98.

The author of *Njáls saga*, like the author of *The Saga of King Magnús and King Harald*, thus believes that the core of the tale, the burning of Njál and his family, could have been told in a formal setting a few years after the actual event. Once again there is an emphasis on truthfulness. In the case of King Harald's Icelandic storyteller, truthfulness earns a royal reward, but in the case of King Sigtrygg, the storyteller lies and loses his head. The latter model may be an indirect way for the saga author to vouch for his own truthfulness, although it is hard to believe that there was much residual truth to be had 280 years after the events described.

Perhaps the most revealing incident of storytelling about Saga Age Icelanders is found in *Fóstbrœðra saga*.[17] When Thormód Bersason goes to Greenland to avenge his foster brother Thorgeir Hávarsson, we are told that at a thingmeeting one of Thorgeir's killers, a certain Thorgrím Einarsson, tells the story of Thorgeir's last stand and death. As in *Njáls saga*, the storyteller is seated formally on a chair, this time in the open air, with a large audience that seems to include most of those attending the meeting. Here too the narration is about current events, but once again the author seems to have believed that there were oral stories about Saga Age characters.

One can of course disallow such references to storytelling by supposing that they are invented as a false authentication of the saga author's fiction. Some scholars have adopted this line, but it seems hypercritical.[18] It is difficult to believe that a number of saga authors would have invented the institution of storytelling if everyone in the reading or listening audience knew full well that no such institution existed. Furthermore, it taxes credulity to believe that what the saga authors told about the Saga Age was the product of simple invention. The invention would have to be remarkably detailed and remarkably well harmonized. We may also ask ourselves what the point of such elaborate invention would have been. As Gísli Sigurðsson points out, Harald Hardrule's Mediterranean adventures are quite implausible, but independent Byzantine sources show that there was some historical basis for the stories.[19]

Apart from the storytelling anecdotes, there are other indications, al-

---

[17] ÍF 6:229–34. The most recent translation is by Martin S. Regal; see *The Complete Sagas of Icelanders*, 2:329–402.

[18] The episode in *Fóstbrœðra saga* is interpreted this way in Heller 1977.

[19] Gísli Sigurðsson 2002, 253–55.

beit less specific, of live oral traditions in thirteenth-century Iceland. Gísli Sigurðsson has mounted a powerful case that the sagas of the East Fjords were orally inspired, not literarily. The narrative variants that they embody suggest not a single, monolithic literary formulation but mutable traditions that could be set down differently by different authors. The problem of saga variants used to be studied on the basis of variant redactions of one and the same text, notably *Ljósvetninga saga* and *Bandamanna saga*, but it has emerged fairly clearly that these are cases of literary variation.[20] With Gísli Sigurðsson's book the focus has shifted to the study of narrative variations found in quite different texts. The implication of this shift is that there was a widespread knowledge of the Saga Age traditions and that depending on the context, they could be used rather freely.

The existence of substantial oral traditions is further evinced by the variation in the genealogical records. These variants are close enough to suggest common knowledge of family relationships but not close enough to suggest that genealogies were transferred unchanged from one text to another.[21] It is therefore fair to surmise that Icelanders in the thirteenth century knew about their Saga Age ancestors and knew how they were related to one another, without reference to written records. It may also be fair to suppose that they knew about their ancestors in a narrative context, because the sagas are by no means dry family records; on the contrary, they are dramatic stories of conflict and intrigue. We could of course imagine that the oral traditions provided only family information and genealogical details and that the dramatic plots were contrived by the saga authors as they wrote. The dramatic effects are so ubiquitous and so recurrent in form, however, that it is hard to believe they were invented independently by two or three dozen saga writers, without precedent in an anterior storytelling style. These effects are more likely to have been inherited storytelling conventions, presumably attached to the cast of characters familiar from Saga Age traditions.

So far, we may perhaps conclude that there were living traditions about kings and leading Saga Age figures and turn next to the ques-

---

[20] Close studies of the variant redactions were made by Magerøy (1956 and 1957).

[21] Björn M. Ólsen published a long series of papers in *ÅNOH* (1904, 1905a and b, 1908, 1910, 1920) in which he argued that the saga genealogies were generally derivative from the genealogies of *Landnámabók*. But see Gísli Sigurðsson 2002, 193–201, and his summary statement, 343–44.

tion of dimensions. How long was an oral story about the Saga Age? It has always been easier to believe in short oral stories than in long oral stories, and that belief was reaffirmed in Carol Clover's paper "The Long Prose Form." She built her case to a large extent on the evidence that long prose stories are hard to document in other oral traditions around the world. Long prose sagas in Iceland, orally performed, would therefore be a considerable anomaly in the larger, international picture. Consequently, Clover is inclined to believe that short narratives dominated the oral tradition and that these short narratives were variously combined at the writing desk to produce long written sagas.

The existence of short narratives in oral form seems to be assured by the Icelandic *þættir*. These *þættir* are even more difficult to date than the sagas because they contain so little ambient information that might shed light on their composition. The best indication is an early collection of some sixteen *þættir* in *Morkinskinna*, the original redaction of which dates from around 1220. The difficulty is that scholars do not agree on the question of whether these *þættir* were already present in the original redaction or were interpolated at a later date. If, however, Ármann Jakobsson is right in his recent book on *Morkinskinna* that the *þættir* were indeed present in the first redaction, then we can say that the short form was fully developed at the dawn of saga writing.[22]

Where did the *þættir* come from? They were presumably not invented as decoration for *Morkinskinna*, because they are fairly ubiquitous in the sagas. The examples in *Morkinskinna* are very well told. In general the author of *Morkinskinna* is an exceptionally good narrator, and it is possible that the excellence of the *þættir* should be attributed to this author. On the other hand, it is difficult to believe that they could be shaped with such uniform skill if there was not an anterior tradition of well-told, anecdotal stories.

The more pressing issue is whether there were also long stories from the Saga Age. The best evidence comes from the young Icelander's recital at King Harald's court, a recital that extends through the twelve days of Christmas. Andreas Heusler calculated that if the allotted time each day was fifteen minutes, the total recitation time would have been three hours.[23] That is a very conservative estimate indeed; it is difficult

[22] Ármann Jakobsson 2002, 42–43, 54, 68–71, 87–88.
[23] Heusler 1941, 205.

to imagine a situation in which the whole court comes to a standstill for the sake of a fifteen-minute recital. Even half an hour would be a modest estimate.

The recitals referred to above in *Fóstbrœðra saga* and *Njáls saga* also seem to presuppose a more extended narrative. Listeners abandon other activities and gather around to devote their full attention to a storyteller. The length of time implied in this setting is particularly apparent in *Fóstbrœðra saga*. Here one of the listeners is able to leave the recital in order to seek out Thormód and apprise him that he is missing a good story. Such a break in itself might amount to fifteen minutes, and yet the messenger is in no apparent fear that he will lose the thread of the story. It appears, then, that such storytelling sessions could be quite long or, at least, could be extended in such a way as to become long.

There are also stylistic reasons for believing that stories could be told at considerable length.[24] Some of the rhetorical practices that characterize the plots of the written sagas suggest as much: narrative dilation, elaborate premonitory devices, parallel actions, a gradual mounting of complex tensions, and a conspicuous taste for retardation. If these ubiquitous devices in the written sagas are a heritage from oral storytelling, then the oral stories must have been of some length. Dilation, retardation, and a gradual buildup of plot are not techniques appropriate to short oral stories. To be sure, they could be attributed to writing authors, but the literary inspiration of such a style is hard to locate. It is not a draft on any of the literary traditions of the Middle Ages—hagiography, chronicle, or romance.

In discussing oral stories we need to ask not only how long they were but also how stylized they were. Were the oral prototypes in some sense factual or informational, or were they narratively streamlined and dramatic? Or were they both? The genealogical accounts, place-name traditions, and colonizing reports are certainly more on the informational side, but there are clear indications of a dramatic style. A strikingly large percentage of the written sagas is accounted for by dialogue.[25] Dialogue is already fully developed in the short *þættir*, which

---

[24] I argue the point in more detail in Andersson 2002, 406–7.

[25] The percentages of direct speech are tabulated in Netter 1935, 17–18. They range from 6–7 percent in *Reykdæla saga* to 24 percent in *Egils saga*, 31 percent in *Laxdæla saga*, 39 percent in *Njáls saga*, and 44 percent in *Ljósvetninga saga*. See also Úlfar Bragason 1986, 47–48. Here the contrastingly low percentages in *Sturlunga saga* are noted, from a low of 5–6 percent to a high of 30 percent in *Þorgils saga ok Hafliða*.

are memorable and easy to retell. If dialogue was characteristic of short oral narratives, it would presumably have been characteristic of long oral narratives as well.

There is a further piece of evidence. The sagas set in the Saga Age and as late as the early twelfth century (*Þorgils saga ok Hafliða*) are distinctly more dramatic than the contemporary sagas set in the late twelfth or the thirteenth century: *Sturlu saga, Guðmundar saga dýra, Þórðar saga kakala, Þorgils saga skarða, Íslendinga saga,* and others. To be sure, these latter sagas have their dramatic moments, but in general they are narratively flatter than the classical sagas.[26] It has usually been assumed that this difference in style came about because the older sagas had passed through an oral filter and were thus stylistically heightened—and indeed it is difficult to find an alternative explanation for the clear distinction between the dramatic older sagas and the more chroniclelike contemporary sagas.

The distinction is by no means a simple one, because the classical sagas, both the oral precursor traditions and the written redactions, will surely have influenced such compositions as *Íslendinga saga*—for example, the prelude leading up to the battle at Qrlygsstaðir.[27] At the same time, there are traditional sagas that are somewhat in line with the chronicle style of the contemporary ones: for example, *Eyrbyggja saga,* parts of *Laxdœla saga,* and *Vatnsdœla saga.* Different authors could therefore opt for different styles. Nonetheless, the stylistic demarcation between traditional and contemporary sagas is quite palpable.

To distinguish between a traditional style and a contemporary style is not, however, tantamount to distinguishing an oral style and a literary style. Literarily composed sagas such as *Íslendinga saga* could imitate oral style, and orally transmitted sagas such as *Eyrbyggja saga* could imitate chronicle style. We must therefore find other ways to explore the permeable boundary between oral and literary style.

Perhaps the best evidence comes from the earliest kings' sagas, Odd Snorrason's *Saga of Olaf Tryggvason* and *The Legendary Saga of Saint Olaf,* which are the subject matter of the first two chapters in this book. That Odd's biography was to a large extent a literary project is clear enough from the fact that it was initially composed in Latin. Odd's book reveals, especially in the middle section, an undeveloped sense of plot

[26] Liestøl 1930, 71–74.

[27] Some of the stylistic points of similarity between the classical sagas and *Sturlunga saga* (mostly thirteenth-century sagas) are reviewed in Úlfar Bragason 1986, 53–58, 61–63, 80–83.

and severe problems in the motivation of the action, yet the final section on the Battle of Svǫld is as consistently dramatic as any account to be found in the classical sagas. Here we find an awkward literary contrivance and a fully evolved oral tale side by side. This mismatch certainly suggests that Olaf's biography was not orally performed as a whole and that the first attempt at a total narrative was a rather clumsy literary experiment.

That impression is reinforced by *The Legendary Saga*, which is a close copy of the largely lost *Oldest Saga of Saint Olaf*. *The Legendary Saga* is compositionally even less satisfactory than Odd's saga. For the most part it simply threads together a series of separate anecdotes extracted from clusters of skaldic verse. But it also provides a brilliant exception, the story of how King Olaf converted the recalcitrant heathen chieftain Dala-Gudbrand ("Kristni þáttr"). The anecdote is a storytelling gem, interpolated into *The Oldest Saga* presumably by the author of *The Legendary Saga* and presumably from a separate source.[28]

Like the story of the Battle of Svǫld, this anecdote bears all the marks of an orally perfected tale, but in one respect it is quite different. It is not a traditional tale about a hero of the North, like Olaf Tryggvason, but a literary invention based on a hagiographic pattern known as the thaumaturgic duel. It shows therefore that oral style (what we think of as "saga style") could be separated from traditional contexts and placed in the service of literary innovation. I return to the implication of this stylistic separability later, but *The Legendary Saga* as a whole confirms the impression left by Odd's saga that the composition of a long biography was initially a difficult project and a strictly literary undertaking, with no support from a single prior oral narrative. It assumes only bits and pieces of tradition, the joining of which was a literary task.

The perfection of a long narrative form was achieved with remarkable speed, however. Both Odd's *Saga of Olaf Tryggvason* and *The Legendary Saga* are compositionally flawed, but as early as 1220—if our dating is reliable—the long narrative form appears fully developed in *The Saga of King Magnús and King Harald* and in *Egils saga*. That there were oral traditions about Harald and Magnús is assured by the recital of the young Icelander at Harald's court, and Egil's adventures must

---

[28] The harmonizing of the hagiographic commonplace with the narrative technique of the sagas is analyzed in Andersson 1988a.

have been handed down in his own family, underpinned as they are by a large amount of verse. But even at this early stage it is impossible to say what is oral and what is literary. The overall biographical form is probably literary, but it is difficult to believe that such brilliant narration would have been possible without a storytelling precedent—for example, the older Thórólf's demise at the hands of Harald Fairhair, Egil's obstreperous youth, the head-ransoming sequence in York, or the grotesquely inflated adventures in Värmland.

The authors of *The Saga of King Magnús and King Harald* and *Egils saga* were primarily storytellers, not chroniclers, but we must remind ourselves that there are also sagas with very little storytelling vitality, notably *Eyrbyggja saga*. Some explanation is needed to account for the greater and lesser storytelling ability in these texts. It would seem that if the Saga Age traditions were uniformly dramatic in their oral transmission, the written sagas that emerged later would be equally dramatic. A possible hypothesis to account for the uneven style is that some, but not all, saga authors were themselves good storytellers and able to transfer their storytelling skills from oral recital to the written page—just as the author of "Kristni þáttr" in *The Legendary Saga* was able to cast a hagiographic commonplace in perfect saga form without the aid of oral tradition. Other saga authors were not skilled storytellers and were condemned to write their narratives in a less dramatic form.

This is a simple distinction with not so simple implications. For one thing, if the same story could be written well by a skilled storyteller and less well by an unskilled narrator, we must conclude that the dramatic style was not inherent in the story or the oral tradition but was brought to the tradition by the teller or writer. The narrative matter itself was neutral; it was the quality of the teller that counted. For another, if the dramatic style of the tradition was not inherent, we must conclude that the form of a given story was not predetermined; a tradition could be told well or badly. There was no such thing as *Egils saga* in the tradition; there was only, so to speak, inert tradition waiting for a skilled narrator to make something of it, orally or in writing.

There has been a long-standing but unverifiable conviction that behind every individual written saga there lies an equivalent oral saga.[29]

---

[29] This was the fundamental assumption in Heusler's theory of the saga (last stated in 1941). See also Liestøl 1930, 114, 117, 135.

This is the assumption from which Gísli Sigurðsson and Tommy Danielsson have liberated us. Danielsson's haunting image of *det muntliga havet,* the open sea of orality,[30] suggests that there is no hard and fast form, only an ebb and flow. A teller or writer dips into the great expanse of tradition and shapes some part of it, but the ocean image is so shifting and amorphous that it becomes difficult to say anything about the tradition. This impasse makes Gísli Sigurðsson and Tommy Danielsson hesitant to dicuss the tradition, but some categories of narrative are so recurrent in the written sagas that they must have some precedent in the oral tradition. I suggest seven such categories:

1. There must have been something akin to biographical traditions, or at least something that could be formed into biography, because the biographical form is so common in the written sagas: for example, in the kings' sagas, in *Egils saga,* in the skald sagas, and in several sagas from the Sturlung complex.
2. There must have been ghost and sorcerer stories, which crop up again and again in the sagas (even though they have no particular function and are unlikely to have been invented). To name just a few, they recur with particular frequency in *Eyrbyggja saga, Harðar saga Grímkelssonar, Laxdæla saga, Grettis saga,* and *Gull-Þóris saga.*
3. There must have been genealogical traditions of a copiousness and complexity that is hard for modern people to imagine.
4. There must have been regional traditions, or traditions about particular families, such as those found in *Egils saga, Laxdæla saga, Ljósvetninga saga,* and *Vatnsdæla saga.*
5. There must have been traditions about lawsuits, which we find almost everywhere and which Tommy Danielsson, in particular, has emphasized.
6. There must have been traditions about armed conflict, which are equally ubiquitous and, if not related in full, are referred to as common knowledge.[31]

---

[30] See note 9 above.

[31] I collected the passages in question in Andersson 1966, but my conclusion—that references to conflict in the written sagas imply that these conflicts were also the subject of oral tradition—was rejected by Klaus von See (1981, 533) and Gísli Sigurðsson (2002, 51).

7. There must have been traditions about place-names, which figure prominently throughout, though nowhere with the same persistence as in *Harðar saga Grímkelssonar*.

All this material would have been available to saga authors in the thirteenth century, but we do not need to assume that it was cast in a particular form. It is more likely that the authors collected and correlated the narrative, choosing whatever seemed relevant to the story in hand. In other words, the selection of narrative material was quite free: the author could not only pick and choose among the narrative incidents and details but could also determine the main thrust of the story to be told. If the written sagas had been carried over verbatim from, or even modeled closely on, the oral prototypes, the general thrust would presumably have been quite similar from one saga to the next, but the sagas as we have them include a number of different modes. Among them I would single out three types that are particularly frequent in the extant texts.

1. There is first of all the biographical mode, which accounts for all the kings' sagas, the bishops' sagas, and those we traditionally refer to as skald sagas. It is also found in a variety of the so-called family sagas, especially the outlaw sagas (*Gísla saga, Harðar saga, Grettis saga*), and in several texts from *Sturlunga saga* (*Sturlu saga, Guðmundar saga dýra, Þórðar saga kakala*, and *Þorgils saga skarða*).
2. A second available mode was the regional or chronicle saga. Among the classical sagas this mode is represented by *Víga-Glúms saga, Reykdœla saga, Eyrbyggja saga, Ljósvetninga saga, Laxdœla saga*, and *Vatnsdœla saga*. In the Sturlung complex the clear and compendious example is *Íslendinga saga*, but we could also assign the early *Orkneyinga saga* and *Færeyinga saga* to this category.
3. A third category is the feud or conflict saga, a mode that is at the center of many if not most of the family sagas: for example, *Heiðarvíga saga, Hrafnkels saga, Hœnsa-Þóris saga, Droplaugarsona saga, Vápnfirðinga saga*, and *Njáls saga*. It is also an important pattern in many of the regional examples such as *Víga-Glúms saga, Reykdœla saga*, and *Ljósvetninga saga*. In the Sturlung collection it is represented by *Þorgils saga ok Haflíða*.

Thus the author of a saga was free not only to choose particular narrative incidents but also to lay down an overall narrative mode or style. Again, it seems unlikely that the mode was predetermined by the oral story, because the modes are so intermixed in the written sagas that they must also have been intermixed in the oral stories. There are no pure biographies, no pure regional sagas, no pure conflict stories. Instead, the modes are usually combined. Thus *Egils saga* is predominantly biographical but also regional and dramatic. *Bjarnar saga Hítdælakappa* is equally dramatic and biographical. *Ljósvetninga saga* is equally dramatic and regional. *Eyrbyggja saga* is regional but also biographical in its treatment of Snorri goði (Snorri the Chieftain). *Laxdæla saga,* regional and highly dramatic, concludes with a biographical focus on Gudrún Ósvífrsdóttir. The emphasis, or combination of emphases, was up to the individual author, and we may surmise that at the oral level the teller exercised the same options. Each teller must have made individual decisions on style as well as matter.

Given that dramatic narration is peculiar to subject matter that seems to have passed through an oral filter for a considerable period of time, dramatic style must have been characteristic of the oral stories as well. The oral traditions, the oral stories fashioned from them, and the ultimate written sagas were all polymorphous, but tellers settled on particular stories and gave them a particular form. Writing authors did exactly the same thing: they chose a particular matter and fitted it to a particular mode. There is, however, no reason to suppose that a given written saga corresponded to any particular oral story, unless we imagine that a skilled storyteller was fond of a particular story, practiced it, and eventually elected to cast it in writing. Thus the oral storyteller and the saga author could conceivably have been one and the same person, but it is equally conceivable that they were quite different people.

The sagas that appeal to modern readers most are the traditional and dramatic feud or conflict sagas. They strike us as being the most literarily polished texts and the most exciting stories. They must have had something of the same effect on early audiences too, but medieval listeners probably had a broader appreciation of the sagas than we do. The sagas about the discovery of Vinland, sagas, which have little narrative verve, would have struck them as interestingly otherworldly, whereas the chronicle and regional sagas, which to our taste are overburdened, would have compensated with an abundance of genealogical and quasi-historical lore close to the listeners' roots and close to their hearts. Even the bishops' sagas would have had a readership among the faithful, and the texts classed as *fornaldarsögur* (legendary sagas) would have had a readership no less than modern fantasy fiction. King Hákon the Old's son Magnús listened to a fictional *Huldar saga on his ship, but he listened to saints' lives and kings' sagas on his deathbed.[32] In short, there must have been a diversity of literary enthusiasms to match the diversity of traditions.

The fundamental principle to be extracted from the work of Gísli Sigurðsson and Tommy Danielsson is that there is unlikely to have been a one-to-one match between written sagas and equivalent oral stories. There was no oral *Egils saga*, but there were probably dozens of stories about Egil and his ancestors, both short and long. These stories would have included the seven types of tradition listed above, among others. There would have been stories about Egil's life, perhaps even summaries of his life. There would have been supernatural stories about shape-shifting, magic, and berserks immune to steel. There would have been genealogical traditions about settlement and intermarriage. There would have been regional stories about dealings in Borgarfjord—for example, Thorstein's dispute with Steinar Onundarson at the end of the saga. There would have been stories about Egil's legal claims and lawsuits. There would have been stories about his duels and conflicts with royalty. There would have been traditions about places: the place where Skalla-Grím fetched up a great stone from the fjord to serve as an anvil, or the place where Egil hid his chests of silver at the end of this life. And, of course, there would have been stories about Egil's poetry.

But these stories and traditions would not have been joined in anything like the form we know until they were united in the biographical structure familiar to us as *Egils saga Skallagrímssonar*. The important point to make here is that the saga authors presumably had almost unlimited options in choosing and organizing the available traditions. The content of the stories was no doubt agreed on by many people, but the selection and ordering of the stories was left to the individual teller or writer who shaped them.

The assumption made in the following chapters is thus that there

[32] See "Sturlu þáttr" in *Sturlunga saga*, ed. Örnólfur Thorsson et al., 2:765–66; and *Konunga sögur*, ed. Guðni Jónsson, 456–57.

were both long and short forms of transmission. In Odd Snorrason's *Saga of Olaf Tryggvason* we find evidence of short anecdotal transmissions unrelated to a larger narrative sequence, but we also find, in the epic finale on the Battle of Svǫld, a fully developed narrative replete with the dramatic devices that characterize the sagas in their full flowering. In *The Legendary Saga* the anecdotal mode is predominant, but here too we find an episode ("Kristni þáttr") that exemplifies saga art at its best. In *The Saga of King Magnús and King Harald* the anecdotal tradition continues to be palpable, especially in the interlarded *þættir,* but the author structures the narrative as a whole in a more decisive and purposeful way by investing it with a political viewpoint. The compositional development is less obvious in the sagas about early Icelanders than in the kings' sagas because the author of *Egils saga* appears on the scene when the compositional problems of the long form have already been resolved. The author depends to a large extent on anecdotal materials underpinned by Egil's verse, but these materials are subsumed in a biographical frame taken over from the kings' sagas and no less controlled by a political outlook than *The Saga of King Magnús and King Harald.*

The author of *Ljósvetninga saga* rejects the tradition of the king's saga in order to trace a regional conflict that is strictly Icelandic. The author of *Laxdœla saga* and that author's imitators return to the model of *Egils saga* by adopting a multigenerational form. But *Laxdœla saga* goes one step further by modeling the core of the story on the Norse legend of Brynhild and Sigurd. In the shorter sagas of the late thirteenth century and in *Njáls saga,* both the biographical form and the generational structure are resolutely abandoned in favor of a drama of ideas. In all these sagas the outcroppings of tradition gradually recede as authorial autonomy and literary innovation become increasingly evident. The old question of whether the sagas, as we have them, are traditional or literary is misleading because the sagas are part of a continuum in which both traditional and literary components evolve over time. The way they combine is a question that must be explored anew for each saga in turn.

CHAPTER ONE

From Hagiography to Hero

Odd Snorrason's *Saga of Olaf Tryggvason*

The Traditions

There is no evidence of professional or quasi-professional saga tellers in Iceland, but there are some indications that historical lore was in the hands of persons with special qualifications. When Ari Thorgilsson began the process of recording Icelandic history in the 1120s, he referred to three of his informants in the very first sentence of his extant booklet: his foster father, Teit, the son of Bishop Ísleif, who was born in 1006; his uncle Thorkel Gellisson; and Thuríd, the daughter of Snorri the Chieftain, who died in 1112.[1] Ari credits Teit with being the wisest man he knew, notes that Thorkel had a long memory, and describes Thuríd as both widely informed and truthful. Elsewhere, Ari says that Teit learned of the arrival of the missionary Thormód in the year 1000 from a man who was actually there.[2] In a third passage he records that at the age of twelve, in 1080, he was with his foster father, Teit, when Hall Thórarinsson—who in turn had fostered Teit and was also possessed of a long memory and truthfulness—said he could remember that when he was three years old, in 999, Thangbrand had baptized him.[3] Thus Ari believed that he had access to secure sources of information going back to the days of King Olaf Tryggvason (995–1000).

The most interesting of Ari's informants may well be Thuríd, Snorri

[1] ÍF 1.1:4.
[2] Ibid., 15.
[3] Ibid., 21.

the Chieftain's daughter, though we know scarcely more about her than her name and that of her otherwise unknown husband, Gunnlaug Steinthórsson. Two redactions of *The Book of Settlement* refer to her as "Thuríd the Wise."[4] A minuscule curriculum vitae of her father, known as "The Life of Snorri the Chieftain," lists Thuríd as the sixteenth among his nineteen legitimate children.[5] Since Snorri died in 1031, Thuríd cannot well have been born much after 1025, and she would have been well up in years by the time Ari consulted her in, let us say, the 1080s or 1090s.

What makes Thuríd interesting is that she was at the center of so much historical information. Her father was a towering figure in the Saga Age, centrally involved in many of the most noteworthy events, but her information would not have been confined to Iceland. Her brother Halldór was in the service of King Harald Hardrule of Norway and was his close companion during Harald's adventurous early years in Constantinople. The story recapitulated in the foregoing introduction relates that an Icelander told of Harald's adventures in the presence of the king himself and explains that he had acquired the story from Halldór in Iceland. Thuríd would have known no less. Halldór is listed as number eleven among Snorri's children and would perhaps have been ten years older than Thuríd. The sagas relate that Halldór fell out with King Harald after their return to Norway and sailed back to Iceland in 1051, when his sister Thuríd would have been in her twenties and avid to hear his tales of adventure.[6] She would therefore have had direct access to information about King Harald and, in addition, King Magnús, with whom Harald shared the throne for some years.

Thuríd would in fact have known about the subject matter in all the sagas described in the following chapters. She would have known about King Olaf Tryggvason in connection with his conversion of Iceland when her father was in midlife. She was born during the reign of Olaf Haraldsson and would have been old enough to hear firsthand reports of his fall at Stiklarstadir in 1030. From her brother she would have known the stories of King Magnús and King Harald, told at greatest length in *Morkinskinna* and reviewed below in Chapter 4. In several of the sagas about early Icelandic heroes her father was a participant:

[4] Ibid., 118–19.
[5] ÍF 4:185.
[6] ÍF 5:LXXXVIII.

for example, in *Heiðarvíga saga*. When he returned to Iceland, Halldór lived at Hjardarholt, the former residence of Olaf Peacock, who had married Egil Skallagrímsson's daughter Thorgerd.[7] Thuríd would therefore have had immediate access to the traditions of the western Icelanders, the Mýramenn (*Egils saga*) and the Laxdœlir (*Laxdœla saga*). In addition, Thuríd's older sister Thórdís was married to Bolli Bollason, the last dashing figure in *Laxdœla saga* and heir to the whole romantic tradition of his family.[8] The story of Gudmund the Powerful in *Ljósvetninga saga* would have been familiar to most people, including Thuríd, because her father, Snorri, and Gudmund were the preeminent chieftains of their age and played major roles in the great finale of *Njáls saga*. Thuríd would thus have had an encyclopedic knowledge of her times going back a century or more and would have been a key figure in the transmission of these traditions down to her death in 1112. During her lifetime the events of the Saga Age would have been quite alive and accessible.

Was Thuríd a teller of tales as well as a custodian of information? We are not told. Nor do we know at what point Saga Age traditions began to take on the legendary dimensions that we know from the sagas of the thirteenth century. But dramatization may have set in quite early; a dispute between Thorgils Oddason and Haflidi Másson in the 1120s appears as a full-fledged saga in the first half of the 1200s, suggesting that literary recasting could be accomplished in about a century.[9] If that interval is anything to judge by, the Saga Age tales told about Egil Skallagrímsson, Gudrún Ósvífrsdóttir, and Njál Thorgeirsson could have solidified into legend by the time Ari wrote in the 1120s.

Ari records enough detail of one such tale to suggest that there may well have been full saga narratives in his day. The story in question emerges as the written *Hœnsa-Þóris saga* in the latter part of the thirteenth century. This is what Ari has to say about it in the twelfth:

There was a great assembly dispute between Thórd gellir, the son of Olaf feilan from Breidafjord, and Odd, who was called Tungu-Odd and came from Borgarfjord. Odd's son Thorvald was present at the house-burning of Thorkel Blund-Ketilsson together with Hœnsa-Thórir in Qrnólfsdale.

[7] Halldór is placed at Hjardarholt in "Halldórs þáttr Snorrasonar," ÍF 5:277.
[8] See genealogy VIII in ÍF 1.2.
[9] Andersson 2002, 398–407.

Thórd gellir was in charge of the prosecution because the son of Thorkel Blund-Ketilsson, Herstein, was married to Thórunn, his niece. She was the daughter of Helga and Gunnar and the sister of Jófríd, who was married to Thorstein Egilsson.

They were prosecuted at the assembly in Borgarfjord, at the place that was later called Thingnes. At that time the law stipulated that killing cases should be prosecuted at the assembly nearest to the place where the deed was committed. They fought there so that the assembly could not be legally convened. Among Thórd gellir's followers Thórólf, the brother of Álf í Dǫlum, fell. Then the case was transferred to the Allthing, and there they fought again. This time men in Odd's following fell, and Hœnsa-Thórir was outlawed and later killed. Others who were present at the burning were outlawed.[10]

Although there are significant discrepancies between this summary and the later saga (discussed in Chapter 9), it is clear that the same plot is being told. The main points are similar enough that the saga was once believed to be an imaginative expansion of Ari's epitome, but it seems more likely that the accounts represent different oral stages in the evolution of the saga.[11] At all events Ari was familiar with some version of the story.

Ari does not tell the story for the sake of a story, however, but only as the background for a legal reform designed to protect the prosecution from bringing a case at a hostile assembly place. The indication that he knew a Saga Age narrative is only incidental, but it is perhaps sufficient to show that he had access not only to wise informants but also to storytellers. He elects to use story only as a source of information, but there would come a time when the narratives as such would arouse the literary interests of the Icelanders.

Ari had some knowledge of Icelandic history and knew something of Norway as well. Chapter 7 of his *Íslendingabók* tells how King Olaf Tryggvason dispatches the Saxon missionary Thangbrand to convert Iceland, without success. Informed of the failed mission, Olaf resolves to take reprisals against the Icelanders in Norway, but two Icelandic chieftains intervene and promise to make a fresh attempt. There follows a detailed account of how this attempt succeeded, an account that

[10] ÍF 1.1:11.
[11] Gísli Sigurðsson 2002, 318–21.

anticipates even fuller versions of the event in *Laxdœla saga* and *Njáls saga*. How much more Ari knew about Olaf Tryggvason is uncertain, but he refers to "kings' lives" that were part of an earlier edition of his booklet.[12] He refers in addition to Sæmund Sigfússon, who also wrote about Norwegian kings. He could therefore have known something about Olaf's birth, youth, accession to the throne, conversion activities in Norway, and fall at the Battle of Svǫld in the year 1000.

The relevant traditions, both Icelandic and Norwegian, would have persisted through the twelfth century, but they did not surface in literary form until the end of that century. For our purposes the most important codification of Olaf's story is Odd Snorrason's *Saga of Olaf Tryggvason*. Odd is known from *The Book of Settlement* and is credited with the authorship of *Yngvars saga víðfǫrla* as well as being mentioned in *Grettis saga*.[13] He was a monk in the Benedictine monastery at Thingeyrar in northern Iceland and appears to have written his saga about Olaf Tryggvason between 1180 and 1200, perhaps closer to 1180. The much later *Greatest Saga of Olaf Tryggvason* states that Odd wrote it in Latin.[14] The Latin original is lost, however, and, apart from a couple of Latin phrases and a four-line ditty, we have only two differing redactions of an Icelandic translation plus a fragment of a third. There is no good evidence on the date of this translation, but perhaps it was made before the composition of *The Oldest Saga of Saint Olaf* from about 1200.[15]

Odd's text is the first to have full saga dimensions. It covers 190 pages in a popular Icelandic edition and 100 pages in an English translation. The form is strictly biographical and is therefore, in terms of literary genres, closely akin to the saint's life, the dominant form of prose narrative in twelfth-century Iceland.[16] The sources for the saga were not unlike the sources available to Ari: at least one short written account, some dramatically preformed oral narrative, and a handful of specialized informants.

We may begin with the informants. Odd does not identify them himself, but they appear in a chapter appended to the main manuscript

---

[12] ÍF 1.1:3.

[13] *The Saga of Olaf Tryggvason*, trans. Andersson, 4–5.

[14] Ibid., 2.

[15] Lönnroth 2000, 263; Andersson 2004a.

[16] On *The Saga of Olaf Tryggvason* as hagiography, see esp. Sverrir Tómasson 1988, 261–79.

(AM 310, 4to) from the second half of the thirteenth century.[17] In this passage the following words are attributed to Odd:

> I was told this story by Abbot Ásgrím Vestlidason, the priest Bjarni Bergthórsson, Gellir Thorgilsson, Herdís Dadadóttir, Thórgerd Thorsteinsdóttir, and Ingunn Árnórsdóttir. These people instructed me in the saga of King Olaf Tryggvason as it is now told. I showed the book to Gizur Hallsson and corrected it with his counsel.

The same information is repeated in *The Greatest Saga of Olaf Tryggvason*, prefaced by this statement: "The brothers Gunnlaug and Odd report that the following people provided most [*Flateyjarbók*: of what they set down and put in narrative form] concerning King Olaf Tryggvason."[18] The same names follow in a somewhat different order and with Ingunn in the form Arngunn. It has been argued that these informants belong only to Gunnlaug, who wrote a much more fragmentarily preserved life of Olaf, and not to Odd, but there is no compelling reason to doubt the evidence of both texts.[19]

We know considerably less about Odd's informants than we do about Ari's. Only two can be identified. One of them is Ásgrím Vestlidason, who was abbot at the north-central monastery at Munkathverá and died in 1160 or 1161.[20] Of particular interest is Ásgrím's early death date. He represents what was known about Olaf Tryggvason around the middle of the century, and his information may in fact go back to the beginning of the century and be more or less contemporary with Ari's. Since he was an abbot, we may surmise that his information would have had a clerical slant.

We know rather more about Ingunn, who is described at some length in Gunnlaug Leifsson's *Jóns saga helga*. She is listed in especially laudatory terms among Bishop Jón's disciples:

> There was also a chaste maiden named Ingunn under his instruction. She was no less accomplished in the aforementioned book skills than the others. She taught many people grammar and instructed anyone who wished to learn. Thus many became well educated under her guidance.

---

[17] *Saga Óláfs Tryggvasonar*, ed. Finnur Jónsson, 247.
[18] *Óláfs saga Tryggvasonar en mesta*, ed. Ólafur Halldórsson, 3:66.
[19] See Bjarni Aðalbjarnarson 1937, 85–86.
[20] Ibid., 86; *Biskupa sögur*, 1:415; *Sturlunga saga*, ed. Örnólfur Thorsson et al., 1:106.

She was much given to correcting Latin books by having them read to her while she did needle work or embroidered or [performed?] other manual tasks with saints' lives [copied? illuminated?], thus making people acquainted with God's glory not only by oral instruction but also with the work of her hands.[21]

Bishop Jón died in 1121, and Ingunn could have been his pupil in his last decade. She may therefore have been contemporary with Ásgrím Vestlidason, though she may also have lived a little longer.

In any case, Odd's interest in Olaf Tryggvason clearly goes back to the middle of his century, when he would have been a child or a very young man. It is also clear that at least some of his sources were clerically colored and would have focused on Olaf as a missionary king. The more secular sources emphasized Olaf's heroic feats: for example, the skald Hallar-Stein's "Rekstefja" and "Óláfsdrápa," perhaps from the late twelfth century.[22] Odd would not have cited them in his original Latin version because of the linguistic gulf, but he surely knew these poems or their sources. There were thus both ecclesiastical and secular strands in his information.

Odd Snorrason had written sources as well. He refers to both Sæmund Sigfússon and Ari Thorgilsson, presumably to the latter's lost "kings' lives." There is in addition a close match between the early parts of his narrative and the narrative found in the historical epitome *De Antiquitate Regum Norwagiensium*, written in Norway by a monk named Theodoricus sometime around 1180.[23] Scholars have argued that Theodoricus's work was also among Odd's sources, but it is equally possible that both Odd and Theodoricus drew on Sæmund and Ari in such a way that their narratives came to resemble each other closely.[24]

Whatever the immediate written sources, they seem to have determined the outline of Odd's saga. The initial phases tell of the death of Olaf's father, how the orphaned infant was smuggled abroad, how he spent years in servitude but came to be fostered and honored in Russia, and how his early military exploits culminated in conversion on the Scilly Isles. The sequel traces his return to Norway and how he

---

[21] *Biskupa sögur*, 1:241.
[22] See *Skj*, IA:543–52 and 573–78; IB:525–34 and 567–74.
[23] *MHN*, 3–68; Th.
[24] *The Saga of Olaf Tryggvason*, trans. Andersson, 6–7.

wrested the throne from Jarl Hákon, how he pursued the conversion of Norway and Iceland, and how an alliance formed among the Danes, Swedes, and dissident Norwegians led to his downfall at the great Battle of Svǫld.

If there were written sources on these matters, what need did Odd have for the informants listed in AM 310, 4to, and *The Greatest Saga of Olaf Tryggvason?* It is apparent that he wished not just to reproduce the brief account he found in his written sources but to expand the story into a much longer and fuller narrative. We might therefore ask where the very notion of a long book came from. It is not easy to point to particular models, but the book culture of the twelfth century, as practiced by Ingunn, for example, surely offered precedents in abundance, whether in the form of Roman epic, European chronicle, or hagiographic compilation. Odd would have been cognizant of a new, more encompassing format; the task was to realize these new dimensions in royal biography. Odd's solution was to some extent impressive and to some extent disorderly.

Assembling the Pieces

In the first twenty-five chapters Odd follows roughly the lead of his written sources, although the narrative of Olaf's escape from Norway, enslavement in the Baltic, and rise to eminence in Russia is greatly expanded over and above the accounts in Theodoricus's *De Antiquitate* and the other synoptic histories (*Historia Norwegiae* and *Ágrip af Nóregs konunga sǫgum*). The explanation must be that Odd's informants had fuller oral versions of this period than could be found in the short written histories. There is also an account of Olaf's early adventures and marriage in Wendland, an episode not foreshadowed in the synoptic histories and more likely to be innovation than tradition. I return to it below.

On the death of Jarl Hákon and Olaf's accession to the throne, the synoptic histories are fairly full, but once Olaf is installed on the throne there is virtually nothing about his Christian mission, merely a summing-up of his successes. Here Odd intervened with a great quantity of anecdotal material in chapters 26–60 of his saga. Since there is no written precedent for this part of the narrative, and since the organization is loosely additive, the section seems most likely to be based on oral anecdotes. We learn of the forcible conversion of the Orkney Islands (chapter 26) and Olaf's first preaching in Norway, attended by divine intercessions that promote his eloquence and silence the heathen opposition (chapter 27). Three chapters (28–30) are devoted to the discovery of the mortal remains of Christian refugees on the island of Selja and to the churches that were built there. This account is closely related to a written "Acta Sanctorum in Selio," which must have been available to Odd in some form.[25]

Three chapters preserved only in a Stockholm manuscript (S22–S24) describe how Olaf converts the people of Hǫrdaland by the political device of marrying his sisters to the local chieftains. He accomplishes the same end in Thrándheim by the less diplomatic device of offering to dispatch the pagans to their gods if they are truly so devoted to them. Another two chapters (32–33) recount Olaf's abortive wooing of Queen Sigríd in Sweden, a miscalculation that will have dire consequences. Chapter 34 adverts to the marriage of the Danish king Svein (Svend Forkbeard) to a Wendish princess. This episode breaks the sequence of missionary activities and is likely to be a later interpolation from *Jómsvíkinga saga*, inspired perhaps by Olaf's marriage project and the role King Svein is destined to play in Olaf's ultimate demise.

Chapters 36–38 return to the Christian mission. Olaf invites a band of sorcerers to a feast and, once they are disabled by drink, burns the festive hall to the ground. He then prosecutes the mission in the far north and hangs the obstinate pagan chieftain Hróald on the island of Godey. Finally, he begins machinations to force the conversion of the chieftains in Hálogaland. At the conclusion of this chapter he unexpectedly approaches Sigríd once again with a renewed marriage proposal, but when she refuses the stipulation that she convert to Christianity, Olaf indignantly slaps her, and the meeting ends in permanent hostility. In this larger sequence the themes of conversion and marriage are interwoven, but there is both a duplication and a contradiction. It appears that Odd was working from two traditions. According to one, Olaf alienated his potential wife by giving her what appeared to be a golden arm ring, which turned out to be only gilded iron. According to the other, he rejected her because she persisted in her pagan convictions. There was thus both a secular story of deceit and an exemplary story of religious irreconcilability. Odd did not attempt to resolve the conflict but let it stand.

[25] *MHN*, 147–52.

A brief chapter (39) notes the construction of Olaf's first great ship, named Traninn (the Crane), and raises the prospect of his marriage to the Danish princess Thyri, sister of King Svein. The following chapters return to an extended narrative of conversion: chapter 40 recounts the conversion of Hallfred Óttarsson and Kjartan Óláfsson in Norway, moments that are later rehearsed in *Hallfreðar saga* and *Laxdœla saga*, and chapter 41 is largely a verbatim loan from Ari Thorgilsson's account of the conversion events in Iceland. Chapter 42 returns to Norway, where Olaf prosecutes his secret plan for converting the chieftains in Hálogaland, but in chapter 43 the theme changes and Olaf suffers a visitation from the demonic god Odin, whose appearance ushers in a series of supernatural occurrences. The first of these (chapter 44) is another story of sorcerers, this time miraculously blinded, rounded up, and executed on a skerry.

Chapter 45 reports the construction of Olaf's second great ship Orm inn skammi (the Short Serpent), but most of the chapter is given over to the final consummation of the plan to convert Hálogaland. He has the chieftain Hárek abducted and persuades him to convert in exchange for the command of four districts. Shortly thereafter, Hárek captures yet another intractable heathen, Eyvind kinnrifa, and turns him over to King Olaf. Though subjected to torture, Eyvind is obdurate and eventually explains that he was begotten by an unclean spirit, is not truly human, and therefore cannot undergo baptism. With that he dies.

A second Hálogaland chieftain, Thórir hjǫrt (hart), turns into the stag embodied in his nickname. Olaf's famous dog Vígi gives chase and kills him but also suffers near-fatal wounds. Only the arts of a Lappish magician, who had once promised Olaf to perform such a service, save the dog's life. Here the supernatural elements have accumulated to such a degree that Odd feels compelled to address their credibility: "The sort of tales about such phantoms and prodigies as have just been related may surely seem less than credible."[26] Odd can attribute to them only a sort of metaphorical credibility as the delusions of the devil: "The matters that we have related with respect to such tales and exempla we do not judge to be true in the sense that they happened, but rather we believe that they appeared to happen because the devil is full of deceit and evil."[27]

[26] *The Saga of Olaf Tryggvason*, trans. Andersson, 97.
[27] Ibid.

In this comment Odd appears to enter into dialogue with both his readers and his informants. He seems in fact to distance himself from the latter, suggesting perhaps that they are more credulous than he. That stance casts him in the role of a passive recipient rather than the author of his own fictions. Some of the informants may indeed have had a more supernatural bent than Odd felt comfortable with, and that says something about the kind of transmission available to him.

Chapter 46 reverts to the marriage strand and relates how Olaf weds Thyri after her marriage to King Búrizleif of Wendland fails because of her objections to a heathen husband. Once more Odd interweaves conversion and marriage plots: Thyri qualifies as Olaf's consort because, unlike Sigríd, she is an ardent Christian. Olaf now returns to his crusade and destroys an idol of Frey in Thrœndalǫg, convincing the Thrœndir to convert. In the meantime, King Svein of Denmark marries Sigríd, Olaf's sworn enemy. We are not told whether Sigríd persists in her pagan convictions after marrying a Christian king, but we may perhaps assume that she does and that Svein is therefore compromised by his new alliance. Once again religious orthodoxy is a subtheme in the marriage patterns, and Olaf's enemies are defined not just as political opponents but also as religious antagonists. The Christian monarch is pitted against a heathen Swede and a Danish king doubly undermined by a heathen ally and a heathen wife.

We will see that the heathen encirclement of Olaf is completed when Jarl Eirík Hákonarson, true to his father's notorious paganism, remains in that tradition and displays a prow ornament of Thor when he makes common cause with the kings of Denmark and Sweden against Olaf. The fourth, somewhat shadowy member of the coalition, Jarl Sigvaldi, is also marked by a long-standing and quite caricatural association with paganism.[28] It may have been, at least in part, Sigvaldi's reputation for pagan treachery that inspired the idea of a pagan plot against Olaf.

If any thematic framework can be extracted from the somewhat random chapters 26–60, it is that after a period of successes against the pagans at home in Norway, Olaf finally succumbs to an international pagan conspiracy. The saga has been compared in other repects to *The Song of Roland*, but it also bears comparison to the extent that Olaf, like Roland, is a tragic Christian champion.[29] His overriding mission is to

[28] Ibid., 20–23.
[29] Lönnroth 1975, 43.

promote Christianity and combat paganism, at home and abroad. Just as Roland is exalted in his final hours, so too does Olaf acquire a heroic profile when his time begins to ebb. As doom gathers, Odd combines both secular and religious intimations. In chapter 49 he commemorates a moment of athletic prowess when Olaf rescues one of his followers from a perilous perch on a cliff face, and in chapter 50 there is a repertory of athletic accomplishments.

Chapters 51–52 complete the religious portrait. The king's follower Thorkel dydrill goes ashore with him one night and witnesses a vision: "There came over him [the king] so great a light that he [Thorkel] said that he could scarcely look at it. Then he said that he saw two figures clad in beautiful garments laying their hands on the king's head. He said that he thanked God that he should see such a vision."[30] Olaf forbids Thorkel to report this event to anyone, but eventually Thorkel does pass it along to King Harald Hardrule: "Many years after the death of King Olaf, when Thorkel was an old man, he told of this occurrence to King Harald, who considered Thorkel to be a truthful man."[31]

Thorkel figures in *The Saga of King Magnús and King Harald* (in *Morkinskinna*) and could have relayed the information to Harald as late as 1050. Harald had many contacts in Iceland, notably Halldór Snorrason, who, as we have seen, returned to Iceland about this time. Ingunn Arnórsdóttir or another contemporary could have heard about the incident around 1100 and passed it on to Odd Snorrason in the middle of the century. The problem for Odd would have been where to locate a no longer datable incident, but he seems clearly to have elected a placement toward the end of Olaf's life as a summation of his favor in the sight of God.

The point is reinforced in the following chapter (52). Here King Olaf takes his place on his highseat, then suddenly vanishes. Only the bishop can see that he is standing in the middle of the hall talking to a man who is likewise invisible. This vision prompts speculation about whether he is really a mortal king or an angel "sent by God and clothed in human flesh to preach the name of the Lord Jesus to many peoples."[32] Odd duly itemizes the "many peoples" and specifies the reasons for a residue of paganism in Norway. The persistent residue

[30] *The Saga of Olaf Tryggvason*, trans. Andersson, 101.
[31] Ibid.
[32] Ibid.

opens the way for a definition of the relationship between the mission of Olaf Tryggvason and the mission of his successor, Olaf Haraldsson. The latter merits the status of a saint, but Odd is at pains to make it clear that the former is not greatly inferior:

> But the present Olaf Tryggvason, after he lost the realm in the great battle that he fought on Orm inn langi (the Great Serpent), was taken away from us so that mortal men cannot know clearly what the nature of his saintliness is. Nor has it been revealed what signs and miracles are connected with him, but no one doubts that he was sent by God. God also made him more outstanding than other kings and admirable in all providential ways. For that reason we must all praise the name of the Lord Jesus Christ for this man, to whom he granted such great power and distinction, in the same way we praise God for King Olaf the Saint.[33]

This passage looks like the final summation, the final exaltation of Olaf before he meets his fate at Svǫld. It is the logical point at which to wind up his career and turn to his last days. The transition begins well enough with the construction of Olaf's legendary ship the Great Serpent (chapter 53), on which he is destined to succumb. But then, as if by afterthought, Odd reverts to his missionary activities. He describes Olaf's appearance and eloquence one last time and, less to the point, recounts how he convenes yet another assembly in Thrándheim, demolishes an idol of Thor, and kills the chieftain Járnskeggi of Yrjar and converts his terrified followers. That this retrospective positioning of a conversion episode is not inspired by chronological considerations becomes clear at the end of chapter 54: "After the killing of Járnskeggi and after the king had entered into a distinguished marriage with the queen Thyri, he repudiated Járnskeggi's daughter Gudrún."[34] Since the marriage to Thyri was reported much earlier, in chapter 46, the present chapter should have been positioned in that context. The following chapter (55) is no less misplaced; it is in fact a duplicate of chapter 37, in which Olaf executes the recalcitrant heathen Hróald on Godey. Chapter 55 identifies Olaf's victim as Hróald in Moldafjord, far to the south, but the descriptions are so similar that the two passages must be variants of the same incident.

[33] Ibid., 102.
[34] Ibid., 105.

How should we account for these supernumerary conversion episodes? It is difficult to believe that Odd broke the dramatic rhythm of his narrative so awkwardly, but it is also difficult to imagine such a clumsy interpolator. It looks as though Odd wrote as he continued to collect material from his oral informants and added these episodes at the last moment, without recognizing that one of them had already been told.

The miniature chapter 56 adds a further conversion episode, perhaps the most bizarre of all. Olaf seizes an unidentified heathen and kills him by inserting a snake into his mouth. The snake then emerges from the man's stomach carrying his heart in its jaws. The following chapter 57 strikes a new note. It tells the tale of an Icelander named Sigurd who, at the behest of the well-known Icelandic chieftain Thorkel trefil in Borgarfjord, kills King Olaf's forecastleman Grím. The king later captures Sigurd and avenges his retainer by loosing his dog Vígi on the culprit.

This incident would have been passed down in Iceland in transmissions that may well have been the source of the rather rich information about Vígi. But we must ask again why it is positioned as an afterthought. The answer may be that it casts a negative light on Olaf, who is in fact harshly rebuked by the bishop and must do penance. There is perhaps a certain logic in recording Olaf's greatest misdeed, along with his greatest deeds, toward the end of the saga. There may also be a connection between this crime and the statement in the last chapter (78) to the effect that Olaf ended his life in a monastery "and devoted himself to God by the inspiration of the Holy Spirit and dwelt in a monastery in Greece or Syria to repent the misdeeds he had committed in his youth."[35]

Chapter 58 again seems out of sequence. It tells the story of how the brothers Hyrning and Thorgeir, who are married to Olaf's sisters, trick the pretender Gudrød (son of Erik Bloodax) and burn him in his house. These brothers were introduced in chapter S23, and their resolute loyalty might have been mentioned then or at some point when Olaf's claim to the throne was still open to challenge, rather than at the end of his reign.

This section of the saga concludes with a humorous encounter with the god Thor (chapter 59) and a conclave of trolls who have suffered

[35] Ibid., 136.

at Olaf's hands (60)—supernatural matters that might well have been included in chapter 43, together with the demonic visitation by Odin. In short, the whole run of chapters from 54 to 60 amounts to a sort of appendix of episodes that Odd failed to include earlier, all the more so because chapter 62 attaches neatly to what was told in chapter 53 about the building of the Great Serpent. Chapter 62 turns to events in Denmark, where Queen Sigríd inveigles her husband Svein into a campaign against Olaf. But before reviewing the conspiracy that brings about Olaf's downfall, we must return to an early chapter in the saga that is key to understanding Odd's compositional techniques.

The indications thus far are that Odd made extensive use of anecdotal material gathered from his informants, but Olaf's first marriage, to Queen Geira, in chapter 10 has no precedent in the synoptic histories and does not look like a draft on oral tradition, because there is no traceable route of transmission. The episode is part of his legendary prehistory, to which there were no ready witnesses who might have made their way to Norway or Iceland.

During his early adventures Olaf finds himself headed for Russia with his fleet but is thrown off course by a storm and brings his ships to anchor in Wendland. His arrival is reported to the widowed Queen Geira by her trusted lieutenant Dixin, who delivers a long speech praising Olaf's appearance and extraordinary qualities and expressing the suspicion that he may be of royal blood. Dixin proposes forthrightly that this man may be the right husband for Geira, and she accordingly offers him magnificent hospitality. As the festivities proceed, Dixin pursues his marriage project, which eventually comes to fruition. But three years later Geira dies, and Olaf, grief-stricken, makes his way back to Russia.

This romantic interlude connects with nothing else in the saga and has the earmarks of a fiction based on the story of Dido and Aeneas, the hero blown off course and romantically entangled with a widowed and commanding queen. The thought is all the more tempting because there is evidence that Virgil's *Aeneid* was known in Odd's monastery at Thingeyrar and was used by his monastic brother and fellow biographer Gunnlaug Leifsson.[36] But such a borrowing would also involve a major contradiction in Odd's working methods. Thus far he has appeared in the light of a rather inept collector of anecdotal lore, at least

[36] Magerøy 1998, 77; Würth 1998, 38, 48, 56, 59, 71, 82.

where his narrative is not supported by the clear outline of a written source. How do we reconcile our poorly organized folklorist with an innovative adapter of a piece of classical literature? The solution is perhaps that Odd was a rather good narrator as long as the action was clearly laid out for him but that he had compositional difficulties when no overall plot line was available.[37]

His difficulties become particularly apparent in his rendering of the conspiracy against Olaf, because he seems to have had before him conflicting versions of this narrative. Queen Sigríd initiates the conspiracy in Denmark, where she convinces her rather passive husband that he has been disgraced by Olaf's failure to consult him before marrying his sister Thyri. A reluctant King Svein finally acquiesces and allows a plan to go forward whereby Jarl Sigvaldi will be induced to lure Olaf to a meeting of the northern kings, with the additional presence of Olaf's Norwegian rival Jarl Eirík Hákonarson. Olaf agrees to the meeting, but in chapter 63 the plot is suddenly suspended to allow for a new motivation.

Queen Thyri now claims that she is owed money by her brother Svein and asks Olaf to collect the debt. Accordingly, Olaf sets out with a great armed force, but on the way he interviews a blind and prophetic farmer who, unaware of Olaf's identity, predicts that Norway is about to lose four great treasures: king, queen, the Great Serpent, and the legendary dog Vígi. Olaf proceeds on his way, not to Denmark to demand payment for Thyri but to the proposed conference of northern kings. The other kings do not appear because, as is apparent from chapter 62, the real plan is to ambush Olaf on his return from Wendland. But why should he go to Wendland? Why does he not stop in Denmark to demand Thyri's money? Was it not the plan to trap Olaf more or less unarmed rather than with a huge fleet?

The question of Wendland is resolved by shifting ground and reinterpreting Thyri's debt as lands in Wendland that Olaf can demand and receive from the Wendish king Búrizleif. Nonetheless, the complex of conflicting motivations, the fictitious conference of kings, and the exact nature of Thyri's debt leaves a residue of puzzling questions. Odd clearly had both motivations in mind, the ambush with a superior force enabled by the alleged conference and Thyri's debt; one is

[37] Thus Odd's telling of Olaf's flight from Norway may have drawn inspiration from the flight of the Christ child from Herod.

found in Theodoricus and the other in the *Historia Norwegiae* and *Ágrip*.[38] But Odd relapsed into uncritical collecting and failed either to make a decisive choice or to harmonize the contradictions in some plausible way. He did, however, reassert the conversion theme by causing Olaf's enemies to lure him with the prospect of a renewed crusade. Olaf must therefore suffer the irony of falling into the trap because of his ardent devotion to the Christian cause.

The Heroic Finale

On the heels of this particularly ill-wrought narrative comes a spectacularly well-told conclusion, the story of the Battle of Svǫld. The high drama of this sequence has already been signaled by the blind farmer's forecast of Olaf's imminent fall. (This sort of anticipation by prophecy, vision, or dream will come to play an almost threadbare role in the classical sagas, in which no doom is left unforetold.) It is reinforced in Wendland when Olaf's men begin to complain of their long absence from home and are generously released by the king, with the author's clear proviso that they are abandoning their lord in his hour of need. This desertion also has the advantage of explaining away sixty of Olaf's seventy-one ships, leaving him with a remnant of eleven ships against the combined navies of Denmark, Sweden, and dissident Norway. The isolated hero faced by insuperable odds has a long history in heroic literature, not least of all in the heroic legends of medieval Scandinavia.

The drama unfolds slowly. The conspirators, eager for action, keep a sharp lookout for Olaf's Great Serpent. Each time a great ship heaves onto the horizon, it is misidentified by one of the lookouts, and Jarl Eirík is obliged to correct the false impression and urge patience. Finally the Great Serpent appears: "When it approached near enough to be made out, they could see splendid dragon heads shining with great brilliance, and it took a long time for the stern dragon to appear. This ship was all adorned with gold and silver, and everyone stared at the great ship as it advanced. Everyone marvelled how long it took before they saw the stern ornament."[39] It is as if the ship unfurls along the

---

[38] *MHN*, 23–24; *MHN*, 117 (or *Historie Norwegie*, ed. Inger Ekrem and Lars Boye Mortensen, 96), and *Ágrip*, ed. and trans. M. J. Driscoll, 32.

[39] *The Saga of Olaf Tryggvason*, trans. Andersson, 120.

horizon, but even in this fine scene Odd is not as careful as he might be; if we keep count of the misidentifications, it turns out that they add up to sixteen vessels in Olaf's squadron rather than the eleven we have been apprised of. The miscount is, however, easily eclipsed by the protracted drama.

It is Jarl Eirík who proclaims the final identification: "Stand up now, for we need no longer dispute whether this is the Great Serpent; now you can meet up with King Olaf Tryggvason." The enemies lying in ambush and all agog for action are suddenly seized by fear, and Eirík affords them little comfort: "This magnificent ship is fitting for King Olaf inasmuch as he is as much superior to other kings as this ship is superior to other ships."[40] The allies now draw lots and determine that the Danes will attack first.

Olaf's men urge him to save himself, but he has the heroic lexicon well in mind: "Indeed I will not flee, because I would rather fight. He is not a proper king who flees from his enemies out of fear."[41] Olaf then orders that his three largest vessels be chained together with the Great Serpent in the middle. When his lieutenant Úlf the Red voices concern that the Great Serpent will project so far ahead of the other ships as to make the forecastlemen in the prow vulnerable on both flanks, Olaf escalates the heroic rhetoric to high disparagement: "I didn't know that I had a forecastleman who was both a carrot-top and a catamite. I had it built larger than other ships because I wanted it to be as much more conspicuous in battle as it is more splendid under sail than other ships."[42]

The Danes also get a taste of the poisoned phrase. When Olaf learns that they are advancing to the attack, he responds derisively: "The forest goats will not overcome us, for the Danes have the courage of goats." After a long battle the Danes are in fact obliged to withdraw "with little of the glory that King Olaf got." Next it is the turn of the Swedes, who are treated to an even larger dose of vitriol than the Danes because they are heathens: "The Swedes will have an easier and more pleasant time licking out their sacrificial bowls than boarding the Great Serpent in the face of our weapons and succeeding in clearing our ships. I suspect that we will not need to fear these horse eaters."[43]

[40] Ibid.
[41] Ibid.
[42] Ibid., 122.
[43] Ibid., 123–24.

Accordingly, after another prolonged struggle, the Swedes too must retreat.

The epic triad closes with a third attack, this time by Jarl Eiríks Norwegians, who are patriotically portrayed as being more formidable. This culminating encounter is suspended temporarily as the surviving warriors on Olaf's ship are catalogued by name. Only then does Jarl Eirík launch his attack in his ship Járnbardinn (a ship with an ironclad prow). As Olaf watches the approach, he turns respectful: "From this contingent we can expect a hard battle. They are Norwegians like us and have often seen bloody swords and many a passage at arms." Jarl Eirík is also credited with an honest motive: "He is not holding a slack course in our direction, and he probably has it in mind to avenge his father."[44] Nonetheless, Eirík is repelled in the first encounter and must put to shore for fresh crews before making a second attempt.

The renewed attack is prefaced by two strategies, one spiritual and the other material. In the first place, Eirík, the inveterate heathen son of a heathen father, vows to accept baptism if he is victorious. He therefore removes the prow ornament representing Thor in favor of the symbol of the cross. In the second place, he appeals to the wise military strategist Thorkel the Tall to devise some means of overcoming Olaf's giant ship. After some demurral Thorkel eventually contrives a mechanism to drop heavy beams on the Serpent, thus causing it to list. As Eirík now advances a second time, Olaf begins to recognize that time is running out: "Thor is now gone from the prow of Járnbardinn, and the holy cross has been put in his place. The Lord Jesus Christ would presumably rather have two souls than one."[45]

Olaf continues to fight with unprecedented valor, and with one final opportunity to document his Christian right-mindedness. His follower, the celebrated archer Einar Thambarskelfir, tries to bring down Eirík but misses the mark with his first two arrows. Eirík is not sanguine about a third attempt and urges a notable archer in his own retinue to shoot Einar. The archer declines, but he does undertake to disable Einar's bow by hitting it with an arrow of his own: "Einar's bow burst apart. When King Olaf heard the bursting sound, he asked: 'What snapped?' Einar replied: 'Norway was snapped out of your hands, lord,'" said Einar. King Olaf became very angry and said: 'God

---

[44] Ibid., 126.
[45] Ibid., 127.

will determine that, not your bow.'" But a short time later he is obliged to concede that God has decided against him: "Great good fortune is on the side of the jarl, and God now wishes him to have the kingdom and the land."[46] Olaf disappears in a heavenly effulgence, leaving friend and foe to wonder whether he has been slain or has plunged overboard and swum to safety, eventually ending up in a monastery in Greece or Syria.

Odd's saga is a snarl of narrative contradictions. Certain passages are well told and likely to engage the reader's interest. Other passages are badly told and jar the reader's instincts about logic, convincing motivation, and dramatic form. Notably the long central narrative in chapters 26–60 gives the impression of a particularly ill-assorted and ill-shuffled collection of anecdotes about Olaf's encounters with pagan opposition, both human and demonic. These moments are organized neither by chronology nor by topography. There is no indication that they were transmitted in connected narrative, and there is at least one indication (the duplicate attempts to convert Hróald) that the tradition was maintained in the form of separate incidents remembered and relayed by separate informants. Odd's recording does not seem to have improved on the random sequence. The final episodes of those chapters in particular look like an afterthought and could have been worked into the body of the narrative in a more persuasive way.

And yet there are passages throughout the text that are narratively convincing. The tale of Olaf's birth and escape to Russia is one such. The story of his marriage to Geira is short but well contrived. The last days of Jarl Hákon after Olaf's return to Norway are cast in memorable form. The conversion sequence in Iceland is better told than any of the conversion episodes in Norway. Finally, the events leading up to the Battle of Svǫld and the battle itself are recounted in a style hardly destined to be improved on in the later sagas. How do we reconcile these narrative high points with the narrative deficiencies so apparent in the core of the saga?

What the well-told episodes have in common, for the most part, is that they are supported by written models. Olaf's birth and escape are modeled on the nativity of Jesus and his flight into Egypt, supplemented by Joseph's sale into slavery, although the thwarted search for the infant at Mjǫrs and the malicious humiliation of Jarl Hákon at the

---

[46] Ibid., 130–31.

residence of Hákon the Old in Sweden are nowhere foreshadowed and look like examples of native storytelling technique. Queen Geira appears to have learned her role from Dido, without the melodrama. Jarl Hákon's last days may well have been narrated in summary detail in Ari's kings' lives, and Ari palpably provided the narrative of Iceland's conversion.

These brief narrative successes are, however, no match for the extended description of the Battle of Svǫld. The battle is staged with the parallelisms, repetitions, and retardations that are destined to become saga idiom in the next century. The staging is complemented by the incisive dialogue and honed disparagement that are no less hallmarks of the later saga. It is a matter not of an occasional rhetorical flash but of a sustained heroic narrative in a style no less grand (and no less sentimental) than, for example, the story of Kjartan Óláfsson's death in *Laxdæla saga*. The techniques for profiling the death of a hero were apparently fully developed and available at the end of the twelfth century. But in what form?

In this case no written model suggests itself. The technique must have been oral. Odd describes Svǫld as the greatest battle in the North, and the stanzas cited in support of the action give some assurance that the battle lived on in oral transmission. It is assumed that these stanzas were not part of Odd's original text, because translating them into Latin would have been too arduous, but it is nonetheless reasonable to suppose that Odd would have known the stanzas and that much of the transmission would have been consolidated around them.

The existence of a tradition and the dramatizing of that tradition in saga style are, however, separate issues. The written model usually adduced for the prelude to the Battle of Svǫld is Charlemagne's march on Pavia in the Monk of St. Gall's *Life of Charlemagne*. But that account stands model only for the repeated misidentifications, not for the pointed dialogue, the biting deprecation of the enemy, and the self-consciously articulated drama of the sequence as a whole.[47] With no evidence of a complete written model, it seems most likely that the narrative was fashioned from oral precedents.

Odd's *Saga of Olaf Tryggvason* is thus a composite of written and oral sources joined with varying success. The written sources are reasonably transparent, but the oral sources confront us with contradictions.

[47] Ibid., 118–20 and note. See Lönnroth 1963, 85.

At their best they are fully developed and highly dramatic, but at their least effective they are small nodes of tradition without larger context, set down in isolation. We may ask what this contradiction tells us about the oral transmissions of Iceland. Perhaps it tells us that we should not limit ourselves to a simple choice between long and short stories, between dramatic narratives and small units of information. Perhaps we should imagine that both types of transmission were available. They stood to be combined, and it was the art of combination that developed over time and ultimately produced finely articulated narratives quite beyond the range of such early experimenters as Odd Snorrason.

CHAPTER TWO

Sanctifying a Viking Chieftain

The Oldest/Legendary Saga of Saint Olaf

There are some indications that the Icelanders had less oral tradition about Olaf Haraldsson than they had about Olaf Tryggvason, although the former ruled longer and later (1015–30) and should have been in more recent memory. The difference may have been that Olaf Tryggvason enjoyed some quasi-official status as the apostle of Christianity in Iceland, whereas Olaf Haraldsson's reputation was cultivated more particularly in Norway.

We have no list of informants for the *gesta* of Olaf Haraldsson, as we have in the case of Ari Thorgilsson and Odd Snorrason, but similarly knowledgeable men and women must have been available to our saga writer.[1] They would have been heir to a rather rich transmission of skaldic verse composed by Olaf's Icelandic contemporaries, but they would also have had oral reports going back as far as the early eleventh century. Snorri Sturluson's prologue to *The Separate Saga of Saint Olaf* refers to Ari Thorgilsson's foster father and informant Hall Thórarinsson, reemphasizing that he was well informed and had a good memory, extending back to the time he was baptized at the age of three, in 999. Snorri goes on to say that Hall traveled abroad and had a partnership with Saint Olaf, as a result of which he achieved great honor and success: "On this basis he was knowledgeable about his [Olaf's] reign."[2] Snorri also notes that Hall did not die until 1089. Some people who had learned from him would therefore still have been alive in the middle of the twelfth century.

---

[1] *Olafs saga hins helga*, ed. O. A. Johnsen, XIX–XXI.
[2] ÍF 27:420.

Another of Ari's informants was his uncle Thorkel Gellisson, whose father Gellir was much involved in King Olaf Haraldsson's negotiations with Iceland and who is mentioned several times in *Heimskringla*. We will see in addition that the prominent Icelander Hjalti Skeggjason is assigned a central role in Olaf's negotiations with Sweden and would have brought firsthand information back to Iceland. Quite a different source of information would have been the petty Norwegian king Hrœrek Dagsson, who was captured and blinded by Olaf and later banished to Iceland to prevent any conspiratorial activity. He spent one year with the western chieftain Thorgils Arason, who was the grandfather of the Gunnlaug who married Ari's distinguished informant Thuríd Snorradóttir. He spent another year with the great northern chieftain Gudmund inn ríki Eyjólfsson, whose family was much involved in King Olaf's plan to annex Iceland. Hrœrek would have had a great deal to tell about Olaf's coming to Norway and would no doubt have cast it in a less favorable light than appears in the sagas. There would surely have been no lack of tradition concerning the later Olaf.

The first written record emerged in the late twelfth century in the synoptic histories, albeit in a form rather different from the sources on Olaf Tryggvason. Only the *Historia Norwegiae* has anything to relate about Saint Olaf's early years. We are told that he was held in high esteem in Russia, but we are not told how he got there.[3] As an exile he is obliged to take to a life of piracy in the Baltic, but he eventually abandons this worldly way of life in deference to his Christian faith. He subsequently forms an alliance with King Svein Forkbeard of Denmark and invades England, but Svein dies a short time later, leaving Olaf to continue his raiding activities in Britain and as far afield as Spain. Ultimately, he joins Svein's son Cnut (the Great) in a renewed campaign against England and distinguishes himself by reducing London Bridge, but for this service he receives no reward. A plan to marry the Swedish princess "Margaret" also comes to nothing when her father decides to marry her instead to King Yaroslav in Russia against her will. Margaret's "wise" but unnamed sister succeeds in easing the tensions by entering a sort of compensatory marriage to Olaf. Sometime later Olaf sails from England to Norway with two ships and four bishops, but the *Historia Norwegiae* fragment breaks off without providing an account of events in Norway.[4]

---

[3] *A History of Norway,* ed. and trans. Carl Phelpstead and Devra Kunin, 23.
[4] Ibid., 25.

For the remainder of the story we must turn to Theodoricus and *Ágrip,* two sources that have virtually no overlap with the *Historia Norwegiae.* It is in fact quite striking that, aside from Theodoricus's brief mention of Olaf's support of King Ethelred in England and his equally brief mention of Olaf's interview with a prophetic hermit, neither text has anything to say about Olaf's birth, refuge in Russia, or early adventures.[5] They pick up the story only after his arrival in Norway, but from this point they have closely matching accounts and chronologies.

Olaf lands on the island of Sæla and shortly thereafter captures the unsuspecting ruler of Norway (under the aegis of Denmark), Hákon Eiríksson. This Hákon is in fact the son of the Jarl Eirík who defeated Olaf Tryggvason at Svǫld. The first winter in Norway Olaf spends with his foster father and mother in Upplǫnd. Thereafter he pursues his conquest and defeats Svein, the son of King Cnut of Denmark and later England, at the Battle of Nesjar. That is the sum total of the information provided on his conquest. It is followed by a very brief statement about how he fostered Christianity and strengthened the kingdom (not remotely comparable to Olaf Tryggvason's long string of conversion activities). Both synoptics then pick up the failed betrothal to Princess Ingigerd of Sweden and Olaf's compensatory marriage to her younger sister Ástríd. With Ástríd he has a daughter (Úlfhild in Theodoricus, Gunnhild in *Ágrip*), who is later married to Duke Otto of Saxony, a story that is developed at considerable length in *Morkinskinna.*[6]

That is the extent of Olaf's initial thirteen-year reign in Norway, according to the accounts of Theodoricus and *Ágrip.* What follows is the story of his demise and death. King Cnut incites the northern chieftains against him, and the tensions are exacerbated when Olaf's follower Áslák fitjaskalli kills Olaf's principal antagonist, Erling Skjálgsson. The upshot is that Olaf must flee Norway and take refuge in Russia once more. King Cnut secures Norway under the rule first of his nephew Hákon and then of his son Svein.

Both Theodoricus and *Ágrip* catalogue Olaf's chief opponents and recount how he returned to Norway to be joined by friends and kinsmen. On the details of the final Battle of Stiklarstadir the sources differ somewhat, but they reconverge on the date of the battle and the first miracles. Taken together, these narratives may serve to convey some idea of the information on Olaf available in the late twelfth century: it

[5] Th, 19; *Ágrip,* ed. and trans. Driscoll, 34.
[6] *Morkinskinna,* trans. Andersson and Gade, 115–23.

would have included the landing at Sæla, the encounter with Hákon Eiríksson in Saudungssund, Olaf's first winter in Upplǫnd, the Battle of Nesjar, some account of Olaf's reign, his marriage, exile, and ill-fated return.

Here I must pause to explain the cryptic dual title *Oldest/Legendary Saga*. It refers to two closely related saga texts. What we call *The Oldest Saga* survives only in six rather short fragments from a version that is estimated to have been written circa 1200.[7] A comparison of the fragments with *The Legendary Saga* suggests that the latter is a slightly abbreviated redaction of *The Oldest Saga* with, as we shall see, two substantial and quite easily isolable interpolations.[8] The comments below therefore refer largely to the text of *The Legendary Saga* minus the two interpolations.

The general outlines provided by the synoptics were not the only source of information for the authors of *The Oldest/Legendary Saga*. Also available was an extensive stock of skaldic verse, from which the author drew no fewer than sixty-three stanzas or partial stanzas. We have seen that the translator of Odd's *Saga of Olaf Tryggvason*, probably not Odd himself, also drew on the skalds but only toward the end of the saga and only to the extent of fourteen stanzas. The biography of Olaf Haraldsson thus marks the first extensive use of the skaldic corpus in the sagas. It may well be that the author of *The Oldest Saga* (the fragments cite six full stanzas) knew the translation of *The Saga of Olaf Tryggvason* and was inspired by this precedent to make fuller use of the skaldic reservoir.

Chapter 11 cites a stanza from the skald Sigvat's "Víkingarvísur" (viking-raid verses) celebrating Olaf's victory at London Bridge. It is followed by ten more stanzas attributed to Olaf himself, but a number of these appear to be misattributed; they belong to a poem about an attack on London by Cnut the Great in 1016.[9] The critical use of skaldic verse had clearly not yet reached the level attained by the author of *Morkinskinna* and Snorri Sturluson. Chapter 13 cites two more half-stanzas from the "Víkingarvísur" on battles fought by Olaf at Canterbury and an unidentified location. In chapters 24 and 25 another stanza and a half from Sigvat's "Nesjavísur" (Nesjar verses) underpin Olaf's

---

[7] The fragments were first edited by Gustav Storm in *Otte brudstykker* (1893). On the later discussion see, Andersson in *ONIL*, 212–13.

[8] The problem is clearly set out in Jónas Kristjánsson 1976.

[9] Finnur Jónsson 1920–24, 1:459.

naval victory at Nesjar. In chapter 46, a stanza from "Hǫfuðlausn" (head ransom) by Óttar svarti (the black) celebrates Olaf's subjection of the Shetland Islands.

But it is not until chapter 56, about halfway through the saga, that the stanzas become dense. In a sequence of six chapters (56–61) there are twenty-two and a half stanzas and a stray line. This sequence is particularly interesting because it is not the customary catalogue of battle stanzas from praise poems but rather a collection of what might almost be described as domestic scenes, involving several skalds shuttling among the Scandinavian monarchs but generally ending up with Olaf. Chapter 57 identifies them as Sigvat (Thórdarson), Óttar svarti, Thórarin loftunga, and Thorfinn munn. Chapter 61 adds Thórd Háreksson (*recte* Særeksson) and Hárek ór Thjóttu.

Chapter 57 tells how Óttar svarti leaves Iceland, visits first with King Olaf of Sweden, and then with King Cnut in Denmark. To the latter he expresses the wish to visit with King Olaf in Norway, but Cnut warns him that Olaf is angered by a love poem Óttar has composed for Queen Ástríd and recommends that he revise certain passages. Óttar presents Olaf with the revised version and, in addition, a panegyric (of which only a line is recorded), and the brash skald is duly forgiven. There follows a completely incidental stanza in which the skald asks the king for a sword. Equally unmotivated is a stanza in which Sigvat expresses his pleasure that Olaf acted as his daughter's godfather and a love stanza attributed to Olaf himself and, according to the prose, addressed to Ingibjǫrg Finnsdóttir, who could be the daughter of Olaf's ally Finn Árnason.

These stanzas have nothing to do with Olaf's reign or royal fortunes and must have been preserved only in the context of the Icelandic skalds. They show that the traditions in Iceland were not exclusively organized around the Norwegian court. They codified the lives of the skalds, too, but it is one of the compositional failings in *The Oldest/Legendary Saga* that these quite separate traditions are not well integrated. Chapter 58 continues in the same style with an exchange of stanzas between Óttar and King Olaf about one of Óttar's love adventures, followed by two peculiarly trivial stanzas in which Sigvat and Óttar commemorate an occasion on which King Olaf sent a gift of nuts to their table. Perhaps the real point of the episode was lost in the transmission. Quite unconnected is another episode in which the king orders Thormód to compose a stanza about Sigurd the Dragonslayer, who is depicted on a hall tapestry. Finally, there is an account of Stein Skaptason, the son of the Icelandic lawspeaker Skapti Thóroddsson, who commits a killing, is pardoned by King Olaf, and eventually runs off to join King Cnut in Denmark.[10] The anecdote goes on to tell how Stein extracted an additional payment from Cnut but lost his favor in the process.

The adventures of Stein Skaptason would, again, have been of interest only in Icelandic circles and would presumably have been transmitted by Stein's descendants. The episode is curiously isolated in *The Legendary Saga* (it is guaranteed for *The Oldest Saga* by fragment 3), but the wealth of such transmissions is bespoken by Snorri Sturluson, who tells us that not only Stein came from Iceland at Olaf's summons but also Snorri the Chieftain's son Thórodd, Gellir Thorkelsson, and Egil, the son of Sídu-Hall.[11] According to Snorri's chronology, they arrived the year after the death of the great northern chieftain Gudmund Eyjólfsson in 1025, and they represented some of the foremost families in Iceland. We will see below why they may have been summoned by King Olaf, but it seems in any event certain that their dealings with the king would have lived on in memory.

The random episodes in these chapters illustrate that the author attempted to fill out the core of the saga with narrative matter available in Iceland. The procedure is not unlike what is found in Odd's *Saga of Olaf Tryggvason,* and the effect is similarly disorganized. The episodes do not combine into a coherent narrative, and there is no attempt at a chronology; the author merely sets down scattered traditions in disconcertingly abbreviated form. Such random recording does not, however, begin as late as chapters 56–61. Egil Hallsson's experiences at Olaf's court are related in chapters 50–52; earlier still, in chapters 40–42, Olaf summons the Icelander Hjalti Skeggjason to act as an intermediary in his dealings with King Olaf of Sweden. These dealings have turned hostile because of competing territorial claims. It seems unlikely that King Olaf would have depended solely on an Icelander for such a delicate diplomatic mission, but it is not implausible that Icelandic tradition would have inflated Hjalti's role in this way.[12]

---

[10] Stein's parentage is not identified here but can be found in *Heimskringla* (ÍF 27:220).

[11] Ibid. Thórodd is mentioned in *The Legendary Saga* (*Olaf saga hins helga,* ed. and trans. A. Heinrichs et al.), chapter 78; Egil Hallsson is mentioned in chapters 50–52.

[12] On the improbability, see Schottmann 1994:541.

The tale is characteristic of saga style to the extent that it credits the protagonist with almost preternatural foresight. Hjalti responds to the summons by traveling directly to Sweden without honoring the Norwegian court with a visit on the way. This apparent affront is destined to pay rich dividends, for Hjalti is received graciously by the Swedish king only because he appears to be uncompromised by any contact with his Norwegian rival. Hjalti is allowed to converse with the king's daughter Ingigerd and avails himself of the opportunity to play the matchmaker, as Dixin did in the marriage negotiations between Olaf Tryggvason and Queen Geira. He praises the Norwegian king to her and suggests that their marriage would alleviate the difficulties between the two countries. Ingigerd is not averse. Hjalti feels encouraged to pursue his representations with her father, who also appreciates the advantages of the arrangement. A meeting between the kings takes place, and the match is concluded. The plan later disintegrates, but Hjalti has done his part brilliantly and returns to Iceland.[13]

Olaf's failed betrothal to Ingigerd is mentioned in all three synoptic histories and would have been common knowledge, but the saga author converts the bare mention of the failure into an intriguing narrative with a display of diplomatic ingenuity and eloquence based entirely on Icelandic transmissions. Indeed, the whole stretch of narrative from chapter 40 through chapter 61 appears to be elaborated on the basis of Icelandic tradition. Chapters 40–43 constitute the story of Hjalti's diplomacy. Chapter 44 again expands the information in the synoptics, telling how Olaf was married to his Swedish rival's second daughter Ástríd, how their daughter Úlfhild was married to Duke Otto of Saxony, and how Olaf fathered an illegitimate son Magnús with his wife's washerwoman, Álfhild.

Chapters 45–46 turn to the beginning of King Olaf's political troubles: King Cnut's demand for tribute and the first stirring of resistance among the Norwegian magnates. This narrative prefaces a fuller account in chapters 47–49 of how a certain Ásbjǫrn Sigurdarson—the nephew of Olaf's chief antagonist, Erling Skjálgsson—kills the king's steward Thórir sel and is condemned to death. The Icelander Thórarin Nefjólfsson is able to delay the execution until Erling Skjálgsson arrives on the scene to effect a settlement. Thórarin Nefjólfsson is described by Snorri as a northern Icelander of no great lineage, but his

---

[13] On Hjalti's mission in general see Johnsen 1916.

diplomatic achievement seems nonetheless to have been preserved in tradition and thus becomes a foundation for this episode.[14]

Chapters 50–52 recount the story of the Icelander Egil Hallsson and his eloquent intervention on behalf of the heathen Gautlander Valgard. Eloquence, it is clear, was an accomplishment that the Icelanders were eager to attribute to their ancestors. Chapters 53–54 relate incidents connected with an otherwise unidentified Dane named Sigurd, who is banished by King Cnut but takes refuge with Olaf. The point of the story seems to be that Sigurd benefits from a miracle performed by Olaf, but there is no indication of how the story got to Iceland. Chapters 55–56 provide a somewhat analogous account of how Thormód Bersason took service with King Cnut but later made his escape to join the service of King Olaf. Three stanzas suggest that the narrative had been passed down in memory. Chapters 57–62 contain the incidents already reviewed above and are, once again, derivative from Olaf's Icelandic skalds. Thus chapters 40–62 overall are a fairly mechanical collection, in no particular order, of narratives available in Iceland.

Chapter 63 returns in earnest to Olaf's political troubles and marks the beginning of the end. But before the conclusion of the story, skaldic stanzas, which are the core source throughout, surface in three more clusters: a small cluster of four stanzas in chapters 62–65; a sequence of six stanzas from a panegyric composed by Thórarin loftunga (praise-tongue) for King Cnut in chapter 70; and a collection of thirteen stanzas in chapters 78–88 relating to the Battle of Stiklarstadir and its aftermath. The first cluster (three stanzas assigned to Sigvat and one to Olaf himself) pertains to the killing of Erling Skjálgsson and expands the information available in the synoptics. The second cluster from Thórarin's panegyric on Cnut is of particular interest because it reemphasizes the international scope of the Icelandic skalds, who were by no means restricted to the Norwegian court. The final group is attributed to three skalds: eleven to Thormód (whose stanzas focus more on Olaf) and one each to Thorfinn and Sigvat.

Despite the king's heroic last stand, the reader may sense reservations as early as Theodoricus's somewhat strained protestations: "Dogged in his pursuit of justice for all, he persecuted no one, oppressed no one, condemned no one except, to be sure, those whose own wickedness and persistence in evil had already condemned them."

[14] ÍF 27:125, 215–18.

As Olaf's death approaches, Theodoricus continues in the same vein: "This man, born in almost the remotest parts of the North, among barbarians and savages, see how he shone forth like a star, how humble he was and how sublime, and this not in a slave's condition, but in the exalted rank of king." And finally: "His purpose was manifest beyond all doubt and free from any uncertainty—to keep wicked men and criminals from persecuting those who were good."[15] There is an undertone of rebuttal in these passages that surfaces explicitly in *The Legendary Saga* (chapter 28) in a statement made peculiarly self-conscious by unremitting alliteration:

> His reputation was uneven as long as he was in this world. Many said he was domineering and autocratic, hard and vengeful, grasping and acquisitive, irascible and difficult, ostentatious and arrogant, and all in all a worldly chieftain. But those who knew him better said that he was mild and humble, good-hearted and amenable, mild-mannered and gentle, wise and popular, reliable and faithful, attentive and dependable, generous and munificent, reputable and right-minded, distinguished and just, good and law-abiding, authoritative and moderate, submissive to the laws of God and good men.[16]

The author completes the balance sheet by stressing Olaf's humility one more time: "And now God allows his glory to shine all the more brightly because he worshipped Him more during his lifetime and humbled himself in corresponding measure to God and men."[17] The emphasis on humility echoes Theodoricus, but the author reveals the other side of the ledger as well and thereby signals a discrepancy in public opinion that is carefully obscured by the Norwegian writer Theodoricus.

Yet *The Oldest/Legendary Saga* does not reveal what may have been the greatest source of detraction from Olaf's reputation in Iceland. That aspect remained for Snorri Sturluson to add into the story a quarter-century after *The Oldest Saga.* In chapter 124 of his *Saga of Saint Olaf* in *Heimskringla,* Snorri takes note of the extremes to which King Olaf went to secure friendly relations with the Icelandic chieftains, but he

---

[15] Th, 21–22, 30.
[16] *Olafs saga hins helga,* ed. and trans. A. Heinrichs et al., 80–82.
[17] Ibid., 82.

goes on to suggest a little cryptically that there was a hidden motive: "In this proof of friendship that the king demonstrated toward Iceland there were other elements that were later revealed."[18]

The revelation comes immediately in the next chapter, in which King Olaf dispatches Thórarin Nefjólfsson to Iceland to propose that Iceland submit to his rule and make him a gift of the island of Grímsey north of Eyjafjord. Thórarin addresses the Allthing (annual assembly), and the first reactions are positive, but when the Eyfirdingar sit down to discuss the surrender of their island, Gudmund Eyjólfsson's brother Einar rises to deliver a memorable political speech:

> I have not said much about this matter because no one has asked me, but if I am to express my view, I believe that the right choice for us Icelanders is not to submit to tribute gifts to King Olaf, or to any such impositions as he has levied against the people of Norway. That will be an infringement not only of our liberty but also the liberty of all our descendants who dwell in this land, and that forfeiture of freedom will never be reversed or loosen its grip on this land. Even if the king is good, as I believe he is, it will continue to be the case, as it always has been when there is a change of ruler, that not all kings are the same—some are good and some bad. But if our countrymen wish to maintain the liberty that they have enjoyed since this land was settled, the right policy will be to give the king no foothold, either in the form of land or in response to demands for tribute that might be understood as homage.
>
> On the other hand, it would be good for those who so desire to send the king friendly gifts, hawks or horses, wall hangings or sails, or other such things as are appropriate. It is a good bargain if we can get his friendship in return. But on the score of Grímsey it should be pointed out that if no food resources are removed, an army of men can be maintained there. And if it is a foreign army and they bring longships to our shores, I believe that many poor farmers will find their doorways rather narrow.[19]

It seems unlikely that Snorri invented this decisive opposition to King Olaf, in particular because it is supported by a stanza attributed to Einar in two manuscripts.[20] The authors of *The Oldest Saga* and *The*

[18] ÍF 27:214.
[19] Ibid., 216. On the narrow doorways, see Taylor 1997.
[20] ÍF 27:XLIX.

Legendary Saga may have known about this crisis of independence as well, but since the saga as a whole is designed to celebrate Olaf, they had good reason to suppress it. If the story of Olaf's attempted annexation was in general circulation, however, it would certainly seem to betoken a mixed view of Olaf Haraldsson among the Icelanders.

So far we have lingered in the central chapters and the traditions underlying them but have scarcely touched on the beginning or the end of the saga. The core narrative has something in common with Odd's *Saga of Olaf Tryggvason* in its composition: both assemble an unarticulated collection of incidental information, although in Odd's case the collection remains clearly focused on the protagonist and his policies, whereas the saga of Olaf Haraldsson digresses into the neighboring realms of Denmark, Iceland, and Sweden.

The beginning and end of *The Oldest/Legendary Saga* are more in line with the structure of Odd's *Saga of Olaf Tryggvason*—both texts start with the birth of the protagonist and conclude with his fall in a great battle—but the resemblance is superficial. Whereas the birth of Olaf Tryggvason is neatly modeled on the nativity of Jesus, the escape from Herod, and Joseph's sale into slavery, Olaf Haraldsson's birth is embedded in a tale of domestic drama and magic typical of hero stories. The regional king of Vík and Vestfold in eastern Norway, a certain Olaf digrbeinn or Geirstadaálf, has an intimation of death and publicizes the coming event. Once dead, he appears in a dream to a man named Hrani, ordering him to enter his burial mound and remove his grave goods. The deceased Olaf instructs Hrani further to place the belt thus acquired around his (Olaf's) daughter-in-law Ásta to enable her to give birth. The remedy succeeds, but Ásta's father, Gudbrand kúla, wants the child exposed, and although his reasons are not clear, his wish prevails. But when a mysterious light appears over the shed in which the child is exposed, he is rescued, baptized with the name Olaf, and raised by Hrani.

In one of the duplications characteristic of the composition of *The Oldest/Legendary Saga* the child is baptized a second time two chapters later, this time by Olaf Tryggvason. He grows up with a precocious intelligence and a sense of imperious self-possession, particularly at the expense of his commoner stepfather, Sigurd sýr (sow). Miraculous birth and precocious development are certain marks of the hero tale. Anne Heinrichs has studied the tale, which is transmitted in a number of variants, in detail and concludes that this variation is indicative of oral proliferation.[21] Whether the proliferation is oral or literary, the tale would seem to be popular in origin, rather than biblical, as in the case of Olaf Tryggvason, although the heavenly light over the shed in which Olaf is exposed may well be a biblical supplement inspired by the Star of Bethlehem.

Olaf's early years are also predominantly secular, though with a certain admixture of the sacred. The *Historia Norwegiae* refers to a period in Russia, but *The Oldest/Legendary Saga* shows no awareness of this phase. Instead, Olaf begins adult life as a viking in the Baltic, then campaigns in England, first against Ethelred and later in league with him. He ultimately joins forces with King Cnut in England with the stipulation that Cnut renounce any claim to Norway. This agreement provides the political justification for Olaf's later conflict with Cnut.

Chapters 12–18 are a poorly integrated enumeration of military successes and intimations of religious devotion. Olaf's prompt attendance at church services is compared favorably with Cnut's dilatoriness. It is also revealed that Olaf wears a hair shirt under his magnificent attire. He fights a series of battles, in the last of which it appears that a host of angels comes to his aid. In more practical terms he captures a jarl and pockets a ransom of 12,000 gold shillings. In the course of further harrying among the heathens he also kills a huge sea monster. Eventually he sails to Sweden, where the Swedish Olaf hopes to trap his three ships in the winter ice, but he manages to keep them afloat by burning pyres around them. In the spring the Swedish king thinks that he has Olaf in his grasp, but a spit of land miraculously splits, allowing Olaf to escape and sail to safety.

More raiding in the West culminates when Olaf's ships are stranded off Ireland. Finding himself surrounded, he advises his men to renounce their viking life, and no sooner have they done so than God refloats their ships and frees them. That miracle is followed by a meeting with a seeress who states that Olaf is bathed in supernatural light and brightness, but the religious buildup is once more cut short by a stray incident in which Olaf kills a great boar. Finally, Olaf sends a servant in royal disguise to a prophetic hermit, who immediately penetrates the disguise and dismisses the impostor. Olaf must therefore appear in person to interrogate the hermit. He learns that he will be not only a temporal king but an eternal king as well.

[21] A. Heinrichs 1989.

The aim of this section is to provide Olaf with a miraculous birth, assemble information on his early adventures, and point the way toward his Christian mission and martyrdom, but the narrative material is jumbled. The circumstances of Olaf's birth are odd and open to distracting questions: What is the nature of Gudbrand kúla's hostility? What causes the delayed and difficult birth? Why should the child be exposed?

The combination of military exploits and religious intimations is similarly awkward; the former are for the most part not fully developed, and the latter seem haphazard. Perhaps the most convincing integration comes with Olaf's miraculous escape from Ireland and his meeting with the prophetic hermit in England, but both these episodes may be literarily dependent on the equivalent passages in *The Saga of Olaf Tryggvason* and owe their form to Odd's superior craft.

Odd is clearly the better narrator. There is drama, ingenuity, and humor in his story of Olaf Tryggvason's birth, escape, and exile, and he manages the transition from religious indeterminacy to Christian commitment more adroitly than *The Oldest/Legendary Saga*, which provides no stages in religious development. Odd also gives a more vivid account of Olaf's return to Norway, however unlikely it may seem that his predecessor would have lured him back. In the case of Olaf Haraldsson, the king apparently lands on Sæla without plan or preparation and overcomes his rivals with little in the way of scenic elaboration. The only exception is the metaphorical moment when Norway is snapped from Svein Knútsson's hands, but that too is most likely to be borrowed from an almost identical episode in Odd's saga.[22]

The discrepancy in narrative craft is no less evident in the sections leading up to the last stands of the two Olafs. Chapters 65–71 describe Olaf Haraldsson's retreat from Norway to Sweden and Russia in the face of King Cnut's onslaught. He remains in Russia for two years, then launches his return (chapters 72–82). The auspices are somewhat confusing. We are told that the Norwegians dispatch deputies to inform Olaf that Norway is without a ruler, but this misinformation is in direct contradiction to the previous chapter (71), in which we are told that after Hákon's death, Cnut had installed his son Svein on the Norwegian throne. This is one of the numerous little confusions strewn along the reader's path, but a more general defect is the author's failure to establish thematic consistency or a dramatic line.

[22] Andersson 2004a, 150–51.

We could argue that the final chapters aim to focus Olaf's emerging saintliness, something that the previous chapters have failed to achieve consistently. In the present sequence almost every chapter includes a miracle or a demonstration of devotion. Olaf heals a child by putting a piece of bread in his mouth, and he declines the service of two heathen berserks (chapter 72). He has a vision in which he surveys the whole world and is pronounced holy by a bishop (73). The standard-bearer appointed by his enemies goes blind, and Olaf predicts the survival of a farmer's two devoted sons (74). His horse stumbles and breaks its legs, but Olaf miraculously resets them; in addition, a drink of water provided for him turns to wine or mead (75). He erects tents and orders masses for the souls of his enemies (76). The two heathen berserks rejected in chapter 72 now convert and join his force (77). Olaf dreams that he has reached the last rung to heaven and orders his men to confess and take communion before the battle (78). One enemy repents of having accepted King Cnut's money and is assigned the task of caring for the wounded (80). Olaf leaves instructions to wash the wounded in the same water used to wash his own body (81). Finally, when he is wounded, he throws away his sword and prays for his enemies (82).

These incidents seem consistent enough to create a valedictory tone, but they are so diluted by other materials that the tone falters. Often enough the result is outright dissonance. Thus Olaf's solicitude for the farmer's sons in chapter 74 is adjacent to a half-humorous anecdote in which Thormód eats a sausage on Friday and responds to a rebuke by saying that it will take more than a sausage to stand between him and Christ. Then, immediately after the transubstantiation of water into wine or mead in chapter 75, Olaf jokes with an Icelander, puns on the name of an enemy (Hrút = "ram" for the slaughter), and kills a hundred men. In these and several other episodes the focus shifts disconcertingly from Olaf to quite incidental figures and diffuses the valedictory effect. This hybrid style differs markedly from Odd's conclusion, in which Olaf Tryggvason holds center stage in almost operatic grandeur.

Not even Olaf Haraldsson's death is scenically realized; here the narrative suffers from the same sort of confusion that besets the saga as a whole. After another quite incidental and inapposite exchange with the skald Thormód (chapter 81) we are told that there was a powerful attack and a stubborn defense. Then, almost incidentally, we are told that the king was killed: "Then it came to pass here that King Olaf lost his life in this battle."[23] In contrast to Odd's careful staging, Olaf Haraldsson dies, in a manner of speaking, offstage. But no sooner is his death reported than he is brought back to life in order to impart some advice on weapons. That opens the way for a reenactment of his death, in tandem with the incidental information that Erling ór Gerdi was the first in the farmers' coalition to fall—"it was also early in the battle that King Olaf fell"[24]—but this time we learn that he had been wounded in the leg by an unnamed relative of Kálf Árnason. In chapter 82 yet a third variant relates that as soon as Olaf was wounded, he threw his sword away and was killed by Thórir hund and Thorstein knarrarsmid; at the same time there was a solar eclipse. It seems clear that the author had several versions of the event in hand but elected not to coordinate them into a single scene.

What we have reviewed thus far is likely to have been in *The Oldest Saga* as well as *The Legendary Saga,* but a consensus holds that two substantial passages in the latter were not in the original text and accrued by interpolation. One of these need be mentioned only in passing: it comprises a long appendix of miracles in chapters 90–107. The reason for believing that these miracles are a later addition is not only that they are a disconnected catalogue but that unlike the saga text up to this point—which is somewhat abbreviated, compared with the six fragments of *The Oldest Saga*—they can be compared with separate miracle transmissions and prove not to be abbreviated.[25] They were therefore not subject to the general revision that converted *The Oldest Saga* into *The Legendary Saga* and must have been added in after that revision was complete.[26]

Of much greater interest is a second interpolation, which appears as chapters 31–36 and 68–69 in *The Legendary Saga.* We have seen by comparison with Odd's *Saga of Olaf Tryggvason* that the accounts of Saint Olaf have little to say about his conversion activities. The author (or reviser) of *The Legendary Saga* must have been cognizant of this lack and tried to remedy it with at least one extended conversion episode. That the episode came from a written source and not tradition is demonstrated by the fact that it appears in Snorri Sturluson's *Saga of Saint Olaf* in

---

[23] *Olafs saga hins helga,* ed. and trans. A. Heinrichs et al., 194.

[24] Ibid., 196.

[25] *A History of Norway,* ed. and trans. Carl Phelpstead and Devra Kunin, xl.

[26] These miracles can be read in Devra Kunin's translation (ibid., 32–74).

largely the same wording, although it seems clear that Snorri did not take it over from *The Legendary Saga*. Rather, both *The Legendary Saga* and Snorri seem to have adopted the same independent conversion tale.[27]

The episode is inserted after two very short chapters (29–30) in which we are told that Olaf restored Christianity completely; thus, the insertion is clearly intended to substantiate this general claim. We learn that the chieftain Dala-Gudbrand in Gudbrandsdal hears of Olaf's mission, summons an assembly, and proposes to intimidate the king with the sight of the local idol of Thor. In a preliminary skirmish, Olaf routs Gudbrand's son, who returns to his father thoroughly chastened. Both Gudbrand and his chief lieutenant Thórd ístrumagi have ominous dreams and resolve to hold a joint assembly with the king.

At the assembly Olaf preaches conversion, but Gudbrand derides a god who cannot be seen—unlike his own god Thor who is on display every day (although on this particular day he must be kept indoors because it happens to be raining). Gudbrand challenges Olaf's God to demonstrate His alleged power by making the sky merely overcast on the following day. On that day the bishop delivers a further exhortation, but Thórd ístrumagi scoffs at the new God and challenges Him to make the sun shine the next day. That night Olaf instructs his men to bore holes in Gudbrand's boats.

Before sunrise on the third day the heathens carry their idol of Thor triumphantly onto the assembly grounds, and Gudbrand delivers yet another disparaging speech about Olaf's God. In the meantime, Olaf whispers to his lieutenant, Kolbein, bidding him smash the idol of Thor with his cudgel while the heathens are not looking. He then delivers a rebuttal about the helplessness of a manmade idol and signals the visible manifestation of his own God as the sun rises brilliantly. When the heathens turn to look at the blinding apparition, Kolbein destroys the idol, and the heathens disperse in consternation. With their boats disabled, however, they have no means of escape and are forced to accede to Olaf's renewed appeal to convert.

Even if there were no other indications that this episode is interpolated, we would have to surmise that it has a separate origin because it is narratively so superior to anything else in the saga. The intricate plotting, the creation of scenic detail, the self-conscious symmetries, and the ironizing speeches have no counterparts elsewhere in the text.

[27] Jónas Kristjánsson 1976; Andersson 1988a.

These compositional niceties are, however, not the direct outgrowth of native narrative practices. The construction of the episode is based on a familiar hagiographic pattern that has been called the thaumaturgic duel, a contest in which the true God vanquishes blind superstition.[28] In this instance the contest culminates in the moment when the mystery of divine invisibility is revealed in the embodiment of the sunrise, the *sol salutis*. The creation is entirely literary, although the narrative contrivances may owe a good deal to native storytelling practices.

What makes the episode compositionally interesting is the evidence that storytelling skills could be applied to any material, whether native or foreign, traditional or literary. Odd fashioned the Battle of Svǫld in all probability with the aid of oral prototypes, but the unknown author of Gudbrand's conversion fashioned the tale on the basis of a hagiographic commonplace. What conclusion should we draw from this narrative flexibility? I noted above that there is no evidence of professional storytellers in Iceland, but that does not mean that there were not more- and less-skilled storytellers. The authors of *The Oldest/Legendary Saga* show no signs of highly developed skills, but the author of this conversion anecdote was an exceptionally gifted narrator.

A further question arises in connection with this narrative gem: What motivated the writer to create a single conversion episode in the apparent absence of any tradition about Saint Olaf's conversion activities? It is as if the author undertook the task of remedying a defective tradition. But the lack of conversion information would have become apparent only when some version of Saint Olaf's saga was committed to writing, making it obvious that a whole phase of his activity was missing. That would suggest that Gudbrand's story was composed with a knowledge of, or even in conjunction with, the written saga. It would hardly have made sense for an Icelander (the level of narrative skill suggests that the author was an Icelander) to compose an isolated conversion anecdote about a Norwegian king unless it was to supplement a larger Icelandic project.

The separate genesis of saga and conversion tale suggests in any case how flexible saga writing was in the early stages. The narrative could be tightened, expanded, or supplemented from oral or literary sources. License to elaborate was in fact a central feature of the art, as we will see in Chapter 4.

[28] Bang 1897; Martínez Pizarro 1985; Andersson 1988a.

CHAPTER THREE

Creating Personalities

The Saga Age Icelanders

King Olaf Tryggvason and King Olaf Haraldsson were remembered as great promoters of the faith and men of heroic dimensions, but it is difficult for a reader of their sagas to assess their personal qualities beyond the accomplishments required by their roles. They occasionally interact with their wives or their followers, though almost never in a way that is revealing about these relationships. Neither thoughts, reflections, principles, nor motivations are developed in such a way as to explain their actions. The reader is not invited to see them as characters impelled by a particular style or inner conviction. And yet, when the Icelanders began to write sagas about their ancestors, it is precisely this personal perspective that we find in some of the earliest texts, in which the actions of the protagonists are consistently viewed as expressions of their personalities. This chapter will deal with five of these sagas: *Víga-Glúms saga, Reykdœla saga, Fóstbrœðra saga, Heiðarvíga saga,* and *Gísla saga Súrssonar.* Each of these stories is predicated on the personal idiosyncrasies of one or more characters. Whereas the sagas of the two Olafs were clearly construed as biographies, the first sagas about Icelanders might better be understood as portraiture. In each case it is the profile of the man that focuses our attention and centers the action. We may not remember episodes in much detail, but the personalities stay with us.

Víga-Glúms saga

At the conclusion of *Víga-Glúms saga* the protagonist earns one of the most unambiguous memorials conferred on a saga hero: "People agree that Glúm was the greatest chieftain in Eyjafjord for twenty years, and for another twenty years none was more than his equal. People also agree that Glúm was the most outstanding among all warriors in this country" (chapter 28; ÍF 9:98). The task confronting the saga author was therefore to justify this reputation and account for Glúm's record in Eyjafjord, a task that does not appear to differ greatly from the mission undertaken by Odd Snorrason and the author of *The Oldest Saga of Saint Olaf*. The approaches nonetheless diverge widely. Whereas the lives of the two Olafs are chronicled in straightforward and extensive detail, the men themselves remain opaque. Glúm Eyjólfsson, by contrast, is primarily a personality and only secondarily a political figure. We learn relatively little about his leadership style but a great deal about his innate qualities. It is therefore clear that at some point in early saga writing the art of characterization came to the fore, a development that is most likely to have been promoted by native storytelling conventions. This hypothesis would account for the fact that characterization is so sparse in the kings' sagas and so conspicuous in the native sagas, with a first great culmination in *Egils saga* (see Chapter 5 below).

In *Víga-Glúms saga,* characterization emerges at the very outset in a testy exchange between Glúm's grandfather Ingjald (son of one of the great colonists in the north, Helgi the Thin) and his son Eyjólf. Ingjald is described as "cantankerous, taciturn, quarrelsome, and stubborn" (chapter 1; ÍF 9:4), and he confirms these traits when his more open and sociable son invites a Norwegian merchant to stay with them. The author seems intent not so much on what happened as on letting the readers know what sort of people we are dealing with. The scene is less an action unit than a psychological moment.

The initial friction is immediately succeeded by a second collision of personalities. Eyjólf is eager to accompany his Norwegian guest Hreidar on his return voyage, but Hreidar is oddly reluctant. It turns out that he has a brother Ívar back in Norway who makes a special point of disparaging Icelanders. Hreidar is therefore afraid that Eyjólf's presence in his house will cause dissension and place him in an awkward crossfire between his brother and a good friend. That is exactly what comes to pass, but the author conceives of the situation as a testing ground for Eyjólf's character. Eyjólf indeed refuses to be drawn into a quarrel and placidly accepts the malicious nickname *hrúga* (heap). His imperturbable good nature eventually wins over the hostile brother Ívar, and he confirms his personal worth by killing a bear. We may, however, note that character comes first in this sequence and the illustrious deed second. The deed itself is confirmed by the tried and true method of killing a berserk, a feat that opens the way for Eyjólf to win the hand of the chieftain Vigfús's daughter. The very inequality of the match testifies to the Icelander's inborn superiority, a theme that figures prominently in the sagas in general.

Once back in Iceland, Eyjólf and his Norwegian wife have four children, including the protagonist Glúm, who, however, is one of the first deceptively unpromising youngsters who people the pages of the sagas: "He was persistently tight-lipped and taciturn, a tall fellow and bushy-browed, with straight blond hair, slight of build and rather slow to mature. He did not attend meetings" (chapter 5; ÍF 9:15). After his father's death, two neighbors, Thorkel and Sigmund, begin to encroach on his mother's land, but Glúm remains listless. Seeing that he is not up to the challenge, he tells his mother, at the age of fifteen, that he wishes to go abroad. In Norway he approaches his maternal grandfather Vigfús, but Vigfús is not much impressed. Glúm continues to behave in an unprepossessing manner until one day a notorious berserk arrives on the scene and proceeds to humiliate everyone in the hall. This moment provides Glúm with the opportunity to follow in his father's footsteps by standing up to the berserk, and in doing so he gains his grandfather's approval and is offered his Norwegian inheritance. But Glúm, like many another Icelandic patriot, prefers to return home and see to his inheritance there.

On his arrival he finds his mother still suffering the depredations of her neighbors, but she bids Glúm be patient until the right time. The neighbors extract the best field on her farm as compensation for a claim of theft against her two favorite slaves, a claim that turns out to be false. Glúm seems at first to be as disengaged as ever, but he suddenly emerges from his torpor, drives trespassing cattle off his land, and speaks his first words to warn the neighbors against future encroachments. He follows up the threat by killing Sigmund and assembling his own relatives in support of his legal case, in which he is victorious. He then banishes the remaining neighbor Thorkel from the district and repossesses his hereditary land at Thverá. The taciturn youngster reveals himself as a thrifty speaker, the stay-at-home who declines to attend meetings becomes adept at organizing his clan and managing litigation, and the listless farmer regains his land in full. Little wonder that chapter 10 begins with the words "Glúm was now accorded great honor in the district" (ÍF 9:35). His position is further enhanced by a good marriage.

It is not specified that Glúm became a chieftain until the very end of the saga, but political problems soon devolve on him. The first is the case of a man who is turned down in his bid for a wife and is understandably resentful when Glúm wins her hand for a suitor who is no better than the first but happens to be Glúm's cousin. Glúm must iron out the case by providing for both men. The second problem he confronts has attracted some attention because it has been judged similar to a story told by Petrus Alfonsi in his *Disciplina Clericalis*.[1] It grows out of a horse match between Glúm's worker Ingólf and a certain Kálf (a not uncommon name meaning literally "calf"). The match turns ugly when Kálf strikes Ingólf with his staff, a stereotypic motif that clearly demands revenge.[2] The upshot is that Glúm kills a calf and persuades Ingólf to announce that he has killed Kálf, although in reality Glúm commits the killing on his own. In due course a killing case is brought against Ingólf, but Glúm quashes it on the ground that the case has been brought against the wrong defendant. This is the first indication that Glúm's newfound presence is combined with a taste for subterfuge. He has become not only a forceful leader but also a scheming master of deception.

Both the element of subterfuge and the element of wordplay recur in the following episode, which has also been the subject of special study.[3] It centers on a great feud between Glúm and Skúta Áskelsson, who marries Glúm's daughter but then repudiates her, thereby causing a rift with his father-in-law. At one point in the ensuing feud, Skúta ambushes Glúm, who makes his escape by apparently leaping over a high riverbank. The trick here is that Glúm, familiar with the terrain, knows in advance that a ledge below the lip of the bank will catch his fall. He throws his cloak into the river, and while Skúta rushes down to the water to spear the empty cloak, Glúm calls out triumphantly from the high ground. Skúta, in turn, makes a clever escape, and for the moment the antagonism ends in a draw.

Aside from the daughter unhappily married to Skúta, Glúm has two sons, the mannerly Már and the ruffian Vigfús. Vigfús's foster father,

---

[1] See Cederschiöld 1890. The story can be read in *The Disciplina Clericalis of Petrus Alfonsi*, 106. The similarity is not so great as Cederschiöld argued because the pun is entirely missing in Petrus Alfonsi.

[2] See Kersbergen 1927, 73–74.

[3] Lotspeich 1903. See also *Víga-Glúms saga*, ed. G. Turville-Petre, pp. xxii–xxxii, Björn Sigfússon in ÍF 10:LX–LXVIII, and Jónas Kristjánsson in ÍF 9:XII–XXI.

a man with a poor local reputation, is suspected of theft, and a charge is brought against him by a certain Bárd. Glúm judges that the man is not worth defending, but Vigfús forces his hand and obliges him to quash the case, to the detriment of his personal popularity. Bárd proceeds to kill the suspected thief, and Glúm regains his popularity by making easy terms. Later, at a horse match, Bárd makes a verbal assault on Vigfús, who consequently kills him and is therefore outlawed, although Glúm protects him in hiding. What characterizes this sequence is Glúm's reasonableness in maintaining order and navigating the shoals of local politics.

This is also his stance in the next conflict, which pits two cousins, Arngrím and Steinólf, against each other because one is suspected of seducing the other's wife. The outcome is yet another killing and a major confrontation, indeed a pitched battle, between Glúm's party and the rival clan of the Esphœlingar. Complicated negotiations ensue, and Glúm temporarily retains the upper hand by shifting the responsibility for one of the killings from himself to an innocent man. Suspicions nonetheless arise, and Glúm is required to swear an oath affirming that he did not commit the killing. He responds with a famously ambiguous oath, which at first deceives his enemies but is later exposed and brings about his downfall. He is subsequently exiled from the district but lives on to become a blind old man. The saga concludes with two more encounters, from which Glúm emerges at least on equal terms. He makes a final attempt to lure the brothers Gudmund the Powerful and Einar, who become major figures in *Ljósvetninga saga,* into stabbing range, but Einar is no less sagacious than Glúm and forestalls the ruse.

As the final statement in the saga makes clear ("Here ends the saga of Glúm"), the story is focused specifically on Glúm and his record in regional politics. It is not the plotting or the composition that makes the saga interesting; indeed, the block composition that recounts a series of fairly separable episodes one after the other is rather reminiscent of the episodic concatenations in *The Saga of Olaf Tryggvason* and *The Oldest/Legendary Saga.* Nor is it the handling of the narrative details, which are a little knotty and difficult to penetrate, that holds the reader's attention. It is rather the character of the hero that brings the story to life. Glúm's tricks, not the narrative line, are the memorable moments. They also provide the continuity of the story, which is predicated on the well-worn male Cinderella theme, a theme that gives the saga its larger unity. Glúm is presumably never in reality a retarded, oafish youngster; he merely plays the part until he finds the right moment to assert himself. He knows and sees all, including the future contingencies. His succession of subterfuges might suggest moral reservations, but the author's final assessment makes it doubtful that Glúm is meant to be seen as a questionable character. The emphasis seems rather to be on his political astuteness and his ability to negotiate difficulties that are thrust on him by others. He is presumably to be viewed as the quintessentially successful chieftain with all the necessary martial and mental skills.

Reykdœla saga

Reykdœla saga has a great deal in common with Víga-Glúms saga, to the point of narrative overlap. They tell of some of the same people in the same region, and it is not unlikely that they were written in the same vicinity. A likely guess at a precise location is the monastery at Munkathverá, which was founded in the middle of the twelfth century. Both sagas deal with a series of local hostilities recorded in separable episodes. The similarities are so great that the two sagas share the episode in which Víga-Skúta attempts, without success, to ambush Víga-Glúm. The narrative correspondence is exact down to the wording, although Reykdœla saga provides rather more information. Because the episode shows certain stylistic differences from both Víga-Glúms saga and Reykdœla saga, it has been thought that an independent story was interpolated into both sagas.[4] We have seen that such an interpolation is plausible in The Legendary Saga of Saint Olaf, but because the stylistic discrepancy is much greater in that case, interpolation seems less likely in Víga-Glúms saga. That two sagas, all unknowing of each other, though from the same region, should incorporate the same independently written episode strains belief and may be a relic of the nineteenth-century conviction that interpolation was routine. The first monograph on Víga-Glúms saga, in the wake of the rhapsodic theory of Homeric composition, posited that the saga was a concatenation of independent stories connected end to end.[5] From such a perspective every episode might be considered in some sense an interpolation. But

[4] See especially Lotspeich 1903.
[5] Theodor Möbius 1852.

given the contiguity of these two sagas and their parallel structure, it would be easier to suppose that one saga copied from the other, and that is the assumption I make.

When the two sagas are compared, it is generally believed that *Reykdœla saga* represents an earlier stage in saga writing because it is artistically less accomplished. Indeed, Dietrich Hofmann offered a compelling argument for a very early date, between 1207 and 1222, whereas *Víga-Glúms saga* is generally dated later, around 1240 or even 1250.[6] I reverse the order and argue that the author of *Reykdœla saga* knew *Víga-Glúms saga* but also knew a great deal of additional local tradition and was therefore inspired to supplement the earlier text. The idea of a supplement is in line with the borrowed episode of the encounter between Víga-Glúm and Víga-Skúta because the author of *Reykdœla saga* offers more, and to some extent different, detail. The effect of my argument is therefore to place *Víga-Glúms saga* no later than the decade 1210–20: that is, just a decade or two after the first Olaf sagas, and at the earliest date generally agreed on for the first sagas about early Icelanders.

As in the case of *Víga-Glúms saga*, we may preface the argument with the final words in *Reykdœla saga*. Having recounted the killing of Skúta, the author concludes with a summary opinion: "Many thought that in Skúta's case his killing had not come about sooner than expected. But still it should be told in all truth that he was a wise man and a great warrior, and many men were no better than his equal no matter how high an opinion they had of themselves, but he did not impress everyone as an equitable man. Now we have concluded this story" (chapter 30; ÍF 10:242–43). The idea of a final evaluation of the protagonist in political and martial terms echoes the conclusion of *Víga-Glúms saga*. The author seems to be telling us that Skúta may not quite measure up to the standard set by Glúm but that he was nonetheless a considerable figure: in other words, that Glúm was not the only figure in the district whose story was worth telling.

The final words also provide a hint of how the narrative as a whole was conceived. A reading of *Víga-Glúms saga*, including the encounter with Skúta, may have suggested that there was a good deal more to tell about Skúta. The author may even have been a descendant of Skúta's, just as the author of *Víga-Glúms saga* is not unlikely to have

[6] Hofmann 1972.

had some connection with Glúm's family. There was thus some incentive to establish Skúta as a counterpoise, to tell the other side of the story. Having resolved to do so, the author also imitated *Víga-Glúms saga* by rolling the action back to the previous generation and telling the story of Skúta's father, Áskel. The decision to do so opened the way for a moral discussion. The concluding words of the saga suggest that Skúta had a mixed reputation that did not allow for a wholehearted espousal of his record, but the memories of Áskel were quite a different matter. Skúta's family, if not Skúta himself, suggested a historical and moral challenge to the supremacy of Víga-Glúm in the North.

Of all the saga protagonists, Áskel is perhaps the most unblemished; he is rather more saintly, in fact, than either Olaf. His rectitude is only enhanced by the fact that he is constantly trapped between unsavory antagonists, whom he tries repeatedly to reconcile. Although the saga authors are notorious for their objectivity and their reluctance to favor one party over another, this author is an exception. The text is almost startlingly explicit in its moral judgments. About Eystein Mánason we learn that "he was a very inequitable man," and his neighbor Mýlaug is no better, being "a rich man, out for himself" (chapter 1; ÍF 10:153). About the thief Hánef we are informed, "Not much good is told of him in this story, and he was a disreputable man," and Vémund kǫgurr Thórisson, the chief villain of the piece, is introduced in the following terms: "Vémund was not reputed to be an equitable man, and because of that Hánef expected that his bid would not be rejected even though he did not always represent the right cause" (chapter 4; ÍF 10:160). Áskel forms his opinion accordingly: "And now Áskel was ill satisfied because it seemed to him that Vémund was a constant source of evil" (chapter 12; ÍF 10:184). And again: "Áskel was angry and he thought that he [Vémund] had greatly overstepped the boundary in this matter, and he said that he committed one outrage after the other" (chapter 14; ÍF 10:194).

Áskel himself is beyond reproach: "Áskel always demonstrated that he had few equals with respect to the justice he observed in dealing with people and the right-mindedness he exercised toward all" (chapter 7; ÍF 10:171). In the final battle into which he is drawn it is specified that he killed no one. He is himself the victim of a fatal wound, but he hides it until his war party is far enough from the enemy to forestall vengeance or a renewed clash. When Áskel dies, he gets a handsome obituary: "People thought this a great loss because he had been a great and popular chieftain" (chapter 16; ÍF 10:202).

Áskel is clearly a "great chieftain" in a sense very different from Glúm. If any saga author is suspect on the ground of Christian bias, it is surely the author of *Reykdœla saga*. By comparison, the author of *Víga-Glúms saga* cuts a definitely Machiavellian figure, with an outspoken taste for political success and no apparent interest in moral quandaries. The contrast between Glúm and Áskel may be entirely coincidental, but it is tempting to believe that Áskel is a reply to the author of *Víga-Glúms saga* and a rejection of the purely political outlook. If the contrast is deliberate, it establishes two moral poles that lay down parameters for other sagas. The largely political, amoral viewpoint seems to have prevailed in works such as *Fóstbrœðra saga*, *Heiðarvíga saga*, and *Egils saga*, but other writers exploited the moral alternative, among them the author of *The Saga of King Magnús and King Harald*. The most probing and complicated moral sense will emerge in *Gísla saga*.

Víga-Glúms saga has more than once been compared to *Egils saga* on the assumption that Egil is the model and Glúm the imitation.[7] But if *Víga-Glúms saga* belongs to the second decade of the thirteenth century, it may very well have the priority. This sequence may in fact be preferable because *Víga-Glúms saga* is clearly the less ambitious work with respect to plot, poetry, and personality. It is perhaps easier to grasp how the author of *Egils saga* elaborated the more modest model than to suppose that the author of *Víga-Glúms saga* shrank the grandiose design of *Egils saga* into a relatively meager and parochial tale. In one respect the author of *Egils saga* may have adhered closely to *Víga-Glúms saga:* namely, in the depiction of a personality unconfined by moral rules. The author of *Reykdœla saga* adopted rules and wrote more about good and evil than about personality, but if Áskel is the most rule-conscious of saga characters, Egil is famously the least; his nature asserts itself in many ways but always from self-interest. Compared with Áskel, who lives the life of principle, Egil is the more fascinating character and the more brilliant creation. The paradigm for his self-seeking, albeit in modest adumbration, may be found in Glúm Eyjólfsson's life of agile self-promotion.

---

[7] *Víga-Glúms saga*, ed. G. Turville-Petre, xviii, xxi; Jónas Kristjánsson in ÍF 9:XXXVII; and *Viga-Glums Saga*, trans. John McKinnell, 11.

Fóstbrœðra saga

The next two sagas to be discussed have traditionally been dated early, but more recently those datings have been challenged, most radically in the case of *Fóstbrœðra saga*. Sigurður Nordal wrote a detailed study of the various lives of Saint Olaf, in which he surmised that there was a lost *Middle Saga between *The Oldest Saga* and Styrmir's largely lost version.[8] He further surmised that passages from *Fóstbrœðra saga* had been interpolated into the *Middle Saga, a position that he maintained in his introduction to the saga in 1943.[9] Since he dated the *Middle Saga circa 1210, the composition of *Fóstbrœðra saga* would necessarily fall a little earlier, perhaps around 1200; it would thus be among the earliest of the native sagas. But Jónas Kristjánsson went over the same ground in a book from 1972 and concluded that there was no lost *Middle Saga and therefore no reason to press *Fóstbrœðra saga* back as early as 1200.[10] On the contrary, Jónas argued chiefly on stylistic grounds that the saga is more likely to have been written at the end of the century, closer to 1300. The stylistic peculiarities include a series of rather baroque physiological descriptions that clash with the standard saga style and the story as a whole. These passages could be interpolations, but there are rather too many of them to make interpolation plausible, and they are more likely to be the author's idiosyncrasy. Nordal noted, however, that they were more in keeping with the learned interests in the twelfth century than with the perfected saga idiom of the late thirteenth century.[11] Other reservations about Jónas's redating have also been raised.[12]

Jónas Kristjánsson nonetheless succeeded in making the dating quite uncertain. The only topical reference in the saga is a remark (chapter 13; ÍF 6:184) that the paneling of a hall was still intact in the days of Bishop Magnús Gizurarson (1216–37). This note could be based on the author's own observation during the period in question, but it could also be based on a report from as much as fifty years later.

[8] Nordal 1914.
[9] ÍF 6:LXXI–LXXII.
[10] Jónas Kristjánsson 1972.
[11] ÍF 6:LXXVI.
[12] Klaus von See (1976; rpt. in von See 1981a, 443–60) argued against Nordal's view that the *Hauksbók* version is an abbreviation but was quite open to an early date of composition around 1200 (1981a, 458). My own view is that it is difficult to imagine that *Fóstbrœðra saga* was composed late in the thirteenth century but independently of *Heimskringla* (Andersson 2000, 7).

Dating indications are difficult to come by, but some general considerations might still favor an early date. The first of these is that *Fóstbrœðra saga* has a certain affinity with the skald sagas, which seem to have been an early product of saga writing.[13] It is about two notable Icelandic figures who were active in the first decades after the year 1000, Thorgeir Hávarsson and Thormód Bersason. The latter we have already met in *The Oldest/Legendary Saga of Saint Olaf,* in which he is cited a number of times. *The Oldest/Legendary Saga* is based on Thormód's verse only here and there, but *Fóstbrœðra saga* is based throughout on Thormód's testimony, in particular a poem he composed about Thorgeir's deeds ("Þorgeirsdrápa"), of which fifteen stanzas are cited. In addition there are a number of stanzas about Thormód's adventures. The technique in the saga is to recount an episode and then record a relevant stanza. This is also the technique used in the early skald sagas, and it is therefore tempting to assign *Fóstbrœðra saga* to the same early period.

One could argue that since there are two protagonists instead of one, the saga departs from the essentially biographical form of the skald sagas, but the difference is superficial. The prominence of Thorgeir in the early phases of the story can be attributed to his close companionship with Thormód and his special status as the subject of Thormód's "Þorgeirsdrápa." It is only his special relationship to Thormód that gives him such a conspicuous role. His adventures are almost always in tandem with those of Thormód, who therefore figures as the central figure throughout. The overall composition of the saga is quite transparent. It tells first of the sworn companions' joint adventures, then of Thormód's erotic entanglements, then of his vengeance against Thorgeir's killer, and finally of his death in the service of King Olaf at the Battle of Stiklarstadir (1030).

The initial adventures of Thorgeir reveal the same sort of block composition that we observed in *Víga-Glúms saga* and *Reykdœla saga;* each episode is separate and is generally closed off with a stanza from "Þorgeirsdrápa." Thorgeir begins his career by taking revenge against his father's killer, Jǫdur. Together with Thormód he eliminates the troublemakers Ingólf and Thorbrand, and, again on his own, he kills the local predator Butraldi. Once more together, the companions have

---

[13] The skald sagas have been omitted from this book because they are discussed thoroughly in Poole 2001.

a bloody confrontation with other claimants to a stranded whale and are able to make good their own claim. Five remaining adventures are attributed to Thorgeir alone, and four of them are documented in Thormód's verse. Only the somewhat autocratic defense of the thief Veglág goes unmentioned in the verse, though it may nonetheless have been alluded to in a lost stanza. The narrative devoted to Thorgeir covers about eighty pages, or roughly half the saga as it is printed in Íslenzk fornrit. It concludes with Thorgeir's fall in a memorable last stand against an overwhelming force led by Thorgrím trolli Einarsson. The remainder of the story tells about Thormód's boldly and ingeniously executed vengeance for his fallen companion in Greenland, carried out at the behest of King Olaf himself.

Not only is the serial arrangement of adventures reminiscent of the block composition especially in *Reykdœla saga,* but the mode of characterization remains the same, with just one modification: whereas *Reykdœla saga* established the villainy of most characters by contrasting them to the saintly Áskel, the author of *Fóstbrœðra saga* uses a uniformly dark palette. The brief personal descriptions discredit everyone, including the protagonists. When Thorgeir and Thormód join forces, it is reported that "they were not popular, and many people did not consider them to be equitable men" (chapter 2; ÍF 6:125). Thorgeir in particular is almost parodistically insensitive, to the extent of registering no reaction at all when his father is killed (chapter 2; ÍF 6:127). On the following page that trait is generalized in terms of an absence of amorous sentiment: "We are told that Thorgeir was not a ladies' man; he said that it was a blight on his valor to cozy up to women. He seldom laughed and he was generally rude to people." Lest we forget, we are reminded a few pages later (ÍF 6:133) that he and Thormód "were indifferently popular." That sets the tone for all the subsidiary portraits.

Their first antagonists, Ingólf and Thorbrand, are introduced in the following terms: "His [Ingólf's] son was named Thorbrand; he was a great warrior, quarrelsome and unpopular. Both father and son were very inequitable men, who made off with the property of others by intimidation and seizure" (chapter 3; ÍF 6:133–34). Butraldi is no better: "He was a vagabond, a big man, powerful, ugly to look at, tough by temperament, a notorious killer, hot-headed and vindictive" (chapter 6; ÍF 6:142–43). Thorgeir's antagonist Hœkils-Snorri earns more or less the same description: "He was a big, strong man, not handsome to look at, with a fierce appearance, unpopular, hot-headed, and with a vindictive disposition" (chapter 12; ÍF 6:178). A certain Thórir, against whom Thorgeir takes revenge for the killing of one of the king's retainers, has only the reprieve of brevity: "He was a great troublemaker, rather antagonistic and unpopular" (chapter 13; ÍF 6:183). Veglág does not get a personal description, but his thievery tells the story. Gaut, with whom Thorgeir quarrels over firewood, is dismissed in the usual terms: "Gaut was a big, strong man, antagonistic and tough" (chapter 8; ÍF 6:157).

The only moment that saves *Fóstbrœðra saga* from being a rogues' gallery from beginning to end is the presence of some humble people who save Thormód's life during his vengeance mission in Greenland, but they are quite peripheral to the plot. The result of this monotony of evil is that the narrative becomes too uniform and unshaded; not even the protagonists Thorgeir and Thormód are granted much in the way of complexity. Thorgeir amounts to no more than his sword and spear, and his words are largely confined to antagonizing his enemies. Indeed, the only words he addresses to his friend and sworn brother are a provocative question, asking which of them could overcome the other (chapter 7; ÍF 6:151)—a challenge that prompts Thormód to take his leave.

Neither composition nor characterization has therefore attained a higher level than we found in *Víga-Glúms saga* and *Reykdœla saga*. The chief narrative resource is trickery—which Thormód exploits to great effect in Greenland—supplemented by the black arts. In Thormód's case, however, trickery seems a less innate quality, less an index of personality, than in Víga-Glúm's case. Thus the saga's general reliance on block composition, negative characterization, and ingenious escapades would seem to place it in the context of the early northern sagas rather than in the company of the narratively more ambitious sagas surveyed in the chapters that follow.

In one respect, nonetheless, *Fóstbrœðra saga* does mark a clear advance over *Víga-Glúms saga* and *Reykdœla saga:* it is fuller, more skillfully articulated, and therefore easier to read than the other two, about which there is something crabbed and difficult to follow. They are not scenically developed and do not capture the reader's inner eye as the episodes in *Fóstbrœðra saga* do. I suggested in the introduction that saga art was to a considerable extent a re-creation of oral storytelling: that is, a recapturing of the oral style that made the narratives captivating for a listening audience. The authors of *Víga-Glúms saga* and *Reykdæla saga* struggle with that re-creation, but in *Fóstbrœðra saga* it is complete. Such scenes as Thorgeir's killing of Jǫdur, Butraldi, and Gaut, and Thormód's killing of Thorgrím in Greenland, bring these moments to life with an adroit deployment of local details, a few understated words, and a few stage properties. The narrative economy of these moments will hardly be improved on in the later texts, although psychology, characterization, and thematic thrust are destined to make impressive strides.

Heiðarvíga saga

At one time *Heiðarvíga saga* was considered to be perhaps the oldest of all the native sagas, partly on the basis of a fragmentary manuscript judged by the paleographers to be from circa 1250 and partly because Sigurður Nordal thought the style undeveloped.[14] More recently, as in the case of *Fóstbrœðra saga*, the early dating has been called into question: Bjarni Guðnason detected evidence that the author stands in debt to *Laxdæla saga* and must therefore have written after the middle of the century.[15] The debt to *Laxdæla saga* is posited chiefly on the basis of an episode in which the girth on a woman's horse is loosened so that she tumbles into a brook. There are several possibilities. *Laxdæla saga* may have borrowed from *Heiðarvíga saga*, or vice versa. The resemblance may stem from the fact that one author had a recollection of the episode from the other saga and reused it (secondary oral tradition). Or perhaps the similarities are not so great as to persuade us of any connection at all; it may be a case of two authors' using a stock scene. Of these possibilities it is the last that seems to me most plausible. Neither saga shows ready signs of literary borrowing, and the possibility therefore remains open that *Heiðarvíga saga* is a very early text.

Still, Nordal's argument that it represents a less than fully developed style is not very persuasive. On the contrary, it could be argued that *Heiðarvíga saga* represents a real narrative advance and is distinctly more modern than the sagas surveyed so far. All three of these are episodically composed; the protagonists pass through a series of dis-

[14] ÍF 3:CXXX.
[15] Bjarni Guðnason 1993, 238–53.

connected or loosely connected adventures; they distinguish themselves repeatedly but succumb in the end, Víga-Glúm to old age and
the others to armed opponents—*Heiðarvíga saga*, in contrast, focuses
on a single, albeit long and drawn-out, conflict between a kin group in
the Northwest and another in the West. It therefore marks the onset of
the full-fledged feud saga and could very well be understood to represent the full blossoming of the native saga.

But before turning to the action, we must take note of a special problem. *Heiðarvíga saga* is preserved in only one medieval manuscript, of
which about a third was lost because that part, sent on loan from Sweden to Denmark, was burned in the Copenhagen fire of 1728, a fire that
destroyed many of the great collector Árni Magnússon's manuscript
treasures. The missing portion was set down from memory by the
scribe Jón Ólafsson, but that telling can be only an approximation and
cannot be used in the same way as the medieval saga texts. Bjarni
Guðnason has adduced reasons for believing that the retelling is quite
accurate, but there are also signs of uncertainty.[16] It is only the last part
that can serve to illuminate the style and narrative practices reliably.

The saga (as retold by Jón Ólafsson) begins, somewhat in the manner of *Fóstbrœðra saga*, with the story of a ruffian and autocrat named
Víga-Styr. (It is curious how many of the early saga protagonists acquire the "killer" prefix: Víga-Glúm, Víga-Skúta, Víga-Styr; even the
emerging hero of *Heiðarvíga saga* is known as Víga-Bardi.) Styr imposes
his will on the district and declines to pay any monetary compensation
for his quite unmotivated killings. Matters are only exacerbated when
he acquires as a gift from his brother Vermund two berserks, whom
Vermund had in turn gotten from the Norwegian ruler Hákon jarl.
Styr, true to form and on the advice of the perpetually crafty Snorri the
Chieftain, kills off the two berserks by trapping them in an overheated
bath. His misdeeds do not go unavenged, however, and he is eventually killed in an entirely unexpected way by the young son of one of
his victims, a certain Gest. Styr's kin group seeks in turn to take revenge, but with a combination of prudence and good luck, Gest is able
to elude his pursuers and come to terms with his chief antagonist. He
lives out his days in high esteem in the Varangian Guard, a body of
largely Norse mercenaries in Constantinople.

The previous sagas discussed in this chapter would presumably

---

[16] Ibid., 32–43.

have passed on to quite distinct episodes, but *Heiðarvíga saga* maintains the narrative line. The family relationships connecting the people in the subsequent chain of reprisal are not altogether clear, perhaps because of Jón Ólafsson's faulty memory, but Styr's kin group is dissatisfied with the failed vengeance against Gest. Snorri the Chieftain, who is Styr's father-in-law, believes that the responsibility devolves on him. He therefore leads an expedition to kill a certain Thorstein Gíslason, who had afforded Gest shelter during his escape from Iceland. But the killing case is only temporarily settled, for the sons of Hárek, whose relationship to Thorstein is not specified, take revenge for him by killing a man named Hall Gudmundarson in Norway. This killing dictates the remainder of the saga because Hall's younger brother is the redoubtable Bardi, who is the center of the action for the seventy pages still to be told.

When news of his brother's killing is reported in Iceland, Bardi consults his foster father, Thórarin, who advises patience and turns out to be a master of the long-range plan. Under his guidance Bardi appeals to the assembly for three consecutive years. The first year there is no response. The second year there is again no response, but everyone praises Bardi's restraint. The third year a hot-headed son of Thorstein Gíslason, who has returned from abroad, delivers a sarcastic and insulting reply. Thórarin now judges that public opinion is on Bardi's side and that it is time to act. His first move is to obtain a sword with special properties.

At this point we can follow the action in the medieval manuscript. It is clearly laid out but is characterized by Thórarin's almost unnatural foresight as he instructs Bardi on every detail of the plan. He tells him precisely which allies to recruit, and Bardi approaches them accordingly. At the same time, it emerges that Thórarin has devised a fiction of lost horses in order to deploy a spy network among their enemies to the south in Borgarfjord. For a moment the action digresses to Bardi's mother, Thuríd, who incites her sons to vengeance with huge portions of meat designed to remind them of the pieces into which their brother Hall was cut. She is also eager to accompany them on the expedition, but Bardi, remaining impassive, contrives to have her slip from her horse into a brook and return home sodden.

Bardi now gathers provisions and is patted down for telltale signs of future wounds by a foster mother who has prophetic gifts. Intelligence arrives from the south to the effect that the sons of Thorgaut Gíslason (Thorstein Gíslason's brother) will be mowing a certain meadow called Gullteig, and Thórarin formulates his plans in greater detail. He explains the most easily defended sites on the heath Tvídœgra, which they must cross to reach Borgarfjord, and then gives precise directions on how to approach Gullteig. In the meantime their enemies are visited by ill omens, but they take no heed and go about their mowing. Bardi and his men make their approach in tight single file so that their enemies will misjudge their numbers until it is too late. Bardi strikes down Gísli Thorgautsson and advises immediate withdrawal, but his companions are disgruntled about such a paltry vengeance; indeed, they continue to resist and dawdle so that Bardi is obliged to fight his rearguard action at the less good of the two defensive sites on Tvídœgra. There are a number of casualties on both sides, though more among the pursuing southerners, but when a very large southern contingent comes into view, Bardi must withdraw. Snorri the Chieftain, also a master strategist, ultimately brings about a settlement that redounds to Bardi's credit, and Bardi goes on to marry a daughter of Snorri's, only to divorce her sometime later. He then travels abroad to take service in the Varangian Guard, where he is destined to fall in battle but in high repute.

Despite the uncertainties of Jón Ólafsson's transcription from memory, *Heiðarvíga saga* ranks high among the early sagas. The meticulous and sometimes repetitive detail of Thórarin's planning, which Nordal considered a mark of primitive narration, can also be viewed as a highly sophisticated use of suspense and drama, familiar to modern readers from mystery stories. Each succeeding scene artfully defers the foregone outcome and draws the reader ever more firmly into the unfolding plot. The characters in the story replicate the author's reticent handling of the plot by maintaining minimum communication with one another. Thórarin, for all his explicit detailing of the plan, tells Bardi only as much as he needs to know at each stage. There is, for instance, no prior knowledge of his spy network until it reports. Bardi, in turn, tells his men only as much as they need to know at any given moment; he also keeps his mother, with her unbridled craving for vengeance, thoroughly in the dark. This exploitation of silence, which is one of the hallmarks of fully developed saga style, can be exampled in the sagas already discussed but not as a constant feature from beginning to end. What sets *Heiðarvíga saga* apart is that it is stylistically so sustained.

Bardi himself participates in the conspiracy of silence to the extent that he is personally opaque. Not a trickster apparently reveling in his trickery, like Glúm or Thormód, he is in fact a consistently serious character. It could be argued that he is hardly a character at all, since he merely executes Thórarin's instructions, but it may be more to the point to consider that he and Thórarin are complementary characters, Bardi no less impressive in his ability to carry out with perfect discretion what Thórarin proposes. The two of them together form an enviable alliance of wisdom and valor, a partnership of values widespread in the sagas. The partnership will eventually shatter in *Njáls saga,* but it underpins the thinking in many of the sagas up to that point.

Although Bardi shares so little of his personality, it can be argued that he is not only one of the most serious but also one of the firmest saga characters. Just as the author reaches a higher level than previous saga writers in sustaining consistency and pace in the overall narrative, so too does Bardi's characterization attain a new level of compactness. He has a mission and the steady determination to carry it through. Even the odd little scene in which he divorces Snorri's daughter because she buffets him with a pillow is indicative of his stern single-mindedness. There are comic inflections in the portraits of Víga-Glúm and Thormód; Áskel is idealized to a fault; and there is something of the travesty about Thorgeir—but Bardi demands respect in his unerring devotion to a cause.

Gísla saga Súrssonar

The first two sagas discussed in this chapter might be termed district or clan sagas. Víga-Glúm defends his ancestral turf against the neighboring Esphœlingar; in *Reykdæla saga,* Áskel strives vainly to contain his combative neighbors, and his son Skúta conducts an ultimately unsuccessful vendetta against Glúm. These regional conflicts obscure more narrowly confined domestic dealings. Glúm has at least an implied relationship with his mother and his son Vigfús, but the author does not probe these relationships. *Reykdæla saga* reveals nothing at all about the family or emotional lives of Áskel and Víga-Skúta. *Fóstbræðra saga* carries this reticence to a new level: on the one hand, Thorgeir has on principle nothing to do with women or kinsmen, and he alienates his sworn brother Thormód; Thormód, on the other hand, is amorous but fickle, but he too has no observable family dealings.

In *Heiðarvíga saga* there is a new and differing perspective. It may still qualify as a district saga, in which the northwesterners in Víðidale are pitted against the southerners in Borgarfjord. It also continues to focus on an individual of heroic stature and exceptional resourcefulness, but Bardi is more deliberately integrated into his family. His most crucial relationship is with his foster father Thórarin, who is not only a profound strategist but is clearly devoted to Bardi's cause. That cause is the maintenance of family status in the form of vengeance for Bardi's brother Hall, but though the family is at stake, it does not have a high profile; Bardi takes sole command and shares as little information as possible. The author focuses on the campaign and offers no insight into the issues or sentiments as they affect family life. Bardi's somewhat sardonic view of his passionately vengeful mother is indicative. It is perhaps no less indicative that our only information about Bardi's married life with Aud is confined to a loveless pillow fight that precipitates divorce.

How does *Gísla saga* fit into this succession of redoubtable warriors and district feuds? We must first attempt to estimate where this saga stands in the chronological sequence, and that is no easy task. It is generally dated in the first half of the thirteenth century, though not early in the first half. Compositionally, it may well be the most elegant of the saga narratives, a quality that militates against a very early date. Yet it is terse and spare, suggesting none of the broader strokes to be found in the more expansive texts such as *Laxdœla saga, Eyrbyggja saga,* and *Vatnsdœla saga,* and it shares with the earlier sagas a focus on a single individual and a strong predilection for recording skaldic verse. Perhaps the best dating index is the probability that *Gísla saga* was known to the author of *Droplaugarsona saga,* for which there is no good reason to assign a particularly late date.[17] A Norwegian prelude that is more fully and ingeniously exploited than the one in *Víga-Glúms saga,* however, may suggest that the author was inspired by *Egils saga,* in which the Norwegian prelude is a major part of the story. A location between *Egils saga* and *Laxdœla saga* might suggest the period 1230–50, but this dating is even more insecure than most.

Whereas *Heiðarvíga saga* dismisses family matters with something approaching disdain, *Gísla saga* makes them central. District politics,

[17] In Andersson 1968, 28–39, I argued for the borrowing of an episode in *Droplaugarsona saga* from *Gísla saga.*

so prominent in the previous sagas, shrink into the background. It is as if the author is suggesting that the fulcrum of events is not in the extended family but rather in what we would now call the nuclear family. This focus is apparent from the very outset in the Norwegian prehistory. The Norwegian prelude to the action confronts us with difficult manuscript and variant problems that have not been resolved, but in the two redactions of the saga, both the longer and the shorter, there is agreement that an ancestral Gísli avenges the death of his brother Ari, who has been challenged and killed by a berserk intent on taking his bride. Gísli carries out the vengeance and marries his brother's intended, thus preserving family integrity.

The pattern is repeated and escalated in the following generation, in which a second Gísli, the protagonist of the story, kills an unwelcome suitor (or seducer) of his sister Thórdís. The situation is complicated, however, by the fact that the suitor/seducer is also a friend of Gísli's brother Thorkel, and, though unwelcome to their father, on whose behalf Gísli acts, it is not clear that the suitor is unwelcome to Thórdís. Family integrity may therefore come at a high cost in family harmony.

The shorter redaction goes on to tell that a kinsman of the slain suitor/seducer named Skeggi aspires to Thórdís's hand, although she is already involved with a certain Kolbjǫrn. Skeggi is turned down and consequently challenges Kolbjǫrn to a duel, but Kolbjǫrn shrinks from the encounter. Gísli intervenes once more to kill Skeggi and later burn Kolbjǫrn with twelve others in his house. At this point the family emigrates to Iceland, but it is already perilously divided: Gísli has killed three of his sister's admirers and a good friend of his brother Thorkel— all in a good cause to be sure, but dire consequences, as yet unforeseen, are soon to be revealed.

In Iceland the settlers marry and settle down in the following configuration:

Gísli ~ Aud (sister of Véstein)
Thorkel ~ Ásgerd
Thórdís ~ Thorgrím

Gísli, his brother-in-law Véstein, Thorkel, and their brother-in-law Thorgrím are thus bound together in a tight kin group. At first the group seems to flourish and enjoy great esteem, but a man known for prophetic gifts predicts that their concord will not last three years.

Gísli, ever the guardian of family solidarity, proposes to strengthen the bond by causing the four men to swear blood brotherhood. The ceremony commences, but at the last moment Thorgrím withdraws, leaving Gísli to resign himself with a fatalistic formula. The family fault lines are beginning to emerge.

They emerge with even greater clarity one day when Thorkel overhears a private conversation between Aud and Ásgerd. The conversation reveals that Aud once had an attachment to Thorgrím and that Ásgerd may have an ongoing attachment to Véstein. When Thorkel overhears this revelation, he bursts out in dire exclamations, forcing the women to devise some remedy. Their remedies are also characterizations. Ásgerd cows the feckless Thorkel into a meek acceptance with a threat of divorce, while Aud gives Gísli a candid report and asks for advice. He has none to give and once more retreats into fatalistic resignation.

Thorkel, who has been a useless farming partner for Gísli but to whom Gísli is loyal because of his sense of family commitment, leaves his brother and goes to live with Thorgrím, while Gísli maintains his close relationship with Véstein. The erotic rift is thus healed by division; Gísli is no longer close to his wife's former admirer, Thorgrím, and Thorkel has put distance between himself and his wife's former (and perhaps present) lover, Véstein. Gísli's dream of a tight-knit family has come to nothing.

The upshot is that Véstein, the alleged lover of Thorkel's wife, Ásgerd, is secretly murdered in his bed during a violent nighttime storm. The long redaction makes it clear that Thorgrím is the murderer, but the short redaction, whether by oversight or contrivance, does not reveal the murderer's identity and has given rise to much speculation about whether the murderer is actually Thorkel himself or the more hard-bitten Thorgrím acting on his behalf.[18]

The aftermath is bloody in the best saga manner but no longer in the tradition of the clan reprisals that characterized the previous sagas. The bloodshed in *Gísla saga* is confined to the family itself. Gísli, bent on avenging his brother-in-law Véstein, replicates the nighttime murder and kills Thorgrím in his bed in what may be the most emotionally charged scene in all the sagas. We must remember that Thorgrím is married to Gísli's sister Thórdís, who therefore shares the bed in

[18] Ibid., 18–28.

which Thorgrím is killed. Not only that, but in a chilling gesture Gísli first touches Thórdís and makes her believe that Thorgrím is initiating love play. As Thorgrím turns toward her, Gísli thrusts a spear through him and then makes good his escape.

The scene is not only chilling but psychologically complex. In the first place, *Gísla saga* is the only saga that allows the reader access to the intimacies of the conjugal bed. It also suggests that Gísli is taking revenge not only for Véstein's murder but also for Thorgrím's former attachment to his wife, Aud. This is surely the sense of his counterfeiting love play: the price of Thorgrím's amorousness is death. At the same time, the scene is the culmination of Gísli's record of offenses against his sister, who has now lost three admirers and, most grotesquely, a husband to Gísli's purblind sense of family honor. The drama culminates when Thórdís overhears an inculpatory stanza recited by Gísli; she wrestles with her conflicting obligations to husband and brother but finally opts for her husband and divulges Gísli's guilt.

Gísli is consequently outlawed and is pursued by Thorgrím's avengers for thirteen years. During this time the relationship of the brothers Gísli and Thorkel also passes through its final stages. It has been strained ever since Gísli killed Thorkel's friend in Norway, but now he has exacerbated the strain by killing the man who is both Thorkel's closest friend and his brother-in-law. Thorkel is clearly more alienated than ever, though Gísli is strangely uncomprehending. He makes repeated appeals for help to Thorkel, who gives him only halfhearted support. Gísli, seemingly unaware of his own culpability, claims self-righteously that he would not have treated Thorkel so badly.

The same myopia governs his response to his sister. He has no appreciation of the wrongs he has done her and is indignant that she should have revealed his guilt to Thorgrím's family. In a famous stanza (chapter 19; ÍF 6:62) Gísli complains that Thórdís does not have the tough-mindedness of the legendary Gudrún, who put her loyalty to kin ahead of her loyalty to her husband. What she does have, however, is a keen sense of conflicting loyalties, a quandary to which Gísli seems quite oblivious. Her dilemma persists: she marries Thorgrím's brother Bǫrk, but when Gísli is finally brought down by overwhelming odds and the leader of the posse reports to Bǫrk, Thórdís tries to kill him in revenge for Gísli. Although she fails in her murderous intent, she divorces Bǫrk on the spot.

There are other killings in the tale: Thorkel falls victim to Véstein's young sons even before Gísli is slain, and one of these avenging sons is killed by Gísli's Norwegian brother Ari at the very end of the saga. But the killings are predominantly within the family. From start to finish the saga narrates not a feud but the disintegration of a family.

How should we explain this new preoccupation with the family? It has nothing in common with the sagas reviewed above, some of which at least must be earlier. The origin of the family focus is suggested outright in the stanza in which Gísli compares his sister to the Gudrún of heroic legend. On the one hand, if the stanza is correctly attributed to Gísli, it may indicate that his story was already shaped in conformity with heroic legend in the oral tradition. On the other hand, the imitation of the legend is so detailed and so consistent that it might rather be viewed as an authorial design. In some of the sagas discussed so far there is not much evidence of a commanding authorial presence, but in *Gísla saga* the narrative is controlled in such a self-conscious way that we may suspect a firm guiding hand.

The family group crisscrossed and undermined by conflicting erotic attractions is clearly modeled on the foursome of heroic legend: Brynhild—Sigurd—Gudrún—Gunnar, a group torn apart by irreconcilable passions. The oath of blood brotherhood, forestalled at the last moment, is modeled on the oath that binds Gunnar, Hǫgni, and Sigurd in the legend. The murder of Thorgrím in his bed intensifies the scene in which Sigurd is murdered in his bed; both victims are lying next to their wives, and there are even verbal echoes.[19] The theme of marital mismatch in the case of Thorkel and Ásgerd echoes the failed match of Brynhild and Gunnar. In sum, the whole focus on the destructive power of erotic passion has precedent only in the story of Brynhild and Sigurd. It marks a shift from the theme of political contrivance to the theme of high emotion, and this shift is most likely to have been the work of an inspired writer deeply versed in the native heroic legends.

That the core of the saga should be credited to one author does not mean that there were no traditions in circulation about Gísli and his family. The adventures of Gísli during his years of outlawry are more

---

[19] It is specified in both texts that the sword or spear penetrates through to the bed. ÍF 6:54: "En með annarri [hendi] leggr hann í gegnum Þorgrím með Grásíðu, svá at í beðinum nam stað." *The Saga of the Volsungs,* ed. and trans. R. G. Finch, 58: "Guttormr brá sverði ok leggr á Sigurði svá at blóðrefillinn stóð í dýnum undir honum." The phrasing in *Vǫlsunga saga* in all probability derives from the largely lost Eddic poem *Sigurðarkviða in meiri, which would have been familiar to the author of *Gísla saga.*

than a little reminiscent of the cultivation of guile especially in *Víga-Glúms saga* and *Fóstbrœðra saga*. Gísli makes narrow escapes with the aid of ingenious tricks: he switches identities with a thrall who is killed in his place; he eludes pursuers by pretending to be a local simpleton; he escapes a house search by hiding under the bedclothes of a notorious harridan who heaps abuse on the searchers and foreshortens their visitation. This is all in the style of Thormód's resourceful trickery during his vengeance mission in Greenland and would have contributed to effective storytelling in the oral tradition. But whereas the tonality of *Víga-Glúms saga* and *Fóstbrœðra saga* verges on the comic, in *Gísla saga* it emphasizes Gísli's desperate plight and constant peril. The episodes do not detract from the melancholy tenor of the story but rather heighten it.

In one respect the author of *Gísla saga* goes well beyond the heroic legend underlying the plot. The hero Sigurd is a notoriously vacuous personality in both his Norse and his German incarnations, but Gísli is a deeply equivocal figure. On the one hand, he has a high heroic profile. The long redaction introduces him with the words "Gísli was a dark man and like the men of great stature. His strength was hard to measure. He was skilled with his hands and a great worker. And he had a peaceable disposition" (chapter 4; ÍF 6:15). His death is accompanied by the words "Here ends the story of Gísli, and everyone agrees that he was the most valorous of men, although he was not in every respect a fortunate man" (chapter 36; ÍF 6:115). His last stand is singled out for special commendation: "Everyone agrees that no more celebrated defense has been mounted by a single man, as far as the truth can be ascertained" (chapter 36; ÍF 6:116).

These passages amount to undiluted praise to the extent that we choose not to blame the lack of good fortune on Gísli himself. But that is the rub: Gísli does bring misfortune on himself because he is a problematical character.[20] At one level he is right-minded and principled, intent on the welfare of his family and zealous in this cause. Yet he is strangely obtuse in his dealings with his sister and brother, both of whom, especially Thórdís, are alive to the web of conflicting loyalties in which they are caught. Gísli is not. He pursues his course of action with no understanding of or regard for the nuances. He is therefore re-

---

[20] I advocated this view in Andersson 1968, 40–42, but it was ably disputed by Vésteinn Ólason 1999.

sponsible for his own demise because of his own emotional shortcomings. Whereas the heroes of the previous sagas can be contradictory in character, to some extent admirable and to some extent duplicitous, the author of *Gísla saga* is the first to explore a psychological fissure and thus to make the vagaries of human nature the real center of the tale.

The chances that the five sagas discussed in this chapter were composed in exactly this order is vanishingly small. My object has been not to argue a particular order but to suggest certain lines of development in saga writing. At an early point in time, most likely between the composition of *The Oldest/Legendary Saga* (ca. 1200) and *The Saga of King Magnús and King Harald* (ca. 1220), the Icelanders redirected their interests from the lives of Norwegian missionary kings to their own early history. This shift is amply attested by the skald sagas, several of which probably date from this period, and from the interlarded Icelandic tales in *Morkinskinna*. The latter in particular reveal an assertive claim to Icelandic eminence by showing off the early Icelandic ancestors to great advantage in Norway. It was then no great leap from a celebration of Icelanders abroad to a celebration of Icelanders at home, where the protagonists of the sagas described in this chapter concentrate their activity.

The kings portrayed in the early royal biographies were clearly perceived to be the most noteworthy, and a similar choice was made from among the early Icelanders. Those Icelanders whose adventures in Norway were recounted had the advantage of being viewed in the context of Norwegians and other foreigners; not surprisingly, they tended to benefit from the comparison and almost always appear in a conspicuous glow. Those at home, not having the benefit of contrast, were viewed more critically. We therefore find in the native sagas a more varied assortment of portraits, among them, self-promoting characters and outright scoundrels as well as men of distinction.

The stories are, however, organized around figures no less worthy of being retained in memory than the kings and jarls of Norway. *Víga-Glúms saga* traces the career of Glúm Eyjólfsson, who comes into his right slowly but ultimately emerges as a great chieftain. *Reykdœla saga* tells the story of the thoroughly admirable Áskel Eyvindarson and his more mixed but nonetheless formidable son Víga-Skúta. *Fóstbrœðra saga* also has a dual focus on the nearly invincible but strangely unfeeling Thorgeir Hávarsson and his more sentimental sworn brother,

Thormód Bersason, who is fickle in love but wonderfully loyal as a companion in arms. The remaining two sagas are also preoccupied with outstanding individuals: *Heiðarvíga saga* with the cool and single-minded Bardi Gudmundarson, and *Gísla saga* with the focused but problematical Gísli Súrsson. In contrast to the sagas of the two Olafs but, as we will see in the next chapter, in analogy to *The Saga of King Magnús and King Harald*, these native sagas exhibit a highly developed sense of character and personality, as well as a strong interest in political interaction and in the complexities of plot. These features, so wanting in the biographies of the Olafs, surely owe much to the oral precedents outlined in the introduction.

CHAPTER FOUR

Defining Political Identities

The Saga of King Magnús and King Harald

If the estimate of 1200 is about right for the dating of *The Oldest Saga of Saint Olaf,* there elapsed some twenty years between its composition and the writing of *The Saga of King Magnús and King Harald,* the first and by far the longest section of the kings' saga compilation known as *Morkinskinna.*[1] These were the crucial years in the development of saga writing, although we cannot know what the exact sequence of literary events was. It is probable that Karl Jónsson's *Sverris saga* was completed in this period, whether by Karl himself or someone else.[2] A saga about the jarls in west central Norway (Thrœndalǫg) known as *Hlaðajarla saga probably belongs to this period as well.[3] Since it is lost, there is no sure way to evaluate the contents, but judging from a passage in the kings' saga compilation *Fagrskinna* which, according to scholarly consensus, derives from *Hlaðajarla saga, the story was exceptionally well told and fully dramatized.[4]

The first sagas about early Icelanders are likely to date from the period 1200–1220 as well. Among them were one or more of the so-called skald sagas, biographies of Icelandic poets, although doubts attach to the dating of some.[5] *The Oldest Saga of Saint Olaf* makes it clear that

---

[1] For a full literary analysis of this text, see Ármann Jakobsson 2002. References to it in this chapter are from *Morkinskinna,* trans. Andersson and Gade (hereafter simply *Morkinskinna*).

[2] See Lárus H. Blöndal 1982.

[3] On this text see Bjarni Aðalbjarnarson 1937, 199–224; and Andersson 1998.

[4] Indrebø 1917, 147–49.

[5] *Gunnlaugs saga ormstungu* is generally considered to be late, although there is reference to an earlier version (oral or written) in *Egils saga.* For a late dating of *Bjarnar saga Hítdœlakappa,* see Bjarni Guðnason 1994.

an abundance of narrative material would have been available for such a project. Two sagas about early Icelanders, *Fóstbrœðra saga* and *Heiðarvíga saga*, have frequently been assigned to the beginning of the century, but, as we saw in the last chapter, these early datings have been contested.[6] *Víga-Glúms saga* and *Reykdæla saga* are also likely to be early. Several of the sagas belonging to the complex known as *Sturlunga saga*—namely, *Guðmundar saga dýra, Sturlu saga,* and possibly *Þorgils saga ok Hafliða*—are also presumed to have been composed in the first two decades of the century.[7] The first two were written not long after the events they describe and are narratively congested, but *Þorgils saga ok Hafliða* already displays saga style in its prime. Whatever the exact sequence of literary events may have been, both the writing of kings' sagas (in *Morkinskinna* and *Heimskringla*) and the writing of sagas about early Icelanders, represented by *Egils saga,* emerge in full flower in the following decade (1220–30).

The Saga of King Magnús and King Harald is the first text in this new blossoming and was hardly improved on in the later kings' sagas.[8] Like the sagas about Olaf Tryggvason and Olaf Haraldsson it is adumbrated in the synoptic histories, but the scope and style of the narrative is so enhanced as to make the idea of derivation from the synoptics or their sources pointless. Not only is the scale greatly expanded, but the form is made more complex in at least two new ways. In the first place, the unknown author subverts the straightforward biographical form employed in the sagas of the two Olafs by writing a dual saga about two kings—a doubling that has important thematic consequences. In the second place, the saga includes no fewer than thirteen fully developed episodic stories (*þættir*), chiefly about Icelandic visitors at the Norwegian court. Such inserts are not altogether new; we saw that *The Oldest/Legendary Saga of Saint Olaf* included a number of episodic incidents more focused on Icelanders than on the protagonist. These incidents were clearly a rich reservoir of tradition but were sometimes poorly integrated into Olaf's biography.

We might surmise that the author of *The Saga of King Magnús and King Harald* confronted a choice: one option was to omit the separate incidents altogether; the other was to develop them more fully and

---

[6] See Jónas Kristjánsson 1972 and Bjarni Guðnason 1993.

[7] See Andersson 2002, 389, 398.

[8] In his edition of *Morkinskinna* (STUAGNL 53:XXXV–XL), Finnur Jónsson considered the text to be an amalgamation of earlier kings' sagas. The most consistent advocate of unified authorship is Ármann Jakobsson (e.g., 2002, 274).

make frank allowance for their separateness. To omit them would have meant forgoing a precious store of narrative material. The author seems therefore to have elected the option of elaborating them, thereby introducing a new narrative form of great intrinsic interest and at the same time using this form as an independent window on the kings of Norway. Literarily, the tales are comparable to the framed stories of the *Arabian Nights,* the *Decameron,* or the *Canterbury Tales,* but there is no scope for the narrators. Instead, the stories are told by the author for the purpose of shedding light on the kings.[9] Indeed, the dual focus on the two kings and the independent stories serves one and the same purpose: to contrast and characterize the kings.[10] This emphasis on characterization is entirely new in relation to the sagas of the two Olafs, which are heir to the stereotypical characterizations of hagiography.[11]

The older biographical form yields not only to a new narrative inclusiveness but also to an unmediated plunge into the central story. Both Olafs had the benefit of quite elaborate nativity sequences, again in the hagiographic tradition, but we are not invited to witness Magnús's birth, perhaps for the good reason that he was not Saint Olaf's legitimate offspring. Instead, the author begins with a quarrelsome domestic scene between King Yaroslav of Russia and his Swedish-born queen Ingigerd. The queen makes an unprovoked and invidious comparison between her husband and King Olaf of Norway, to whom she was once betrothed. Yaroslav reacts angrily and slaps her. She in turn can be dissuaded from divorce only when her chastened husband agrees to foster King Olaf's illegitimate son Magnús.

We became acquainted with Ingigerd in Chapter 2. She is the Swedish princess who should have married Olaf Haraldsson but whom her father married off to Yaroslav in a fit of pique. Ingigerd has maintained her first loyalty to Olaf, however, and the rather novel prologue to the saga of Magnús serves both to reduce the stature of his Russian foster father and to emphasize his relationship to Olaf, whose intended queen now becomes the boy's chief protectress under dramatic circumstances. The author thus succeeds in combining drama with an implied repatriation of Magnús in his Norwegian heritage. Compared with the minimal note in chapter 72 of *The Legendary Saga* ("King Olaf . . . left his son behind to be fostered by King Yaroslav") the new narrative and scenic

[9] Ármann Jakobsson 2002, 87–88.
[10] See Ármann Jakobsson 1997, 136, and 2002, 82.
[11] On the hagiographical model, see Sverrir Tómasson 1988, 260–79.

vigor is startling.[12] Magnús grows up at the Russian court as a hyper-active boy of great physical accomplishments, who, like Olaf Trygg-vason before him, gives early evidence of his mettle by killing a curmudgeonly courtier who has given cause for offense.

At this point the author inserts a long, semi-independent tale that offers an explanation of Magnús's return to Norway. It is not, strictly speaking, one of the *þættir* because the protagonist is not an Icelander but rather a self-made Norwegian saltmaker named Karl. Moving up the economic ladder (a theme in this saga), Karl undertakes a trading voyage and ends up at the Russian court, where he is treated with great suspicion because his fellow Norwegians are known to have betrayed King Olaf. Magnús, however, is quick to intervene on Karl's behalf, grasping instinctively that he must maintain good relations with his Norwegian people. Karl spends the winter at the Russian court, but in the spring he is dispatched with a well-stuffed purse to identify and win over those Norwegian chieftains who may be ready to promote Magnús's right to reclaim the Norwegian throne from the Danish rulers who have displaced Saint Olaf. During his circuit of Norway, Karl is captured and imprisoned, but he makes his escape in swash-buckling style and is able to convey the necessary information back to Russia. In the meantime, a delegation of Norwegians under the lead-ership of the Throendalǫg chieftain Einar thambarskelfir approach Magnús and secure his return to Norway.

Although the story of Karl the saltmaker is unusually well told and entertaining, certain logical problems suggest that it may have been re-cruited for a plot in which it originally had no place.[13] Was the recall-ing of Magnús to Norway really the work of Yaroslav with the agency of Karl, or was it rather the work of Einar thambarskelfir on behalf of his countrymen? But such questions are obscured by the thoroughly en-gaging narrative of a self-made man turned secret agent. The author's skill is not confined to a new level of narrative verve, however. The story is also designed to make a point about Magnús's fitness for the throne. He befriends a Norwegian man of the people and reveals very early that he has a special link with his native country. Whereas Olaf Tryggvason and Olaf Haraldsson were monarchs merely by grace of di-vine destiny, Magnús displays physical, intellectual, and diplomatic

[12] *Olafs saga hins helga,* ed. and trans. A. Heinrichs et al., 174.
[13] Louis-Jensen 1977, 80–81.

qualities that predestine him for the throne. The Olafs qualify themselves by dint of religious zeal and are almost ceremonially designated
by prophetic hermits, but Magnús has real political qualifications.

He nonetheless faces a difficult task once he assumes the reins in
Norway. He rules a country divided between staunch loyalists on the
one hand and, on the other, the party of western chieftains who de-
fected from Saint Olaf and submitted to Danish rule. At first Magnús
makes a brave effort to treat these parties evenhandedly, but the loyalists soon come to resent the consideration granted the defectors.
Their murmurings undermine Magnús's good intentions, and he begins to share their grudge against the chieftains who betrayed his father and to adjust his policy accordingly. Political harmony is on the
brink of collapse until a group of some conciliators intervene. They
draw lots to determine who will be their group's spokesman, and the
task falls to the Icelandic poet Sigvat. Sigvat fulfills his obligation by
composing a poem known as "Bersǫglisvísur" (unvarnished verses),
of which sixteen stanzas are recorded in the saga. The poem begins in
the style of a traditional praise poem but transitions gradually into an
admonition urging the king to deal justly with his people.

Once again an Icelander appears in the role of an incomparable
diplomat, as Hjalti Skeggjason did in the saga of Saint Olaf, but in this
case the effect is quite different. In the earlier saga the stanzas recited
by Sigvat and others were scattered about as a supplement, sometimes
with questionable relevance. In this saga the poetry is absorbed into
the political drama. We might ask whether a string of sixteen stanzas
does not strain the license of digression in a prose narrative, but as they
are recited, we sense the mounting tension of the conciliators, who listen nervously to the increasingly unvarnished tonalities of the poem.
We participate in Sigvat's apprehension as he boldly takes issue with
the royal will, trying to strike just the right balance between explicitness and deference. We also follow Magnús's train of thought as he bal-
ances his own prerogatives against the justice of what he is hearing.
His sense of justice prevails; he restores equity, and the political crisis
is averted.[14] Everyone emerges triumphant from what could have
been a civil disaster.

In this episode, then, the verses are not a supplement but an integral
part of the unfolding conflict. The author has boldly expanded not only

[14] See Ármann Jakobsson 1997, 204.

the narrative role of the episodic tale but also the role of the inserted stanzas, which number no fewer than 153 in the saga as a whole. A separate study could be devoted to the author's new technique for making the skaldic stanzas relevant, but given the superabundant material, the example provided here will have to suffice. Sigvat's recital consolidates Magnús's position as a ruler sensitive to the will of his people and able to compromise in order to achieve political stability.

It should be noted in addition that the episode is not designed solely to illustrate Magnús's royal qualities. The political initiative is not his alone but is shared with the people. In the first place, Magnús occupies the throne only because he is called to it by the people, represented by a delegation of twelve countrymen. In the second place, when peace is threatened, the remedy is offered in the first instance not by the king but once more by the people, this time represented by Sigvat. Is it only happenstance that Sigvat is an Icelander? The delicate negotiation between royal will and popular sentiment looks as though it could be inspired in the mind of the Icelandic author by the political institutions of his own country, the supremacy of law and the popular assembly as the instruments of reconciliation.

Sigvat's poem may originally have been prompted by a narrow issue, but with time it could have taken on more abstract political overtones in the Icelandic imagination. It may have been recast as a general statement about popular and royal prerogatives. In retrospect it may have looked like a political parable. As such, it illustrates a shift of interest from the king's person in the sagas of the two Olafs to the king's role in a larger political dynamic in *The Saga of King Magnús and King Harald*. Indeed, the episode is summarized in a single sentence reflecting the viewpoint of the people: "From then on King Magnús was so dear to the Norwegians that the people loved him with all their hearts, and he was called Magnús the Good."[15] Thus the saga turns out to be as much about the popular perception of the king as about the king himself. The king makes his way not by imposing an ideology, as the Olafs did, but by reaching an accommodation with the people.

Magnús pursues the same policy in Denmark: "He cultivated the people and made his dispositions with due regard for law and decency."[16] As a consequence he is accepted as king of Denmark at a pop-

[15] *Morkinskinna*, 109.
[16] Ibid., 112.

ular assembly in Viborg. But trouble soon surfaces in the person of a certain Svein Úlfsson, the grandson of the Danish king Svein (Svend) Forkbeard and nephew of Cnut the Great. Magnús generously appoints him jarl in Denmark but is ill rewarded when Svein—known as Svend Estridsen in Denmark—displaces him on the Danish throne. Magnús retaliates with raids in Denmark and then goes on to raid in Wendland.

At this juncture the author inserts a long digression on the marriage of Magnús's half-sister Úlfhild to an unknown Duke Otto of Saxony. The point of the digression seems to be a celebration of Úlfhild's great wisdom in reconciling Duke Otto with an equally apocryphal Emperor Otto (the German emperor at this time was Henry III). Following the digression there is a similarly detailed account of Magnús's campaign against the Wends and his great victory on Hlýrskógsheath (Lyrskovshede) despite overwhelming odds.[17] This narrative seems designed to display Magnús's military abilities but also to emphasize that he fights under the auspices of Saint Olaf, who appears to him in both waking and sleeping visions.

In the sagas of the Olafs the reader is not necessarily disposed to interrogate the author on the function of every episode in the larger economy of the story, but in *The Saga of King Magnús and King Harald* that line of questioning is justified. Each episode seems calculated to develop an aspect of Magnús's personality or competence. Úlfhild illustrates the hereditary intelligence of the family; Saint Olaf appears twice to confer semidivine authority on Magnús's campaign; and Magnús's performance in battle demonstrates that his own accomplishments do not fall short of his heritage or privilege. His success continues on his return to Denmark, where he wins two victories over his rival Svein Úlfsson and reinstates himself as king.

Having done so, he asserts an earlier claim to the throne of England against Edward the Confessor, but Edward responds in a long and passionately reasoned letter justifying his own claim. In a history replete with royal prerogatives it may come as no small surprise to the reader that Magnús acquiesces. He sees the justice of Edward's position and concludes as follows:

> He said that in truth his realm was sufficiently large provided that God would allow him to rule it. He said further that the only thing he would

---

[17] On this episode, see Danielsson 2002b, 209–35.

increase by killing such a chieftain and godly man as King Edward was his chance of losing what was worth a great deal more, to wit, his hope and trust in almighty God.[18]

Here we come to a provisional resting place and a first summation of Magnús's character: an eloquent testimony to his political moderation and internalized sense of God's will. The prior histories of Olaf Tryggvason and Olaf Haraldsson afforded very little insight into their personalities, but the author of *The Saga of King Magnús and King Harald* writes a narrative chiefly focused on character, a saga in which action is subordinate to portraiture. The transition is prerequisite to the creation of the extraordinary characters in the later sagas, and, more immediately, it prepares the way for the portrait of King Harald, who now steps onto the stage.

Harald is cut from a different bolt of cloth. We met him at the end of *The Legendary Saga* (chapter 83), wounded at the Battle of Stiklarstadir and ferried abroad.[19] Like his nephew Magnús he resides in Russia for a time, although why uncle and nephew apparently never meet at the Russian court is not explained. He subsequently gains command of the elite Scandinavian Guard in Constantinople and is credited with the most remarkable adventures found anywhere in saga literature, but that story remains to be told in retrospect.[20] For the moment we learn only that he returns to Scandinavia and presents himself to Magnús disguised as his own messenger and urging that he be well received. He is duly granted a cordial reception, and only then does the author embark on the story of Harald's adventures.

The first meeting with Magnús, in which Harald disguises his identity until he has been assured of getting what he wants, establishes his style. He is a man of multiple guises and infinite guile, and he is destined to become a chameleon king. Unlike his moderate nephew, he is ambitious and deceitful. In Constantinople too he has made his way by disguising himself and using the pseudonym Nordbrikt, which is difficult to decipher. At every turn he outwits the Byzantine general with whom he is charged to cooperate. As a result, he gains sole credit for a series of brilliant victories, in which he prevails by dint of ingenious stratagems too improbable to relate here but uniformly illustra-

---

[18] *Morkinskinna*, 128.
[19] *Olafs saga hins helga*, ed. and trans. A. Heinrichs et al., 196–98.
[20] On Harald's Varangian adventures, see Sigfús Blöndal 1978.

tive of his profound resourcefulness. He eventually runs afoul of the Byzantine emperor and empress but outwits them too and makes an audacious escape by ship over the chains designed to block sea traffic on the Golden Horn. In the meantime he has accumulated an immense treasure and sent it back to Russia for safekeeping.

Having made his fortune and married a Russian princess, Harald is ready to lay claim to a share of the Norwegian throne, but before doing so he holds a parley with Svein Úlfsson in Denmark. Svein proposes an alliance against Magnús, but Harald, though he does not reject such a league out of hand, wishes to ascertain first whether Magnús will acknowledge his claim. Magnús is quite amenable, but, true to his respect for public opinion, he decides to defer to "the advice of his magnates and the wishes of his countrymen."[21] The latter dismiss Harald's request in no uncertain terms, thus making it clear that they perceive no bond between themselves and the adventitious claimant. Harald therefore returns to Svein and forms an offensive alliance with him.

Faced with this joint campaign, Magnús seeks a compromise. Harald is willing but must first find a way to detach himself from his ally Svein. By this time it will not surprise the reader that he opts for deceit: he stages a mock attempt on his own life, blames it on Svein, and departs without further ado. An official conference between Magnús and Harald now results in an even division of the realm with some few prerogatives reserved for Magnús. One stipulation is that Magnús will have mooring precedence, but no sooner has the agreement been concluded than Harald attempts to breach it. Magnús, however, stands his ground and maintains his prerogative. The reader is informed that this is only one example of the "problems that created dissension between the two kinsmen."[22]

The structure of the saga now emerges clearly. The first part has established Magnús's character; the second part, Harald's. It remains for the third part to study them in tandem as they undertake to rule Norway jointly. The first three episodes of this section (chapters 15–17) show off Magnús's special generosity of spirit; the fourth (chapter 18) provides an explicit contrast between Magnús's openness and Harald's jealous nature. The point is driven home in chapter 21, in which

[21] *Morkinskinna*, 151.
[22] Ibid., 157.

the poet Arnór jarlaskald recites panegyrics for both kings. To begin with, there is a little difference over the matter of precedence: that is, over whose praise poem should be delivered first. The difference is resolved in Magnús's favor, but Harald interjects rude comments during the recitation. At the conclusion of both declamations Harald feels belittled: "I can see the difference between the poems. Mine will be soon forgotten and no one will be able to recite it, but the poem composed about King Magnús will be recited as long as the North is peopled."[23] We cannot know whether this evaluation is correct or simply a product of Harald's jealous nature because, whereas some stanzas of Magnús's poem are preserved, not a single stanza of Harald's survives, as he indeed is alleged to have foreseen.[24]

The technique of invidious comparison persists in one of the best-known semiindependent tales in *Morkinskinna*, the story of the Icelander Hreidar. This naive and ungainly visitor at the Norwegian court, whose merit emerges only over time, is befriended by Magnús and persecuted by Harald. It is clear that only Magnús is perceptive enough to appreciate the promise that lies concealed under Hreidar's unprepossessing exterior. The story is a parable not only of two kings but also of two nations. Whereas the apparent rusticity of the Icelander is deceptive and disguises true character, we are given to understand that the lordliness of a Norwegian monarch can be either positive (Magnús) or negative (Harald). The story concludes with Magnús's gift to Hreidar of an island off the Norwegian coast. Hreidar's delighted response is telling: "With that I will link Norway and Iceland."[25] But Magnús is wise enough to foresee difficulties in such a project and buys back the island from Hreidar with a handsome sum of silver.

The moral would seem to be in line with Einar Eyjólfsson's speech cited in Chapter 2: a recognition that the most prudent arrangement between Norway and Iceland is a relationship at arm's length. The association between Iceland and the mother country is also the implied subject of a number of other episodic tales: for example, the famous story of Audun and his polar bear.[26] These tales are thus not only about

---

[23] Ibid., 167. For an edition and translation of Arnór's poem, see Whaley 1998, 113–18.

[24] On the irony, see Ármann Jakobsson 2002, 96.

[25] *Morkinskinna*, 179. On the significance of this episode, see Ármann Jakobsson 2002, 102, 181, 241.

[26] *Morkinskinna*, 211–15.

the dashing exploits of Icelanders abroad, and the saga as a whole is not only about Einar Eyjólfsson's salutary warning that "there are good kings and bad kings." Rather, both the episodic matter and the saga conspire to comment on the interaction between Iceland and Norway. Both have a broad political focus, a focus that persists in the sagas discussed in following chapters. It persists as well in the account of Magnús's somewhat premature death.

The death scene includes a final and symptomatic conversation between the kings. Magnús asks his coregent for some consideration for his friends, but Harald is noncommittal, commenting that his first responsibility is to his own friends. Here Einar thambarskelfir injects the corrective that his first responsibility is rather the welfare of the kingdom—in effect, a summation of Magnús's rule. Magnús goes on to urge Harald to be content with the rule of Norway and lay no claim to Denmark because of his prior agreement with the Danish king, but Harald demurs. In turn he asks what became of the great treasure he gave Magnús when they divided the realm. Magnús points out the faithful followers on whom he has bestowed the treasure and concludes: "Surely the loyalty and valor of a good man is better than a heap of money."[27]

Magnús's death thus encapsulates a political program, emphasizing the importance of the people, the sanctity of foreign treaties, and the obligation to reward loyal service. Einar thambarskelfir reemphasizes the program when he refuses to participate in Harald's seizure of the Danish throne and states rather that it is "much more fitting to bring the body of his foster son King Magnús north to Norway for burial and return him to his father Saint Olaf than to go to war abroad and covet the realms and possessions of other kings for no good reason."[28]

Einar thambarskelfir thus becomes one of the protagonists of the fourth and last part of the saga, which is the story of Harald's sole rule during a twenty-year period traditionally dated 1047–66. Einar is the focal point of regional separatism in Thrœndalǫg and maintains a tense relationship with the king, who ultimately contrives to have him assassinated. Magnús's diplomacy and conciliation thus give way to Harald's policy of foreign adventurism, tyranny, and regional conflict.[29] The hostility between Thrœndalǫg and the central monarchy,

---

[27] Ibid., 182.

[28] Ibid., 185.

[29] Ármann Jakobsson (e.g., 1997, 141, 273) takes a considerably more positive view of King Harald.

which led to the downfall of Saint Olaf, reemerges and will remain the red thread of Norwegian politics down to the reign of Hákon Hákonarson in the thirteenth century.

Domestic antagonism is embodied not only in the person of Einar thambarskelfir but also in the heroic figure of Hákon Ívarsson, who lends Harald outstanding military service. A largely lost *Hákonar saga Ívarssonar*, which is most likely to have been written after *Morkinskinna*, seems to have associated Hákon with an effort at peacemaking between King Harald and Thrœndalǫg, but the effort leads to nothing.[30] Harald's treatment of Hákon is no better than his treatment of Einar. Having married King Magnús's daughter Ragnhild to Hákon with a promise to make him a jarl, Harald reneges on the promise and eventually fights a campaign against Hákon. In both the story of Einar thambarskelfir and the story of Hákon Ívarsson, Harald's most palpable characteristics are deceitfulness and unreliability in domestic politics. Nor does he distinguish himself in foreign affairs. His failure to heed Magnús's recommendation to forgo any claim to the Danish throne entangles him in a prolonged conflict with Denmark, and at the end of the saga his insatiable ambition motivates him to lead a fatal expedition against England.

This final sequence recapitulates several of the issues already broached. When King Edward the Confessor dies and is succeeded by Harold Godwinson, Harold's brother Tostig believes he has an equal claim, and when he is driven into exile, he appeals to Svein Úlfsson in Denmark to form an alliance for the conquest of England. Svein, however, adheres faithfully to King Magnús's principle of nonintervention rather than reverting to his uncle's Cnut the Great's, policy of conquest: "We can choose moderation more in line with our modest ambition than with the success of our kinsman Cnut the Old."[31]

Tostig takes angry leave of Svein and applies next to King Harald in Norway. Harald falls an easy prey to such representations and prepares the campaign against England. His arrival there is accompanied by numerous ill omens, but he presses ahead and after an initial victory is able to take York. During the night Harold Godwinson arrives with a great army and is admitted within the walls of York, despite the commitments made by the townspeople to the Norwegian king. The next day, as the armies confront each other, a small troop of En-

[30] On *Hákonar saga,* see Fidjestøl 1982, 16–17; also Poole 1991, 67–68.
[31] *Morkinskinna,* 262.

glishmen advances to parley with Tostig and offer him a third of the English realm, but since they offer King Harald nothing (except seven feet of burial plot), Tostig loyally declines. When Harald inquires into the identity of the well-spoken leader of the group, Tostig identifies him as Harold Godwinson himself, who is now beyond reach. In the ensuing battle the Norwegians are overwhelmed, and King Harald falls.

The differing responses to Tostig's overtures in Denmark and in Norway underline once again the superiority of sound domestic policy over foreign interventionism. The parley that Harold Godwinson in disguise conducts with Tostig is surely an irony at King Harald's expense, since he has made a career of disguise and deception. Now, at the last moment, the tables are turned against him. The overall moral must be that a king who lives by the sword will die by the sword.

Looking at the saga as a whole, we may first admire the clearly articulated narrative structure, which subdivides neatly into a section on the formation of Magnús's character, a section on the formation of Harald's character, a contrastive study of their joint rule, and a final moralizing tale of Harald's autocracy and demise. Odd's saga of Olaf Tryggvason was also clearly structured as a history of Olaf's rise, royal mission, and tragic fall, but its central section is randomly organized, and *The Oldest/Legendary Saga of Saint Olaf* is poorly organized throughout. No such weakness inheres in *The Saga of King Magnús and King Harald*, which is no less anecdotal but arranges the anecdotes in a meaningful sequence. Moreover, they are almost all fully developed, intrinsically interesting, and relevant directly or indirectly to the larger political theme.

In the sagas of the two Olafs the oral informants were close to the surface of the text and in some sense intrusive. Magnús and Harald's saga also rests on the contributions of oral informants, some of whom are mentioned by name. The author tells us that at the great Battle of Hlýrskógsheath, King Magnús was accompanied by a man named Odd Gellisson, "who told some parts of these events."[32] This Odd cannot be identified in the genealogies, but it is chronologically conceivable that he was the son of Gellir Thorkelsson, who figures in Saint Olaf's service in *The Oldest/Legendary Saga* and who would therefore have been associated with Magnús's cause. Gellir was Ari Thorgils-

[32] Ibid., 118 and 424 n. 8. See also Danielsson 2002b, 218–28.

son's grandfather and one of his informants. Magnús's story could thus have been handed down in the circle of learned men and women with whom we have already become acquainted.

Much more palpable are the oral sources of information on King Harald. The numerous Icelandic poets who visited his court would have returned to Iceland with an abundance of stories, but more central still would have been Halldór Snorrason, who was Harald's chief lieutenant on his Mediterranean campaigns. Chapter 40 of *The Saga of King Magnús and King Harald* tells us how the Icelander who had learned the story of these campaigns bit by bit from Halldór in Iceland recited the story in the king's presence.[33] We have seen too that Halldór was the older brother of Thuríd the Wise, who was one of Ari's chief sources. Halldór would therefore have been in the network of tradition bearers. One of the episodic tales in the saga tells the story of his personal relations with King Harald, relations that confirm the duplicity that Harald exhibits in the saga as a whole.

There are other identifiable sources in the saga, but the author has managed them in such a way that they no longer obtrude as they did in the sagas of the Olafs. The authors of the latter sometimes write as if they had taken fieldnotes and then copied them into their books. In *The Saga of King Magnús and King Harald* there are no unfiltered notes. All the sources have been dramatized and converted into story, just as the 153 skaldic stanzas (or partial stanzas) and the semiindependent tales have been seamlessly integrated into the narrative.[34] The source materials no longer project oddly along the way but have been recast in such a manner that we see only the author, not the informants. This advance marks the advent of mature saga style.

The author achieves the effect by shifting from a largely cataloguing procedure to a theorizing structure. The authors of the sagas about the two Olafs appear to have collected whatever they could find on the lives of their kings and to have set the material down in roughly chronological order. Their aim is biographical in a narrow sense. The author of *The Saga of King Magnús and King Harald* retains the biographical principle but is more interested in the question of character. The result is an exploration of how the differing characters first reveal themselves, how they interact, and how they remain true to form to the end.

[33] *Morkinskinna*, 222–23.
[34] On dramatic staging in *Morkinskinna*, see also Ármann Jakobsson 2002, 94.

Magnús has the advantage of growing up at a Christian court in Russia, where he demonstrates physical prowess and precocious wisdom. On his return to Norway he shows a willingness to be guided by the people and prudent advisers. In particular, he has the instinct of evenhandedness and extends his benevolence to all his countrymen equally. At the same time he is neither gullible nor easy to trick, as he proves in his dealings with the Danish king Hǫrðaknút, who tries to maneuver him into a deferential protocol.[35] If he sins at all, it is in the direction of generosity and trust, as when he appoints the ambitious Svein Úlfsson jarl over Denmark. During the Wendish campaign he proves himself to be a wise and farsighted general, valiant in combat but also sound in his religious devotion to Saint Olaf. His foreign policy in dealing with Edward the Confessor in England is marked by sympathy and a desire to promote peace. This narrative is thus not a piecing together of biographical notes but a political portrait of a Norwegian *rex justus*. Whether the author was familiar with that medieval concept, the king who first and foremost serves his people, is uncertain, but the text suggests a positive presumption.

King Harald's early years produce quite a different picture. His adventures in the Mediterranean characterize him as brave but grasping, secretive, ingenious to the point of duplicity, and learned in the arcane arts. If Magnús is established as a *rex justus*, what are we to think of Harald? Despite his extraordinary intelligence and resourcefulness and his military daring, he can lay no claim to representing a political ideal. This impression is only escalated in the period of joint rule and in the twenty years that Harald rules alone. The episodes in these sections confirm that he is ambitious and deceitful, notably in his dealings with Svein Úlfsson and Hákon Ívarsson. He is also jealous and given to personal antagonisms when he feels that his preeminence has been slighted. Finally, he is less than faithful to his own commitments, including those to his nephew Magnús.

It is evident that the saga is not just about contrasting personalities but also about competing ideas of kingship. The narrative effectively pits a self-serving king against a king who is devoted to peace and the people. That is to say, the author not only shifts the focus from biography to personal portrait but also, by the expedient of pairing the portraits, writes a study of what a king should be. The narrative is

---

[35] *Morkinskinna*, 111.

controlled by a guiding idea, an idea that emerges with particular clarity in the contrasting operations of foreign policy: Magnús's moderation in acquiescing to King Edward's claim in England, and Harald's overeager expansionism in both Denmark and England. Harald succumbs to his own ill-conceived ambition, making it clear that the model of peaceful coexistence is to be preferred.

We have already seen how Icelandic interests stand out in the sagas of Olaf Tryggvason and Olaf Haraldsson. In the former the very selection of subject matter may be determined by the Icelanders' wish to celebrate the king who brought them Christianity; the latter suggests a dependence on the Icelanders in the king's service. We may go on to ask whether in the saga of Magnús and Harald the obvious advocacy of a peaceful and moderate foreign policy also springs from Icelandic concerns. In Chapter 2 we saw that Norwegian ambitions to annex Iceland seem to have gone back to the days of Olaf Haraldsson, and we will see in the next chapter that the years just prior to the writing of *The Saga of King Magnús and King Harald* (ca. 1220) were characterized by a tense conflict between Norway and Iceland. Given that background, it would not be surprising to find an Icelandic writer around 1220 advocating restraint and moderation in Norway's foreign policy, most particularly in the matter of territorial expansion.

If, however, the saga is so politically focused, we may ask whether the author was simply recording traditions, as the biographers of the two Olafs did, or whether the motivation was rather to devise a political argument and then imagine a narrative in support of the argument. Given the great abundance of known traditions and the familiarity of the saga's potential readership with such traditions, it seems unlikely that the author was cutting anything from whole cloth. Indeed, the greatly expanded use of skaldic authority to underpin the narrative suggests an eagerness to adhere to tradition. The narrative itself therefore continues to be traditional, but it is invested with argument and meaning in a new way. The conception is now authorial. *The Saga of King Magnús and King Harald* marks the onset of a narrative art that is more tightly controlled and authoritatively interpreted than before. The initiative has passed more decisively from informant to author.

CHAPTER FIVE

Political Ambiguities

Egils saga Skallagrímssonar

The continuity between the kings' sagas discussed above and *Egils saga* has often gone unnoticed because they have traditionally been assigned to different genres and are therefore not studied together. It could be argued, however, that *Egils saga* merely inverts the paradigm established in the kings' sagas. The latter are overtly about Norwegian kings but covertly about Iceland's position in relation to Norwegian royalty. *Egils saga* is overtly about an important Icelandic family and its most celebrated scion but also centrally about a series of Norwegian kings and how they interact with Iceland.

The very selection of Olaf Tryggvason as the protagonist of the first extended Icelandic saga may have been dictated by his crucial role in sponsoring the conversion of Iceland. In the Icelandic reworking of the Latin original the addition of Icelandic stanzas also makes it clear that Olaf's permanent place in history, especially his apotheosis at Svǫld, was secured by Icelanders. The same point is made in the saga of Olaf Haraldsson, whose memory is chiefly maintained by Icelanders and whose diplomacy during his lifetime owes not a little to Icelandic initiatives. Olaf's designs on Iceland are as yet suppressed, but the potentially tense relationship between Iceland and the Norwegian crown emerges quite palpably in *The Saga of King Magnús and King Harald,* not only in the separate tales (*þættir*) but also in a quite unmistakable set of recommendations about Norwegian foreign policy. *Egils saga* shares this preoccupation but no longer resorts to indirection, as the author of *Morkinskinna* did by shifting the focus to the Norwegian king's relations with Denmark and England. Instead, the author focuses explicitly on the relations between three ninth- and tenth-century Norwegian kings and the Icelanders of the colonial and postcolonial generations.

One of the features that seems to set *Egils saga* apart from the royal biography is the protracted prelude about Egil's ancestors in Norway. The earliest kings' sagas focus on individual kings and provide very little in the way of a prehistory. The author of *Egils saga* could have adopted the same strategy and begun with Egil's birth in Iceland, but instead the story reverts to Egil's grandfather in Norway, a technique that later becomes so standard in the sagas about early Icelanders that it is taken for granted, almost as a genre marker. In literary-historical terms it is, however, revolutionary, and it is exploited more deliberately and to greater effect in *Egils saga* than in any later saga.

Thus the saga is not only about the great poet and hero Egil Skallagrímsson; it is also about the colonization of Iceland, the founding of a nation. In the course of re-creating this historical moment it offers a theory about how the settling of Iceland came about. The theory is simply that a number of eminent Norwegians were driven abroad by the aggression and territorial expansion of the first sole monarch of Norway, Harald Fairhair, in the late ninth century; that is to say, Iceland is the product of Norwegian tyranny. There was probably an earlier account of the career of Harald Fairhair available to the author of *Egils saga*.[1] It became part of the history of an important Icelandic family, but the author also gave King Harald's career a definite slant.[2]

The early chapters tell the story of how Harald "enslaved and subjected" the Norwegians (chapter 3; ÍF 2:8). Some of the petty kings in the West try to resist, but they are either killed in a losing battle or obliged to flee. Harald seizes all the land, "both inhabited and uninhabited, even the sea and lakes," so that all who remain must submit and become his tenants:

Because of this enslavement many men fled the land, with the result that many desolate places were settled far and wide, both to the east in Jämt-

---

[1] See Jónas Kristjánsson 1977 and Berman 1982.

[2] *Egils saga* is often attributed to Snorri Sturluson, but it provides a portrait of King Harald so different from the one in *Heimskringla* that Wieselgren (1927, 166–68) thought it could not be by the same author. Vésteinn Ólason 1968 provides a very helpful survey of the problem. See also Holtsmark 1971, 105; Jónas Kristjánsson 1977; Óláfía Einarsdóttir 1990, 294–97; Baldur Hafstað 1995, 29–31. For a succinct overview of the research on *Egils saga*, see Capelle and Kramarz-Bein 2001. The most recent advocate of Snorri's authorship is Torfi Tulinius 2004.

land and Hälsingland and to the west, the Hebrides, Dublinshire, Ireland, Normandy in France, Caithness in Scotland, the Orkney Islands, Shetland, and the Faroe Islands. And at that time Iceland was discovered. (Chapter 4; ÍF 2:11–12)

Thus the discovery and settlement of Iceland are directly linked to Harald's tyranny and suppression of inherited freedoms. One of the Norwegians who is wise enough not to oppose Harald outright is Egil's grandfather Kveld-Úlf, who declines to take service with the king, as does his son Grím (later Skallagrím). But a second son, Thórólf, finds it dishonorable to equivocate and is eager for the distinction conferred by royal service. He therefore prepares to join the king despite his father's presentiment that Harald will be the ruin of the family.

The first major narrative strand is accordingly the story of how Thórólf takes service with the king. At first he enjoys great favor and is granted the franchise to collect tribute among the Lapps, but two lesser courtiers, with whom Thórólf is at odds over an inheritance, slander him to the king, whom they are eventually able to persuade that Thórólf is withholding payment. Thórólf is in fact the soul of rectitude and cannot believe that the king will listen to slander, but he is wrong. Harald ultimately launches an attack on his residence and delivers the fatal blow in person. It is a story of innocence abused and unrequited service.

In the aftermath Thórólf's brother, Skallagrím, again refuses to serve the king, with whom he parts on furious terms. Skallagrím and his father then take dire revenge for Thórólf's death by killing two of the king's henchmen with their followers and, for good measure, the two sons of the king's foster father, before escaping to Iceland. Harald in turn takes indiscriminate revenge against Kveld-Úlf's kinsmen and friends by imposing unspecified penalties (we may suspect the loss of life or limb) or forcing them to take refuge in the wilderness or abroad.

This initial account of the relations between Egil's clan and Norwegian royalty is unambiguous. It portrays a king who is as uncompromising as he is ambitious, brooks no resistance, and is adamant in imposing his will. In the process he reveals himself to be choleric, accessible to slander, and given to vindictive retaliation. We are a long way from the religious zeal of the Olafs or the principled but flexible statesmanship of King Magnús. In dealing with Harald Fairhair it is vain to strike a neutral posture, as Kveld-Úlf does, and no better to opt for faithful service, as Thórólf does, because the king is apparently subject to the paranoid streak characteristic of tyrants. As it turns out, however, later encounters between Egil's family and royalty tell a less one-sided story.

Before turning to these encounters, we may follow Skallagrím to Iceland, where he settles and raises two sons, Thórólf (named for his deceased uncle) and Egil. They differ in every respect, in complexion as well as personality. Thórólf is handsome, athletic, sociable, valiant, and popular, much like his uncle, as the author explicitly states. Egil is precociously big and strong but also dark, ugly, and contentious in his childhood games. These qualities are hardly counterbalanced by an early demonstration of fluency and poetic skill. The incidents of his youth foretell the willfulness of later life: he goes unbidden to a feast, kills an older boy in an athletic dispute, then kills his father's overseer in revenge for his father's killing of Egil's foster mother in a werewolf fit of the kind that afflicts the dark side of the family and gave Kveld-Úlf (evening wolf) his name. Egil's premature verbal skills are a variant of the *puer senex* topos used in earlier sagas to signal Olaf Tryggvason's predisposition for Christianity and Magnús's early political sagacity. The topos is hagiographic, but in Egil's case it is inverted for use in a pre-Christian Iceland. The underside of the convention is used to show that Egil is destined to be difficult and self-assertive to a rare degree.[3]

When the time comes, Thórólf, like any promising young man and many a future Icelander, wishes to go abroad and see the world. Everyone agrees that Egil, given his personality, should not accompany his brother, but Egil once again displays his willfulness by forcing himself on an unwilling Thórólf.[4] Once in Norway, Thórólf, eager like his uncle for royal recognition, gains the favor of Harald Fairhair's successor, Erik Bloodax, with the gift of a ship. As in the case of the older Thórólf, the relationship begins auspiciously, but it soon deteriorates because of Egil's mischief. He kills King Erik's steward Bárd at a drunken feast, albeit with some provocation, and makes good his escape after killing several other men. The brothers' Norwegian host

---

[3] On Egil's complex personality, see in particular Lie's long but absorbing essay (1946, 145–248; rpt. 1982, 5–108). See also Grimstad 1976; Clunies Ross 1978 (rpt. 1989); Finlay 1992; Vésteinn Ólason 1998, 107.

[4] Eysteinn Þorvaldsson 1968 and Torfi Tulinius 1994, 116–19, suggest that Egil's insistence is already motivated by an attraction to his brother's wife, Ásgerd.

notes that Bárd probably got his just deserts but that Egil takes after his family in not being sufficiently wary of the king's wrath, which weighs heavily.

Despite a temporary reconciliation, the relationship is permanently compromised, especially because of the animosity of Erik's wife Queen Gunnhild, who is notorious in this and other sagas as a sorceress.[5] With Egil no longer persona grata in Norway, the brothers set out on further adventures, ending up in the service of King Athelstan in England. Here Thórólf falls in the great Battle of Vínheath (Brunanburg), and Egil, after a particularly theatrical display of grief, is reconciled by King Athelstan's equally dramatic munificence. He returns to Norway, marries Thórólf's widow Ásgerd, and becomes embroiled in a long-standing and complicated quarrel over Ásgerd's inheritance, to which we must return.

For the moment it suffices to note that Egil brings a court case against his opponent Berg-Qnund but that his claim is blocked by King Erik and Queen Gunnhild. Erik vows to kill Egil, but Egil turns the tables and kills one of the king's men. As a result, he is outlawed in Norway, but before departing he wreaks extraordinarily incommensurate revenge by killing not only Berg-Qnund but Erik's son, his foster son, and twelve others. Finally, he literally adds insult to injury by leveling a magic curse against king and queen in the form of a "scorn pole," a pole planted and topped with a horse's head.

Egil now returns to Iceland, but the interaction is not over. Gunnhild makes use of her magical arts to lure him back to her husband's court, now located in York because Erik has been forced to yield the Norwegian throne to his brother Hákon. Egil survives the reunion only by dint of his friend Arinbjǫrn's devoted and forceful diplomacy. Arinbjǫrn advises him to compose a praise poem in honor of Erik, and when the king refuses to be mollified, Arinbjǫrn goes so far as to say that Erik will have to fight them both. Contrary to all reasonable expectations, Erik allows Egil to depart unharmed, though without an official reconciliation.[6]

The relationship between Egil and Erik is quite different from the

---

[5] On Queen Gunnhild, see the fine essays in Sigurður Nordal 1941; and A. Heinrichs 1996.

[6] This episode has baffled critics perhaps more than any other in *Egils saga*. See Bley 1909, 50–53; Reichardt 1929; Lie 1946 (rpt. 1982); Nordland 1956, 80–87; Kristján Albertsson 1976; Vésteinn Ólason 1990.

one between the older Thórólf and King Harald. Erik emerges as a somewhat passive figure, a bit easygoing and even incautious in having accepted the overtures of Egil's brother Thórólf so readily. He seems indecisive and submissive to his wife's repeated admonitions; his posture in Egil's confrontation with Berg-Ǫnund is tentative; and his conciliatoriness at York after the killing of both his son and foster son seems incomprehensible.[7] In general, he appears to be a rather weak character who leaves the real initiative to Gunnhild.

How does Egil compare? The reader is in no doubt when invited to compare Egil's grandfather, father, and uncle with Harald Fairhair, but in the case of Egil himself the advantage is not so clear. The author provides a good deal of personal information, much of which speaks against Egil: he is willful, reckless, deaf to warnings, violent, intemperate, and relentless in pressing whatever he perceives to be his prerogative. In legal dealings he regularly abridges process by challenging his opponent to a duel, and in overt hostilities he kills almost randomly.

Bearing this in mind, we may now turn to Egil's relations with a third Norwegian king, Erik's successor Hákon Adalsteinsfóstri (foster son of Athelstan), also known as Hákon the Good. Egil, relentless as ever and still determined to make good his claim to Ásgerd's inheritance, approaches Hákon for another hearing. Given the service he has performed for King Athelstan, he may well believe that he has some claim on the favor of Athelstan's foster son. Hákon gives a measured reply:

> I have been informed that my brother Erik, and Gunnhild along with him, would say that you have quite overshot the mark in your dealings with them. It would seem to me that you might rest content even if I do not get involved in this matter, although Erik and I are not so fortunate as to be of one mind. (Chapter 63; ÍF 2:198)

Hákon puts his finger on the central flaw in Egil's character, his excess, but he nonetheless allows him to bring the case before a court. True to form, Egil quickly tires of the process and challenges his antagonist, Berg-Ǫnund's brother Atli inn skammi (the short), to single combat. He emerges victorious by dispatching his enemy with a grotesque bite to

---

[7] Bley 1909, 52, but cf. Hines 1992, 26–28.

the throat (confirmed by an ingenious reading of one of his occasional stanzas).[8] The rules of combat then allow him to possess himself of the lands that are, according to his claim, Ásgerd's portion.

Quite a few years later, after a time of great prosperity in Iceland, Egil returns to Norway to visit his friend Arinbjǫrn. When he learns that the assets he had won in a previous duel with a certain Ljót have been confiscated by King Hákon's stewards, he lapses into deep dejection. Arinbjǫrn, though pessimistic, offers to intercede with the king, but he gets an unfriendly reception in part because the king suspects that he is still allied with the family of his brother and rival, Erik Bloodax. Arinbjǫrn must concede his failure, and Egil is so embittered that Arinbjǫrn sees no recourse but to pay Egil out of his own pocket. Egil immediately cheers up, undeterred by the fact that this time his claim is at the expense of his friend.

This final encounter with royalty reveals a king, perhaps benefiting from the fact that he was a Christian before his time, who is both perceptive and reasonable, although he is not infinitely complaisant. Egil, on the other hand, is unreformed and resorts to implacable dudgeon if he does not get every penny that he thinks is his due. The reception given him by King Hákon offers a perfect opportunity for accommodation, but compromise is not in Egil's character, and the opportunity is lost. After a few more extraordinary adventures (to which I will return), Egil retires to Iceland and a further career of willfulness on the domestic front.

The backbone of this saga is an extended tale of Icelander and king, such as we have in the incorporated *þættir* of *Morkinskinna*.[9] It might be viewed as a highly elaborated version of the tales in *The Saga of King Magnús and King Harald,* in which an Icelander typically confronts King Harald Hardrule. Hreidar illustrates this type (see the previous chapter), but an even more apt example is the story of the troubled relationship between Halldór Snorrason, the son of Snorri the Chieftain, and King Harald. Halldór, the same sort of demanding and self-assertive Icelander as Egil, is one of the very few antagonists to get the best of this king. We may ask how the rivalry of Icelander and king,

---

[8] Jón Helgason 1957. The episode so aroused Bley's indignation that he thought it could not have been written by Snorri, whom he considered the main author (1909, 233–37). The idea that different authors could have been involved in the composition of the saga was raised again in Sveinn Bergsveinsson 1983.

[9] Vésteinn Ólason 1990, 67–68.

adumbrated in *Morkinskinna,* came to be the core of *Egils saga.* Part of the answer may lie in the political tensions between Iceland and Norway in the period 1215–20, just before the time during which it is assumed that *Egils saga* was written.[10]

In 1215, according to the Icelandic annals, two chieftains in southern Iceland, Sæmund Jónsson and Thorvald Gizurarson, set the prices on goods offered for sale by (presumably) Norwegian merchants, as seems to have been customary.[11] But the matter must have been contentious to merit mention at all in the annals. The aftermath was in any case a flaring up of hostilities. The following year, 1216, the son of one of the chieftains, Pál Sæmundarson, went to Bergen in Norway and was subjected to such abuse that he decided to go north to Thrándheim (Trondheim).[12] On the way his expedition was apparently overtaken by a storm, and all hands perished. When Pál's father learned of this, he was outraged and blamed the men of Bergen for his son's death. In 1217 he therefore retaliated by raising a force of five hundred men (six hundred, if we calculate by long hundreds) against another group of Bergen traders and extracted a large indemnity from them, despite the attempts of his brother Orm to pacify him.[13]

It was now the turn of the Norwegians to retaliate. Having spent the winter in Iceland, they prepared to return home in the summer of 1218, but before doing so, they killed the unoffending Orm and his son Jón. Bjǫrn, the son of the second chieftain, Thorvald Gizurarson, took revenge by dragging a Norwegian, said to be related to one of the merchant leaders, out of a church and killing him.[14] In 1219, the Icelandic annals note, no ship came to Iceland from Norway, and this has been understood as an embargo imposed by the Norwegians as the next move in the conflict.[15]

In the meantime, Snorri Sturluson had gone to Norway, where he spent two years with Jarl Skúli and was given a court title by King Hákon and Skúli. In 1220 he prepared to return to Iceland, at a time when feelings were running high against the Icelanders; there was

[10] The political situation is clearly outlined in Meulengracht Sørensen 1992, 121–27, 146–47. See also Sand Sørensen 1980, which views the saga as a defense of traditional institutions against the emergence of centralized monarchy.

[11] *Islandske annaler,* ed. Gustav Storm, 124, 183.

[12] *Sturlunga saga,* ed. Örnólfur Thorsson et al., 1:254.

[13] Ibid., 1:255; *Konunga sögur,* ed. Guðni Jónsson, 52.

[14] *Sturlunga saga,* 1:255–56; *Konunga sögur,* 69.

[15] *Islandske annaler,* 125, 185, 326; Jón Jóhannesson 1974, 241.

even talk of raiding in Iceland during the summer, though cooler heads advised against it.[16] The plan is confirmed in a stanza by the skald Gudmund Oddsson in *Hákonar saga Hákonarsonar*, where the initiative is attributed specifically to Skúli.[17] The plan did not materialize, but it is indicative of the political tensions. Around 1220, when *The Saga of King Magnús and King Harald* was written, the relations between Iceland and the Norwegian crown would almost necessarily have been a paramount issue in both camps.

This is also the time when Norwegian aspirations to annex Iceland resurface. According to *Hákonar saga Hákonarsonar*, the king himself intervenes against the plan to attack Iceland, and the jarl acquiesces. Instead it is decided to dispatch Snorri, who is given the title *lendr maðr* (district chieftain), to reestablish peace. The nature of the mission is explicit—"This was the first time that the jarl brought up the idea that Snorri should bring the country [Iceland] under King Hákon's rule"— but for the moment the idea does not bear fruit: "Snorri made no headway with his countrymen, but he also did not press the issue. Nonetheless the merchants enjoyed peaceful conditions at this time in Iceland."[18]

This interaction is of particular interest in a discussion of *Egils saga* because Snorri Sturluson is, more often than not, considered to be its author.[19] His authorship, no matter how likely, cannot be proved and is therefore not assumed here, but the issues would have been just as clear to any other author working in the same time frame.[20] Still, Snorri's hypothetical authorship makes it particularly inviting to inquire into the saga's point of view on relations between Iceland and the Norwegian king. If we had only the first section, on the relationship between Harald Fairhair and Kveld-Úlf's sons, we would probably not hesitate to view the text as an anti-Norwegian tract, but later interactions are more ambiguous. It might in fact be argued that there is a gradual improvement in the Norwegian kings and a compensatory decline in Egil's dispositon, from early recklessness to relentless self-interest. If these lines of development are to be seen in the context of

[16] *Sturlunga saga*, 1:262.

[17] *Konunga sögur*, 69.

[18] Ibid., 70–71.

[19] Among the many discussions, see Bley 1909; Wieselgren 1927; Sigurður Nordal in ÍF 2:LXX–XCV; Hallberg 1962; Holtsmark 1971.

[20] Óláfía Einarsdóttir 1990, 94–97.

outstanding political issues between Iceland and Norway, it is not at all certain that Iceland has the better of it.

One way to evaluate the contest is to explore the legal case in Norway with which Egil is so persistently preoccupied, the matter of his wife's inheritance. This case was the subject of a classical analysis by one of the founders of Old Icelandic studies, the law professor Konrad Maurer in Munich. Maurer focused on two legal cases in *Egils saga:* the first involving the older Thórólf's inheritance, and the second concerning Egil's entitlement to half of his wife Ásgerd's inheritance.[21] Only the second concerns us here, because it bears on the legitimacy of Egil's claim and the justification of his conduct.

The central question is whether Ásgerd herself is legitimate and entitled to half her family inheritance. She is the daughter of a certain Bjǫrn Brynjólfsson and Thóra Haraldsdóttir, nicknamed *hladhǫnd* (lace hand), whose marriage history is unorthodox. Bjǫrn woos Thóra but is rejected by her brother. He then abducts her and marries her in Shetland, but since the legal formalities have not been observed, Bjǫrn is outlawed in Norway. Eventually, he brings Thóra to Iceland and takes up residence in Skallagrím's household, where Thóra gives birth to Ásgerd. The legal troubles are ultimately settled with Thóra's family in Norway, but Thóra dies, leaving her husband Bjǫrn and daughter Ásgerd. Thórólf (the younger) sues for Ásgerd's hand in marriage and is accepted. In the meantime, Bjǫrn marries a second wife, Álof, by whom he has a second daughter, Gunnhild. The family situation is thus as follows:

$$\text{Thóra} \sim \text{Bjǫrn} \sim \text{Álof}$$
$$\text{Thórólf} \sim \text{Ásgerd} \quad \text{Gunnhild}$$

Subsequently Thórólf also dies, and his brother Egil marries his widow. When Bjǫrn dies too, the question of his inheritance arises. Does it belong to the half-sisters Ásgerd and Gunnhild equally, or does it belong exclusively to Gunnhild, whose legitimacy is not in doubt? This question precipitates a prolonged legal dispute.

Initially, Bjǫrn's son-in-law Berg-Ǫnund (married to Gunnhild) ap-

---

[21] Maurer 1895. Bley (1909, 1–26) attacked Maurer's analysis of the first case vigorously but not his understanding of the second. More recently, Auður Magnúsdóttir 2001, 101–9 has also dealt with the first case.

propriates the whole inheritance. Egil, with the aid of Arinbjǫrn, disputes the issue at a law assembly, but Berg-Ǫnund, secure in the friendship of King Erik and Queen Gunnhild, is unyielding. Egil offers single combat, only to be faced down by king and queen. He subsequently kills Berg-Ǫnund in an ingeniously staged night attack, and the inheritance passes to Berg-Ǫnund's brother Atli inn skammi (the short) under unclear circumstances.

Some years later, Egil resubmits his claim to King Hákon, who agrees to let the law take its course. Egil summons Atli to another assembly at the Gulathing and pursues his claim, but as the complications mount, he again resorts to single combat. This time he kills Atli and makes good his claim.

The case raises many questions. Is the marriage of Bjǫrn and Thóra legal, so that Ásgerd is a legitimate heir? Maurer argues that in the first instance the marriage is not legal, but the further question is whether it can be legitimized in retrospect through the reconciliation of the families. To this question Maurer replies that it probably can. In the process can Ásgerd be made a legitimate heir? Again, the answer is that she probably can.[22] There are many other questions as well, but Maurer's legal analysis as a whole would seem to suggest that Egil's claim is just. This was in fact not the question that Maurer posed; he was more intent on establishing in principle whether *Egils saga* conforms to ascertainable law. Neither the saga author nor Maurer had clear sources. The saga author was dependent on a familiarity with thirteenth-century Norwegian law and possible memories of earlier law. Maurer was dependent on later lawbooks in his effort to discern what might have been the law in the tenth century.

What is interesting about the case is precisely that it raises so many questions that are so difficult to answer. If the saga author had been strongly partisan in Egil's favor, the ready solution would have been to make the case perfectly clear. Why raise the issue of Ásgerd's legitimacy at all? The intention can only have been to introduce maximum complications and to make the issue as opaque as possible, leaving the reader to puzzle out the probabilities. This intention would seem to be equally true of the psychological complexities. Egil may have a just cause, but does he pursue it prudently? The kings may be in a difficult position, but do they acquit themselves reasonably? The case leaves us

[22] Maurer 1895, 101, 114–16, 108–9.

with more questions than answers and no clear point of view. Such indeterminacy may be one indication of an equivocal and neutralizing authorial stance.[23]

The picture does not gain in clarity during Egil's last adventures. Before returning to Iceland he undertakes a mission to collect taxes owed to King Hákon in the Swedish province of Värmland, imagined by the West Scandinavians to be remote and trackless. Egil's exploits in this frontier region are almost grotesquely hyperbolical. It is a story of sinister plots and repeated ambushes. At the first way station his host seeks to disable Egil and his companions with drink, but Egil downs everything put before him and asks for more. When his companions are in danger of succumbing, he drinks their share as well, and when he can hold no more, he disgorges the liquid onto his scheming host.[24] The following morning he compounds insult with injury by chopping off the host's beard and gouging out an eye. What is the reader to make of this more than Pantagruelian display? But it is only a prelude. In a later ambush Egil confronts odds of thirty to four by tying a broad, flat rock to his chest for protection and single-handedly killing nineteen men. After such feats it is almost anticlimactic that he should complete his perilous mission successfully.

Once back in Iceland, Egil lives out his last years in a style that is both comic and tragic, and no less excessive than his foreign adventures. He becomes friendly with his fellow poet Einar Helgason, with whom he can discuss their common literary interests. But one day Einar leaves a precious ornamental shield and, before riding off, notifies the household that it is a gift for Egil. When Egil learns of the gift, he is so outraged by the implied demand that he compose a poem to acknowledge the shield from Einar that he vows to kill him. Only the fact that Einar has put a safe distance between them preserves his life.

The tragedy of Egil's advancing age is that he loses two sons. His response is a melodramatic resolution to starve himself to death, a fate from which he is saved by his daughter's tricking him into drinking milk and offering him the alternative of composing a memorial poem. But even in this extremity there may be a comic intonation, because we

[23] About the first case, Auður Magnúsdóttir (2001, 103) notes that the issue is a matter of interpretation and is not intended to be clear to the reader. On other forms of ambiguity in the saga, see Torfi Tulinius 1994.
[24] For an ingeniously metaphorical reading of this somewhat notorious scene, see Looze 1989, 134–35.

cannot be sure that Egil is not complicit in his daughter's ingenious plan to save him.[25]

The depletions of age do nothing to diminish Egil's willfulness. He eventually cedes his residence at Borg to his son Thorstein and goes to live with his stepdaughter, but when Thorstein becomes embroiled in a quarrel with his neighbor, Egil appears at the assembly, hijacks the legal proceedings, and exiles the intrusive neighbor without any form of compensation for his lost property. Again, we may suspect that Thorstein and Egil are technically correct, but, now as before, Egil's self-assertiveness knows no bounds. He delivers a denunciatory speech in which he states that his antagonists originally received their land from his father and must therefore, in effect, forfeit it on demand. The legality of that proposition is doubtful, and the situation is shot through with irony. It emerges that Egil, given the opportunity, is more autocratic than the kings with whom he has disputed most of his life.

Egil's last years are not devoid of gloom. He becomes old and blind and is a nuisance to the women around the house. Several stanzas look back to better days, but even here a morbid humor persists. As Hermann Pálsson and Paul Edwards translate one of the half stanzas:

> My bald pate bobs and blunders,
> I bang it when I fall;
> My cock's gone soft and clammy
> And desire is not on call.[26]

One trait that suffers no decline, however, is Egil's malice. He proposes to take the two coffers of silver given him by King Athelstan and scatter the coins on the assembly plain in order to provoke a wild scramble for easy money and a riot of fisticuffs. This plan is averted, but he rides off, guided by two slaves, and throws the silver into a waterfall or swamp. No one is sure of the exact location, and the secret is well kept because Egil, for all his blindness, kills the two slaves and hides their corpses.[27] With this bizarre parody of the killing of Hjalli and

---

[25] On this the most famous of Egil's poems, see especially Sigurður Nordal 1924; Ralph 1976; and Harris 1994. On the comic intonation, see Andersson 2000, 3. See also Lönnroth 1996, 19–22.

[26] For a close study of these verses, see the memorial and valediction to Egil in Lie 1989. The *Egils saga* translation by Hermann Pálsson and Paul Edwards, 235, is slightly recast to accord with Lie's reading.

[27] On this episode, see Bjarni Einarsson 1977.

Hǫgni to preserve the secret of the Niflung treasure in the heroic poems of the *Edda,* Egil's life concludes.

The antiheroic finale is something new in saga writing. The lives of Olaf Tryggvason, Olaf Haraldsson, and even Harald Sigurdarson end gloriously in battle. The moment is profiled by a rich exploitation of doom and valor to underscore the personal distinction of the kings and the tragic nature of their demise. King Magnús's death also appears in high relief against a backdrop of religious and political devotion. These figures are heir to the great heroic tradition. But Egil stands apart. His life is not so much grand as it is extravagant, and the extravagance increases as his life advances. The heroic model is no more foreign to the sagas about early Icelanders than it is to the kings' sagas, but *Egils saga* is a conspicuous exception. Seeming to recoil from the tragic mode, it projects Egil rather as a comic figure whose exploits are parodic and morally ambiguous. This is an entirely new tonality and requires explanation.

We have seen that Egil's legal dealings leave him in something of a twilight. His conflicting personal qualities have the same effect. He is a man both of larger-than-life abilities and burlesque deficiencies. If we imagine him in an era of tensions between Iceland and Norway, we must ask ourselves how readers and listeners would have interpreted this decidedly mixed portrait. It seems clear that King Magnús was cast in an idealized mold as the best possible Norwegian king, but Egil is not depicted in such a way as to qualify him as the ideal Icelander.

Until 1220 there had been a highly inflammatory and bloody dispute between Norwegian merchants and two Icelandic chieftains, resulting in a Norwegian threat to make incursions into Iceland and, finally, a delegation led by Snorri Sturluson to persuade his countrymen to submit to Norwegian rule. This situation could not have failed to raise the consciousness of what it was to be Icelandic. That consciousness is already richly attested in *The Saga of King Magnús and King Harald,* in the form of interlarded stories about Icelandic interactions with King Harald Hardrule of Norway. This saga, with its dual focus, not only made room for a larger Icelandic presence but also departed from the panegyric model in the sagas of the two Olafs to set up a didactic contrast between two antithetical kings, Magnús and Harald. We can only suppose that Harald's aggressive and expansionist policies would have been anathema to Icelanders under the threat of Norwegian annexation, and that Magnús's preference for peace and sound domestic policy would have been warmly received. The author of *Egils saga* may have learned the art of contrastive portraiture from the models in *Morkinskinna,* but rather than contrasting two kings, this saga contrasts a legendary Icelander with successive Norwegian kings.

How would contemporary readers and listeners have understood the contrast? The reception in Iceland would to some extent have been governed by a prior knowledge of Egil, whose reputation was surely writ large in native tradition. Icelandic readers and listeners may have had a largely predetermined response to Egil, who was known to them as a heroic figure and a great poet. They would have been drawn to the special focus on Egil's contest with the Norwegian crown, which he not only survives but appears to win. They would have found their view of Egil's heroic stature confirmed and even exalted in its opposition to royal power. Perhaps not particularly alive to Egil's problematic personality in the text, they may simply have delighted in the burlesque aspects.

But we may postulate a second audience, the Norwegian audience.[28] That the book business was binational in this era is illustrated by the fact that the Icelandic sagas of Olaf Tryggvason and Olaf Haraldsson are preserved chiefly in Norwegian manuscripts.[29] Icelandic saga writers must therefore have been aware that they were writing for both audiences, and in a period of some antagonism this dual exposure must have posed special problems. The author of *The Saga of King Magnús and King Harald* responded by giving the Icelanders a larger role and making recommendations about royal policy. The author of *Egils saga* went a step further by shifting the focus from the lives of kings to the history of an Icelandic clan, the Mýramenn, whose distinction is the subject of the final chapter. This history became the platform for the theory that Iceland was settled as a refuge from Harald Fairhair's tyranny and that the exiles attained still greater eminence in their new home.

How would the Norwegians have responded to this rather subversive transformation of their history? Since Egil was born in Iceland and was no longer one of theirs, presumably they would have appreciated the equivocations built into his portrait. They would have perceived the subversions more in terms of Egil's personality than in terms of

[28] See Jónas Kristjánsson 1977, 471–72; Meulengracht Sørensen 1977, 768 (trans. and rpt. 1989, 158–59).
[29] See Stefán Karlsson 1979 (rpt. 2000).

Norwegian history. Where the Icelanders saw ancestral pride and heroic resistance, the Norwegians may have seen inflated claims, ridicule, and patriotic self-delusion. In this way the author could satisfy both audiences. Displacing the tragi-heroic mode of the sagas of the two Olafs, *Egils saga* might in fact be said to mark the true onset of the rhetoric of neutrality that came to be seen as a hallmark of saga writing.

In the earlier sagas I have tried to isolate what was dictated by the sources and what was transmuted by authorial intervention. In the sagas of the two Olafs the sources are still quite palpable and in some measure dominate the writers, who probably saw themselves not least of all as conveyers of tradition. In *The Saga of King Magnús and King Harald* the balance changes. The authorial strategy of contrast and a new political orientation came to dominate, but the sources are still quite visible in the stanzas, the independent tales (*þættir*), and "The Storytelling of an Icelander" (chapter 40). In *Egils saga* the stanzas are also much in evidence, though differently represented in different manuscripts. In the standard edition there are seventy stanzas in three extended poems and another sixty occasional stanzas, but in this case they are less documentary and more literarily illustrative. The author may have been more dependent on the traditions in which the stanzas were embedded than on the stanzas themselves. Those traditions must in turn have been quite extensive. They were presumably passed down in the family of the Mýramenn, and there can hardly be much doubt that the author, whether Snorri or another, belonged to or was attached to that family.

How such traditions would have originated is illustrated by Egil's conversations with Einar Helgason. The author comments:

> Egil asked Einar a lot about news from Norway and about his friends, and about those he could reasonably expect to be his enemies. He also asked a lot about the men in power. In return Einar asked Egil about his earlier travels and his great deeds. Egil liked this talk and became voluble. (Chapter 78; ÍF 2:268)

Einar would thus have been a further reservoir of information about Egil's life and adventures and would have bequeathed the narrative to others independently.

The traditions were no doubt abundant, and we may wonder

whether they were handed down in some particular form. Miraculous as it may seem to us now, it appears that in the thirteenth century people still knew a great deal of Egil's verse by heart. They would also have known stories and would have told them both anecdotally and at length, presumably in many forms. It is difficult to believe that our author relied on a single canonical form, because the text is so dominated by an idiosyncratic viewpoint and a complex system of ambiguities. What the author produced seems not to have been a known tradition but a tightly controlled and independently articulated version of a tradition.[30] There may have been a number of other versions in circulation as well, but *Egils saga* as we have it is a text on which the author stamped such a commanding narrative authority that it made competing transmissions irrelevant.

[30] This view is generally in accord with Bjarni Einarsson 1975 without necessarily subscribing to all the literary borrowings proposed there. See also Jakobsen 1985.

CHAPTER SIX

Turning Inward

Ljósvetninga saga

Scholars have traditionally distinguished between kings' sagas and sagas about early Icelanders. I depart from that tradition with a view to tracing a continuity from three kings' sagas and five native sagas through the transitional *Egils saga* to the full-blown and justly famous middle and late thirteenth-century sagas about early Icelanders. I postulate that *Ljósvetninga saga* is symptomatic of the turning point—not that in itself it marks the turning point but only that it illustrates the shift. It was almost certainly not the first saga with a predominantly Icelandic focus. Some or all of the so-called skald sagas, devoted to the amatory and other adventures of the skalds Bjǫrn Hítdœlakappi, Gunnlaug Illugason, Hallfred Óttarsson, Kormák Ǫgmundarson, and Thormód Bersason, could have been written before 1220.[1] Like *Egils saga* they pendulate between the royal courts of Scandinavia and Britain and the domestic scenes of Iceland. *Reykdœla saga,* which has the same exclusively Icelandic focus as *Ljósvetninga saga* and comes from the same northern region, has been dated persuasively between 1207 and 1222.[2] In other cases the dating is uncertain, but *Víga-Glúms saga, Fóstbrœðra saga,* and *Heiðarvíga saga* could also be early.

A similar dating problem is posed by *Ljósvetninga saga,* which has traditionally been assigned to the middle of the thirteenth century or a little later. I have argued that the evidence points to an earlier date, perhaps in the 1220s, and I maintain that dating here.[3] *Ljósvetninga*

---

[1] On the skald sagas in general, see Poole 2001.
[2] Hofmann 1972 (rpt. 1988).
[3] Andersson and Miller 1989, 78–84. See also Böðvar Guðmundsson et al. 1993, 107; and Monclair 2004, 55–58.

saga, like *Reykdœla saga,* refers to some words spoken by a certain Thorvard Thorgeirsson, an important man in the North who died in 1207: "Thorvard Thorgeirsson was subsequently in the habit of saying, whenever there was a ruckus, 'Let's try the Veisa grip.'"[4] That these rather trivial words should have been quoted fifty years after Thorvard's death seems unlikely. It would make better sense to quote them within living memory of his death in 1207, as the case appears to be in *Reykdœla saga.* A further criterion is that *Ljósvetninga saga* seems to have borrowed an episode from *Morkinskinna* (ca. 1220) rather than *Heimskringla* (completed perhaps ca. 1230–35).[5] It is therefore likely to have been written before *Heimskringla* displaced *Morkinskinna* as the authoritative history. Moreover, *Ljósvetninga saga* provides no historical prelude from the period of colonization, as *Egils saga* does so amply and as later sagas do almost routinely. The composition of *Ljósvetninga saga* may therefore antedate this standard narrative practice. It plunges directly into the main action, as does *Morkinskinna.*

Literary arguments bearing on the author's compositional skills also point to a relatively early date. Although such arguments are indecisive because levels of skill depend as much on the genius of individual authors as on positioning in the literary evolution, we have nonetheless seen a significant gap in compositional level between the sagas of the two Olafs (1180–1200) and *The Saga of King Magnús and King Harald* (ca. 1220). *Ljósvetninga saga* in some ways harks back to the former.

This question is connected with an important problem in the textual transmission of the saga. There is a shorter redaction (*A*) and a longer redaction (*C*), which differ particularly with respect to three semi-independent tales included in *C* but not found in *A*. This discrepancy has been the subject of a long-standing debate; some scholars have believed that the original had no trace of these episodes, which must therefore have been interpolated at a later date, while others believe that the episodes were part of the original but were dropped in the abbreviated version represented by *A*.[6] I adopt the latter view here, but the very fact that doubt could arise suggests the sort of loose, episodic composition found in the central portion of Odd's *Saga of Olaf Tryggvason* and in most of *The Legendary Saga of Saint Olaf.*

[4] Andersson and Miller 1989, 213. The words refer to the manhandling of a certain farmhand at the farm Veisa.

[5] *Morkinskinna,* trans. Andersson and Gade 19–20.

[6] See Erichsen 1919; Björn Sigfússon 1937; Magerøy 1956; Borggreve 1970.

The episodes in question can be considered integral, as contributing to the general disparagement of the protagonist Gudmund the Powerful. Or they can be regarded as interpolations because they are not essential to the narrative and awkwardly reintroduce Gudmund and the important figure Ófeig Járngerdarson (although Ófeig was duly introduced in chapter 1, and Gudmund has been at the center of the action in the first four chapters). These compositional lapses and the episodic quality of the narrative have had the general effect of placing *Ljósvetninga saga* in the forefront of the "*þáttr* theory," the view that the sagas are composites of smaller entities. As the story progresses, however, the plot becomes more streamlined.[7] The first four chapters explain the origin of the prolonged conflict between two regional groupings, Gudmund and his Mǫdrvellingar on the one hand and the Ljósvetningar on the other. Chapters 5–21 (C version) tell how Gudmund prosecuted his vendetta against the Ljósvetningar down to the killing of Thorkel hák, who had joined in slandering him, and how he concluded his life. Chapters 22–31 recount the persisting feud between Gudmund's sons Eyjólf and Kodrán and the next generation of Ljósvetningar.

It is the first four chapters that are the most difficult and most likely to be a stumbling block for uninitiated readers. They plunge us into a legal tangle as knotty as what we found in *Egils saga*, though the English-speaking reader will find the difficulties here alleviated by William Miller's commentary.[8] Legal density is characteristic of the sagas about early Icelanders, and we may begin by asking why the reader is so abruptly confronted with these opaque matters. We could speculate that *Egils saga* made them fashionable and that later writers followed suit, but it is more likely that legal cases figured prominently in the underlying oral traditions and were therefore a part of the narrative transmissions for which the Icelanders were well prepared.[9] *Sturlu saga* notes that the early legal dealings of the late twelfth-century chieftain Sturla Thórdarson are the first thing known about him, and it can hardly by doubted that this record was strictly oral.[10] *Egils saga* offers negative confirmation. After Egil's return to Iceland the text reports: "Egil lived at Borg for a long time and became an old man, but

---

[7] Bååth [1885]; Danielsson 1986, 36–37.
[8] Andersson and Miller 1989.
[9] This is the fundamental proposition in Danielsson 2002a, e.g., 276, 282, 299.
[10] Andersson 2002, 391.

there is no mention of his having disputes with men in this country, nor are we told of duels or killings after he settled here in Iceland" (chapter 78; ÍF 2.257). Disputes, both legal and lethal, seem to have been the stuff of tradition.

Ljósvetninga saga so resolutely cuts the colonial cord tying Iceland to Norway that the gesture seems almost overtly separatist, although connections with Norway do figure briefly at the end of the story. It is as if the author wished to make the point that the story is about Iceland and not about the mother country. There is only a passing statement to the effect that Jarl Hákon Sigurdarson ruled Norway at the time and welcomed a certain Sǫlmund into his service when Sǫlmund was exiled from Iceland because of a killing that resulted from the early legal contentions in the saga.

Hákon tries to facilitate Sǫlmund's premature return to Iceland by sending gifts to both the Mǫdrvelling chieftain, Gudmund, and the Ljósvetning chieftain, Thorgeir.[11] Neither chieftain wants the gifts or the obligations they entail, but they agree to share the unwelcome responsibility. That has the dire consequence of putting Thorgeir at loggerheads with his sons. Given the political tension between Iceland and Norway around 1220, we could imagine that the author intends a critique of Jarl Hákon's intrusion into regional Icelandic affairs, but that probably presses a small point too hard. It is more likely that the dissension between Thorgeir and his sons in the prelude signals the general theme of family discord that runs through the saga as a whole.

Since there is no colonial or Norwegian prelude, as in *Egils saga* and so many others, we might ask what model was available for such an unmediated plunge into local politics as we find in *Ljósvetninga saga*. The likeliest candidates may be *Sturlu saga* and *Guðmundar saga dýra*, two regional sagas centering on important chieftains at the end of the twelfth and beginning of the thirteenth century, and both dated to the period 1200–1220. These sagas also focus exclusively on internal Icelandic matters and thrust the reader directly into complex local dealings without establishing a historical framework. *Sturlu saga* is located in western Iceland and *Guðmundar saga dýra* in Eyjafjord, the same northern region in which *Ljósvetninga saga* is set. At this time there was a great deal of interaction between North and West, and there is no rea-

[11] Andersson and Miller 1989, 125.

son to doubt that the author of *Ljósvetninga saga* would have had access to both the earlier sagas.

We observed in Chapter 4 that around 1220 the author of *The Saga of King Magnús and King Harald* made impressive strides in personal portraiture, much exceeding what could be found in the sagas of the two Olafs. The author of *Ljósvetninga saga,* like the other authors of early native sagas, is focused on the task of depicting qualities of character and personality. Assuming that the episodic matter in chapters 5–12 is part of the original composition, we can in fact conclude that the point of this narrative is to define the personality of Gudmund the Powerful.

The first little story begins with a short statement on the grand style to which Gudmund is accustomed. He not only has a great "spread" but entertains lavishly, encouraging long-term visits by distinguished young men who are given nothing to do but keep him company. In other words, he apes royalty by maintaining something comparable to a king's retinue, a practice quite out of harmony with the Icelandic farmwork ethic. One may also wonder in passing whether the idle young men in his company gave rise to the later charges of homosexuality against Gudmund.

Into this resortlike atmosphere breaks a promising young fellow named Sǫrli Brodd-Helgason, intent on paying court to Gudmund's daughter. His visits cause rumors, and Gudmund reacts by sending his daughter away to live with his brother Einar. Notwithstanding, Sǫrli persists and eventually initiates a marriage proposal. Gudmund rejects the proposal, not because the young people are ill matched but because of the gossip they have occasioned. The unsuccessful swain is referred to Thórarin Nefjólfsson, whom we encountered in Olaf Haraldsson's diplomatic service, and Thórarin cleverly capitalizes on Gudmund's political and ancestral vanity to arrange the marriage. We are thus introduced to a chieftain who exhibits grand habits of mind and inflated ambitions but is also flawed by these weaknesses and can therefore be manipulated by those who understand his shortcomings and are able to exploit them.

The second preliminary story likewise focuses on Gudmund's vanity and affectations of grandeur. He is in the habit of riding around the district with a retinue of thirty men and thirty horses, staying for a week with each of his various constituents to transact business. Like his retinue of young men, this custom looks like a parody of royal privilege, since it seems modeled on the royal rounds of the Norwegian king (*veizlur*), based on his right to hospitality and entertainment throughout the realm.[12] But the custom weighs heavily on the local farmers, to whose hardship Gudmund seems oblivious. When the matter comes to the attention of the northern leader Ófeig Járngerdarson, he devises a remedy that is tailored to the abuse and makes the necessary point: Ófeig too gathers a following of thirty men and thirty horses and proceeds to spend Easter week with Gudmund, who is obliged to replenish both his supplies of hay and food. On his departure, Ófeig explains the parallel, and Gudmund takes the point, although he is not enthusiastic about this packaging of the truth. The anecdote illustrates again how Gudmund is blinded by his vanity and ambition, but also how his arrogance can be foiled by a bold and decisive response.[13]

The third preliminary story is closely related to the second. It too circumscribes Gudmund's authority and assigns Ófeig Járngerdarson an important role in the opposition. It seems clear that to the east of Eyjafjord in Reykjadale, where Ófeig was at home, there must have been a focus of oral tradition hostile to Gudmund. That the stories illustrating this hostility belong to the core of the saga and are not interpolated as an afterthought is borne out by a famous episode in chapter 21—in which Ófeig again discountenances Gudmund[14]—and by the whole second part of the saga, which pits the people around the lake Ljósavatn east of Eyjafjord against Gudmund's sons. This regional contention is the essence of the saga, a replication in miniature of the great contention between eastern Norway and Thrœndalǫg which is central in *The Saga of King Magnús and King Harald*.

The action of the third story is precipitated by a troublemaker named Brand, who becomes the responsibility of the eastern chieftain Thorkel Geitisson and, as a result of violent acts, the target of Gudmund's prosecution. Thorkel tries to effect a reasonable settlement, but Gudmund, true to form, insists on his sole prerogative to decide the terms. Though in a much inferior position, Thorkel temporarily thwarts Gudmund's prosecution and then joins forces with Ófeig to win the hand of Gudmund's niece, thus becoming Gudmund's in-law and blunting the

---

[12] Björn Sigfússon 1934, 195.

[13] Magerøy (1959) considered the anecdote to be a fiction based on an episode in *Guðmundar saga góða*.

[14] This is a moment not infrequently cited as a high point in saga art. See Liestøl 1930, 83–84; Andersson and Miller 1989, 199.

prosecution permanently. Just as the previous story concluded with the comment that Ófeig's reputation was greatly enhanced ("People thought that Ófeig's reputation had grown greatly because of these dealings with Gudmund"), so this story ends with the triumph of Thorkel Geitisson: "Thorkel captured all the honor." Or again: "Thorkel went home with his wife and was judged to have gained greatly in this affair."[15] In this all-or-nothing game the reader may easily deduce that Gudmund's reputation suffers correspondingly.

It is evident that these three stories make the same point in several iterations: Gudmund has all the political clout and all the resources, but he also has character and personality defects that can be exploited by less powerful adversaries with sounder principles.[16] The stories are object lessons in the abuse of power and the limits of autocracy. In this dimension too the saga is reminiscent of the contrast between an overweening King Harald and the principled King Magnús.

At this point it is useful to recall that in the earliest sagas about Olaf Tryggvason and Olaf Haraldsson the anecdotal material was scattered somewhat randomly; especially in the central section of Odd's saga, the incidents were not coordinated in such a way as to create a thematic texture. It therefore marked a significant advance in compositional technique when the author of *The Saga of King Magnús and King Harald* clustered symptomatic episodes at the beginning of the text so as to preface the main action with full portraits of the protagonist kings. The author of *Ljósvetninga saga* carries the technique a step further, using the stories that were in circulation about Gudmund in such a way as to make the protagonist's shortcomings quite palpable.

The portrait is overtly hostile. King Harald Hardrule and Egil Skalla-grímsson were problematical characters, but each has had his defenders.[17] The author of *Ljósvetninga saga*, however, not content with ambiguity, made the underside uppermost. This attention to personal failings becomes one of the more remarkable features of the Icelandic sagas. After the initial hagiographic, and consequently uncritical, portraiture of the two Olafs, saga protagonists become rather more indeterminate, as we saw in Chapter 3. There are no clear-browed Beowulfs, Rolands, or Cids but only flawed heroes who lend an inter-

---

[15] Andersson and Miller 1989, 144, 161.
[16] See also the reflections of Danielsson 1986, 36.
[17] On King Harald, see Ármann Jakobsson 2002, 196–202; on Egil, see Vésteinn Óla-son 1998, 107.

rogatory quality to their narratives. That the three stories illustrating Gudmund's shortcomings are merely prefatory is emphasized by their relative brevity in comparison with the major narrative that follows: the account of Gudmund's extended feud with his detractors to the East.

If this is not the first feud narrative in the sagas, it is certainly one of the best, rich in subterfuge and indirection. It begins with a classical allusion, a reenactment of the "quarrel of the queens" in the legend of Brynhild and Sigurd.[18] This legendary dispute is, in the first instance, about which woman has the more distinguished husband, but from it emerges also the false charge that Brynhild has slept with Sigurd, an accusation that bears bitter fruit. The quarrel in *Ljósvetninga saga* has a similar structure. Gudmund's wife Thórlaug is seated next to Geirlaug, wife of the chieftain Thórir Helgason. A serving woman of Geirlaug's acquaintance unthinkingly serves her first, but Geirlaug, perhaps in a tone of false self-deprecation, defers to Thórlaug, saying that she is not Thórlaug's equal—except perhaps in the distinction of her marriage. Thórlaug is clearly taken aback and counters that surely no one has a husband more distinguished than her own Gudmund.

Geirlaug now launches the thunderbolt, stating that Thórlaug might indeed be right if Gudmund were really a man. The implication is that he is homosexual, a deadly charge in the Old Icelandic value system. Thórlaug responds that Geirlaug must surely be the first to make such a charge, but Geirlaug retorts that it is common knowledge and identifies her immediate sources as a certain Thorkel hák and her own husband Thórir. This interview, like its legendary prototype, thus recapitulates both the theme of marital preeminence and the theme of sexual defamation.

Thórlaug feigns illness and convinces Gudmund to leave the wedding feast. On their way home she reports her conversation with Geirlaug. The accusation relayed by Geirlaug is not one that Gudmund can counter with protests or bland denials. He therefore seeks counsel from his foster father, who advises him to litigate aggressively against Thórir Helgason's constituents so as to exact fines and raise a war chest from which to defray the compensations that the law will impose for the killings that Gudmund clearly contemplates.

The women's quarrel in *Ljósvetninga saga* is not well motivated, and

[18] Andersson and Miller 1989, 165 n.75.

it is not at all clear why Geirlaug would choose to publicize the accusation against Gudmund on this particular occasion. The legend of the contending queens nonetheless provides a suggestive context for the saga. It has the effect of equating Gudmund with King Gunnar, a figure of more ceremonial status than proven mettle, rather than with the great hero Sigurd. Since Sigurd stands accused of having slept with Gunnar's queen, Brynhild, in the legend, it falls to Gunnar to avenge his sexual honor, but he becomes the fomentor rather than the executor of the vengeance. He appeals first to his brother Hǫgni to kill Sigurd, and when Hǫgni pleads the impediment of blood brotherhood with the intended victim, Gunnar incites his younger brother Gotthorm to do the murderous deed. Gudmund similarly plays the role of the machinator rather than the champion. He is in fact ultimately stymied in his plot against Thórir Helgason because he is unwilling to face him in single combat. That an association with the somewhat feckless Gunnar is deliberate is suggested by the thematic continuity with the prefatory stories in which Gudmund aspires to the trappings of a quasi-royal entertainment in his district. Gudmund is the farmer who would be king, and his pretentions are fraught with irony. In differing ways, *Ljósvetninga saga* thus plays off both heroic legend and the tradition of the kings' sagas.

There is no need to rehearse Gudmund's plot against Thórir Helgason and Thorkel hák in detail, but it is set out in a dramatic and artful sequence. No one quite knows what is afoot, although the atmosphere is heavy with apprehension. On the surface, Gudmund succeeds: Thórir is condemned to three years of lesser outlawry on a trumped-up charge, and Thorkel hák is eventually killed when Gudmund and his followers gain access to his house through the betrayal of a scurrilous hireling. But the success is only ostensible; in truth, Gudmund's enemies carry the day. Thórir Helgason, like Gudmund's antagonists in the preliminary stories, is inferior in resources but has the moral upper hand and emerges from the contest unblemished: "He went home to his farm at Laugaland and dwelled there until old age and was held in high esteem."[19]

Gudmund's attack on Thorkel hák does conclude with Thorkel's fall but also, more to the point, with the undoing in perpetuity of Gudmund's reputation. He allows his men to do the fighting while he him-

[19] Ibid., 187.

self shrinks back, giving Thorkel one last opportunity to reformulate the charge of homosexuality:

> Thorkel received multiple wounds because there were many against one, and even though his intestines were exposed he was no less fierce. Gudmund danced away and tumbled into the milk vat. Thorkel saw what happened, laughed, and said: "I imagine your ass has slaked itself at many streams, but I doubt it has drunk milk before."[20]

The triumph of word over weapon is borrowed from the rhetoric of heroic poetry, and it seals Gudmund's fate. By shrinking from combat he has lent credence to the charge against him, which implies cowardice as well as sexual deviation. Thorkel's witticism will be Gudmund's memorial. He is able to live on and retain his standing, but he will not be able to eradicate the accusation, which will continue to haunt his literary legacy.

Readers will inevitably wonder, in the literal way we have of interrogating texts, whether the charge against Gudmund is "true" or not, but that may be beside the point; it may simpy be a metaphorical rendering of the maximum disparagement available in this culture. There are references to the accusation of homosexuality in *Qlkofra þáttr* and *Njáls saga*, but for the most part—not least of all in *Njáls saga*—Gudmund is represented as a powerful and influential chieftain uncompromised by personal detractions.[21] Why then did the author of *Ljósvetninga saga* produce such a damaging portrait? Whatever the motivation, it is a triumph of malice. Outright scoundrels abound in the sagas, but Gudmund's is the fullest portrait of a high-profile politician undermined by the personal failings of cowardice, unscrupulous ambition, and a possible secret life that inspires public disapprobation. The saga sketches not the fall of a mighty man from power and fortune but rather the retrospective exposé of a figure thought to have a secure place in history. The satire directed against Norwegian kings in *Egils saga* can, it appears, be leveled against indigenous statesmen even more explicitly.

That the animus in the saga is regional in nature and not solely a per-

---

[20] Ibid., 193.
[21] Ibid., 86–88. On the historical background of Gudmund's emergence as a powerful figure, see Björn Sigfússon 1934.

sonal attack on Gudmund is borne out by the sequel. Gudmund is succeeded in Eyjafjord by his older son, Eyjólf, who is cast in much the same mold as his father, and a popular younger son named Kodrán. In the same generation the leadership of the Ljósvetningar, some dozen of whom figure in the action, falls to Thorvard Hǫskuldsson, who is described as a "wise and even-tempered man, well along in years."[22] Eyjólf at first tries to mend relations with the Ljósvetningar, but a paternity case that he takes over in his capacity as chieftain soon pits him against a certain Brand Gunnsteinsson and the other clansmen from Ljósavatn. These antagonists in turn fuel the hostility by keeping the matter concealed from their moderate leader, Thorvard. Passions become inflamed to the point of a pitched battle in which, notably, Kodrán is killed, and several other casualties are suffered.

The battle does not have the epic dimensions we find in modern fiction, but it does unfold in some detail, complete with discussions of strategy, maneuvers and countermaneuvers, recruiting anecdotes, an abundance of dialogue, and details of individual combats. Since pitched battles are in fact not the stuff of the classical Icelandic sagas, the degree of articulation in this case stands out. In other sagas about early Icelanders, small encounters involving perhaps a dozen men are the rule. By contrast, indications of numbers in *Ljósvetninga saga* are that the Mǫdrvellingar see seventy Ljósvetningar riding against them and that these seventy are later reinforced by another seventy led by Thorvard Hǫskuldsson; at the same time it is clear that the Mǫdrvellingar have superior numbers. The total number of combatants may therefore be imagined as lying between three and four hundred, a figure that seems quite exaggerated for the Saga Age. Large-scale battles with hundreds of participants are in fact features of the kings' sagas rather than the classical Icelandic sagas. The battles fought at Svǫld, Stiklarstadir, Hlýrskógsheath, and Stamford Bridge are cases in point, and it seems not unlikely that the author of *Ljósvetninga saga* is modeling his battle on these precedents, suggesting in effect that Icelandic history had moments to rival those of greater Scandinavia. What makes the dimensions doubly implausible, however, is that only three deaths and three wounds are actually reported.

When the fighting breaks off, there remains the matter of a legal settlement. As elsewhere in the Icelandic sagas, it is a question of mus-

[22] Andersson and Miller 1989, 203.

tering support on both sides for the confrontation at law on the assembly plain, a civil replication of the military clash. As usual, Eyjólf and his Mǫdrvellingar have greater resources than the Ljósvetningar, who, apart from their numerical inferiority, are threatened with internal dissensions. The killer of the popular Kodrán, a certain Hall Ótryggsson, not only is a target for the enemy but also is threatened with ostracism by his own allies. In addition, a certain Hrafn Thorkelsson, who has performed poorly in the battle, now becomes an object of opprobrium. But Thorvard Hǫskuldsson, who at first was kept in the dark about the gathering storm, emerges as a forceful leader and ensures the solidarity of the Ljósvetningar. He responds to the proposed expulsion of Hall by stating in the aftermath of the battle: "I wish to invite everyone to my farm this evening, first and foremost Hall Ótryggsson, who has suffered and purged shame on our account; we are in this together." Similarly, when Thorvard's son mocks Hrafn for his cowardice in battle, Thorvard repairs the breach laconically by saying "Hrafn shall be seated next to me."[23] Thorvard thus curtails the potential disintegration of his party and restores the unity of his cause.

Having secured the domestic front, he goes on, with a series of maneuvers as bold as they are ingenious, to block Eyjólf's prosecution and force a negotiated settlement on his more powerful opponent. As a result of this settlement, Hall is condemned to full outlawry, goes to Norway, distinguishes himself, takes service with King Harald Sigurdarson, and is ultimately killed by a kinsman of the Mǫdrvellingar. Thorvard himself is exiled for three years and goes on a pilgrimage to Rome. On his return he learns that Eyjólf has flouted the legal settlement and killed his brother Thórarin. Despite this provocation he invokes the moral authority of St. Peter and elects not to return to Iceland, where his presence would only exacerbate the feud. These concluding notes could have been read by a partisan author as a final triumph for the Mǫdrvellingar, but the author clearly belongs to the other camp. Instead of emphasizing the final acts of Mǫdrvelling vengeance, the aftermath highlights Hall's valor and Thorvard's dedication to peace.

The thematic thrust of the second part of Ljósvetninga saga conforms to the first part. In both generations the author erects a contrast between a dominant chieftain with unrivaled resources and a disadvan-

[23] Ibid., 222.

taged but courageous resistance group. It is almost a foregone conclusion that the powerful chieftain will prevail, but that is not the point the author wishes to make. The reader's attention is focused rather on the conduct of the antagonists and their moral stature. The winners are discredited—in Gudmund's case, with palpable malice—and the losers are exalted. It is the losers who display political acumen and forceful policy, as well as religious humility. Thus the saga is finally not about victory and defeat but about qualities of mind and spirit. In this sense it represents a continuity with *The Saga of King Magnús and King Harald;* it too operates with moral oppositions to advocate norms of conduct. The innovation lies not in a new thematic texture but in the transfer of an inherited texture from a Norwegian scene to an Icelandic scene.

This transfer was by no means inevitable; other sagas that were written in the same general area and at approximately the same time do not exhibit a similar synthetic viewpoint. One of these is *Reykdœla saga,* perhaps the most loosely composed of all. It celebrates Áskel as an inexhaustible exponent of good will, but it does not portray a gallery of sharply defined characters akin to Gudmund, his brother Einar, Thórir Helgason, Thorkel hák, and Thorvard Hǫskuldsson. Nor does it establish political or moral categories. *Víga-Glúms saga* is of considerably more interest in this regard—the protagonist is an impressively resourceful and cunning personality—but it too fails to establish character contrasts or some form of moral ledger. Glúm's opponents parade through the saga without offering political alternatives.

Both *Reykdœla saga* and *Víga-Glúms saga* seem more bent on providing a record of regional conflicts than on analyzing political conduct. The triumph of *Ljósvetninga saga* is that it imposes a thematic perspective on the conflicts and invites the reader to abstract certain general principles of conduct against the background of a regional feud. It is not so much a record as an assessment of actions and events, and it is perhaps the first of the native sagas to succeed in the project of generalizing about the feud traditions inherited from the Saga Age. It justifies the supposition underlying the following chapters: to wit, that the sagas could capture such traditions in an interpretive framework.

CHAPTER SEVEN

Gilding an Age

Laxdœla saga

Laxdœla saga, like Ljósvetninga saga, is a regional saga, set in the inner reaches of Hvammsfjord on the west coast of Iceland, to the north of the area settled by Skallagrím in Egils saga. Like Ljósvetninga saga it too is organized by generations, but whereas the author of Ljósvetninga saga seems determined to avoid the colonial period in order to focus on the internal politics of Iceland in the first half of the eleventh century, the author of Laxdœla saga dwells fondly on the age of settlement (870–930). Ljósvetninga saga embraces two generations, but Laxdœla saga reaches seven or eight generations back in time and gives special weight to the founding matriarch Unn the Deepminded.[1]

In its extended prehistory, Laxdœla saga appears to be modeled on Egils saga.[2] The Norwegian ancestor of the Laxdoelir, Ketil flatnef, replicates the fate of Egil's grandfather Kveld-Úlf: both abandon their lands under the expansionist pressure of King Harald Fairhair, but neither reaches Iceland. Kveld-Úlf dies at sea, and Ketil flatnef settles in Scotland while his sons Bjǫrn and Helgi go on to Iceland. The preeminent figure, however, is not Ketil but his daughter Unn, whose son Thorstein becomes king over half of Scotland. After Thorstein's death at the hands of the faithless Scots, she prepares her departure in secret and sets sail with immense wealth. She makes landfall first on the

---

[1] The exact number of generations depends, of course, on where one begins counting. See van Ham 1932, 3; Beck 1977, 385; Bjarni Guðnason 1999, 9.

[2] The verbal echoes proposed by Einar Ólafur Sveinsson in ÍF 5:XLI and Hermann Pálsson (1986, 76, 102–4), are inconclusive, but it is difficult to believe that the author of Laxdœla saga did not know Egils saga.

Faroe Islands and marries off one of Thorstein's daughters, who becomes the progenitor of the greatest family in the Faroes. Unn then goes on to Iceland and colonizes the foot of Hvammsfjord, where she imposes her will on her brothers, along with everyone else. Her favorite is a grandson, Olaf feilan, whom she marries off at a regal wedding feast before herself succumbing at a ripe age and seated upright in a memorable posture.[3]

What we learn about Unn is that she is commanding and enterprising, lavish and imperious, generous and hospitable on an unparalleled scale, gracious to the acquiescent, and dignified to the very end. Because her son Thorstein has been king of Scotland, she is in fact a queen mother, and she acts the part. We may wonder whether the author is responding to Harald Fairhair's sole monarchy in Norway by establishing quasi-royal credentials for the founders of Iceland, or whether regional rivalry has led to an emulation of Skallagrím's grandiose colonization to the south in Borgarfjord.[4] Skallagrím also disposed with a sovereign hand, and his precedent is invoked in no uncertain terms by Egil in defense of his son at the end of *Egils saga.* Status is at the heart of both sagas.

Unn is only the first in a series of queenly figures in *Laxdœla saga.*[5] Since the author had a real predilection for mythic patterning, we might surmise that Unn owes something to the archetypal colonizer Dido. We observed that Odd Snorrason may have harked back to Dido in contriving Queen Geira's marriage to Olaf Tryggvason, but it was as much the passion as the hegemony that caught Odd's fancy. In *Laxdœla saga* it is only the political dimension that grips the author, a woman's extraordinary leadership qualities and statecraft.[6] An erotic preoccupation was reserved for later generations.

Although Unn favored her grandson Olaf feilan, it was Hǫskuld, a great-grandson, the son of her granddaughter Thorgerd, who was destined to carry on the grand tradition. He is something of an enigma, but he is central to the story. After his father's death, Hǫskuld becomes a distinguished and popular man, although he seems to owe much of

---

[3] On the royal resonance of this posture, see Ármann Jakobsson 1997, 96–97; Würth 2001, 299.

[4] On the royal aspirations in *Laxdœla saga*, see Ármann Jakobsson 1998, 365–66, 379 and Bjarni Guðnason 1999, 9–10.

[5] On the figure cut by Unn, see Bouman 1962b, 113–20; and Helga Kress 1980.

[6] On the author's knowledge of Odd Snorrason's saga, see in particular Heller 1976, 53–64, 91.

his success to the lasting bonds forged by his father. We also learn that he is a retainer at the court of Hákon the Good and that he spends alternate winters at the Norwegian court and at home at Hǫskuldsstadir, but we are not told how this arrangement comes about. We learn next that he marries a woman named Jórunn, who is described as beautiful, very self-assertive, and highly intelligent—rather more information than we get about Hǫskuld himself. Nonetheless, he emerges as "powerful, steadfast, and quite wealthy," so that his condition is very honorable and prosperous (chapter 9; ÍF 5:18). How exactly he attains such status is, again, not specified, but he considers that his housing is not on a level with his social standing.[7] He therefore buys a ship and sails to Norway, ultimately for the purpose of acquiring building timber. But first he meets up with a Russian merchant and purchases an exceptionally beautiful and costly slave woman, whose only defect appears to be that she is mute. Hǫskuld takes her as his mistress.

Only then does he make his way to King Hákon, who bestows on him a gift of the necessary building timbers. Once more we may be a little surprised to learn so little about the clearly special relationship between King Hákon and his Icelandic retainer, but when Hǫskuld prepares to leave, Hákon heaps more gifts on him (a gold ring and a valuable sword) and pays him the high compliment of saying that he will indeed be difficult to replace—though exactly what service Hǫskuld has rendered to deserve such princely treatment is not revealed.

Back in Iceland, his mistress gives birth to a son named Olaf (later "Peacock"), and the predictable tension between wife and mistress ensues, obliging Hǫskuld to find housing for his mistress and son at some distance from his residence. The boy is later given in fosterage to a wealthy, if unprepossessing, neighbor. Crucial to the main plot is that the mystery of the beautiful mistress is eventually revealed. One day Hǫskuld overhears her talking to her son, in Irish, and realizes that she is not mute. She turns out in fact to be Melkorka, daughter of the Irish king Mýrkjartan. Thus royalty surfaces once more in the family: Unn is the mother of a Scottish king, and the boy Olaf is the grandson of an Irish king.

---

[7] On the peculiar vacuity of some of the characters in *Laxdœla saga,* see Kersbergen 1933, 56–57; Schildknecht-Burri 1945, 44; Njörður P. Njarðvík 1971, esp. 73; Cook 1992, 48–50.

To be sure, Hǫskuld also has status as the favorite of a Norwegian king, but unlike Unn he is something of a cipher. His life in both Iceland and Norway is shadowy; we are told nothing of his dealings in the district (the sort of narrative so prominent in *Ljósvetninga saga*) and nothing of his ostensible military service in King Hákon's retinue (the sort of narrative richly illustrated in *Egils saga*). The only domestic action is a dispute with his half-brother Hrút over their inheritance, a dispute that is not to Hǫskuld's credit and that he must eventually settle at his wife's behest. We know that Hǫskuld is affluent, but there is no indication of how the wealth accrues. Indeed, the only moment in Hǫskuld's life that is scenically realized is his purchase of Melkorka. It is as if he lives only in the reflected glory of his Irish princess.

That glory redounds even more directly to his son Olaf, who is not only of royal blood but is later offered the throne of Ireland. Accordingly, Olaf greatly outshines his father both at home and abroad. His mother arranges passage for him, and he duly appears at the Norwegian court. Here he becomes the instant favorite of Queen Gunnhild, who, far from being allotted the role of wicked sorceress as in *Egils saga*, is the soul of unselfish solicitude.[8] When she learns that Olaf is of royal Irish extraction, she outfits him magnificently for a voyage to Ireland, declaring jointly with her son King Harald Graycloak that "no more promising man had come from Iceland in their days" (chapter 21; ÍF 5:53). We may again wonder what justification there is for such a judgment, since Olaf, like Hǫskuld, has no record of accomplishment.[9]

This time, though, we do not have long to wait for vindication. Olaf, at the threshold age of eighteen, takes over full command of a vessel manned by sixty seasoned warriors. When they appear to have lost their bearings in a fog, Olaf sides decisively with a minority of one against the other shipmates, judging that the advice of one expert is preferable to that of a majority of fools—not a democratic sentiment but the voice of a firm military man.[10] On the coast of Ireland, Olaf is again a commanding presence. When the local Irish militia wish to treat his stranded vessel as a prize for the taking, he lines his men up at the gunwales and faces the enemy down. It is chiefly Olaf's appearance that intimidates the Irish:

[8] Wolf 1994, 725.

[9] Ármann Jakobsson 1998, 372; Bjarni Guðnason 1999, 15.

[10] Hermann Pálsson 1986, 100–101; Ármann Jakobsson 2002, 189.

Olaf advanced to the prow. He was outfitted with a byrnie and wore a helmet with gold filigree. He had a sword at his side with a gilded hilt and carried a hooked spear that was beautifully ornamented. Before him he carried a red shield on which a lion was depicted in gold. When the Irish saw this equipment, they were overcome by fear and thought the prize was not so easily taken as they had supposed. (Chapter 21; ÍF 5:55)

This thoroughly anachronistic chivalric scene epitomizes the early phases of *Laxdœla saga,* in which appearance is everything.[11]

King Mýrkjartan himself eventually arrives on the scene, allowing Olaf to identify himself in perfect Irish. Invited to the royal court in Dublin, the king's grandson renders distinguished military service against unspecified vikings. The service is merely reported, not described, but it is sufficient to qualify Olaf as Mýrkjartan's successor, as Mýrkjartan informs the court at the conclusion of the campaign: "I wish now to offer him my throne as my successor because Olaf is better qualified as a leader than my sons" (chapter 21; ÍF 5:59). Olaf gives eloquent thanks but prefers to return home. On the way, he stops off again in Norway and is once more overwhelmed with gifts, including a ship, and offers of high office if only he will consent to remain, but he elects to repatriate fame and fortune in Iceland.

He is now ready to settle down. His father proposes that he marry Thorgerd, the daughter of Egil Skallagrímsson, and thus form an alliance with the great clan of the Mýramenn in the South. At this point the regional aspirations of the Laxdœlir and Mýramenn, of *Laxdœla saga* and *Egils saga,* would seem to merge, but Thorgerd is not so easily persuaded. So strained are the social ambitions in this text that she dismisses the potential king of Ireland as "the son of a slave girl." It is only when Olaf, once more magnificently garbed, sits down and converses with her for a day that she is won over. Again, the personal magnetism of the Laxdœlir prevails.

Not content with making the greatest match in Iceland, Olaf sets about constructing a magnificent new house called At Hjardarholt (at Herd Woods). So vast is his wealth that when he moves, the parade of his domestic animals forms an unbroken line from the old home to the new.[12] Sometime later Hǫskuld dies, and Olaf stages a splendid memo-

---

[11] On this fondness for display, see van Ham 1932, 47; Heller 1976, 75–77, 83–86; Ármann Jakobsson 1998, 358–60.

[12] Bouman (1962b, 121) calculated the distance at five kilometers.

rial feast, the second largest ever held in Iceland and attended by no fewer than 1,080 guests. The expenditures and superlatives seem inexhaustible, but now, quite suddenly, the tone changes.

The contentions in *Ljósvetninga saga* were in a sense horizontal: that is, they were played out among contemporaries, between Gudmund and his enemies in the first generation and between Eyjólf and Thorvard Hǫskuldsson in the second generation. *Ljósvetninga saga* represents a synchronic view of history; *Laxdœla saga,* a more diachronic view: a succession of periods with differing characteristics, a golden age and an iron age. In the earlier age there is peace and plenty, almost spontaneously. Heroic reputations are made without a sword's being visibly lifted, and fortunes are made effortlessly by simply appearing at foreign courts. Money grows like the self-sown fields of Norse mythology. As we look back at the lives of Hǫskuld and Olaf, we are likely to retain chiefly that Hǫskuld acquired an Irish princess (a trophy concubine) and that Olaf built a magnificent home (a trophy house). In this history, early Iceland is seen in terms of peerless feasts, voyages for fame and fortune, marital unions of the best and most blessed, priceless apparel, royal receptions, and universal esteem.

The break comes between Olaf's generation and the following generation of his son Kjartan and foster son Bolli. At first the earlier pattern promises to persist: Kjartan keeps company with the most eligible woman in Iceland, Gudrún Ósvífrsdóttir, and seems to have an unspoken understanding with her. He asks her to wait three years for him, then goes abroad, is splendidly received by King Olaf Tryggvason, and becomes romantically involved with the king's sister Ingibjǫrg. In short, the magic of the Laxdœlir is not a whit diminished. But when Kjartan returns to Iceland, he discovers that Gudrún is married to his foster brother Bolli. He himself contracts a somewhat pro forma marriage to a certain Hrefna, but what follows is a gradual deterioration of relations that culminates in Bolli's killing, at Gudrún's behest, of his own foster brother, Kjartan.

Important here are not so much the narrative details as the reversal of the earlier patterns and a supervening gloom. In place of an international round of foreign courts, we find a focus radically contracted to Iceland. Instead of the unquestioning recognition conferred on traveling Icelanders, we find an atmosphere poisoned by suspicion and bitter resentment. In place of perfectly arranged and perfectly successful society matches, we find only marital dissension. Substituted for the priceless gifts of earlier generations are ill-fated gifts that carry a curse: a magnificent headdress intended for Gudrún but given to Hrefna instead; a splendid sword bestowed on Kjartan but later stolen and thrust into a swamp. Instead of unbreachable family solidarity we encounter hostility and death, notably the rift between Kjartan and Bolli. In lieu of the legendary feasts of yore we are treated to a wedding feast for Kjartan and Hrefna rent by quarrels and hard words. The sumptuous attire and ostentatious display of Olaf Peacock and his ancestors is replaced by a regal headdress that is never worn at all.

This part of the narrative is predicated on two tragic myths, one recurring in earlier sagas and the other chiefly in Eddic poetry. The first is characteristic of the so-called skald sagas about early Icelandic poets who had, or were reported to have had, complex erotic relationships.[13] Three of these sagas (*Bjarnar saga Hítdœlakappa*, *Hallfreðar saga*, and *Kormáks saga*) were probably written early in the thirteenth century, and the fourth (*Gunnlaugs saga ormstungu*) is referred to in *Egils saga*, so that at least an oral version was known in the early part of the century. The pattern in these sagas is to focus on a poet who becomes betrothed to a woman in Iceland, then goes abroad for a specified period and either fails to return on time or is maliciously declared dead by a rival, who proceeds to marry his intended. When the poet returns to discover this state of affairs, a feud ensues.

In *Laxdœla saga* the element of malice is downplayed. Bolli does not explicitly falsify the situation, but he does tell Gudrún that Kjartan is involved with King Olaf's sister and should not be expected soon. He also capitalizes on the delay by courting Gudrún, even though he, along with everyone else, knows that Gudrún and Kjartan are a predestined couple. This betrayal may be less egregious than those in the skald sagas, but it is implicit, and the sequel is worked out in even greater tragic detail.[14] The author intensifies the emotional alienation between the rivals in greater depth than the skald sagas and explores the psychological strains between the half-unwilling marital partners more fully. This performance is remarkable because the early, golden-age phases of the narrative have given no inkling that the author is capable of such rich emotional and psychological registers.[15]

[13] On the erotic complications, see Finlay 2001, 232–71.
[14] On the characterization of Bolli see Bååth [1885], 69–70; van Ham 1932, 68–71; Drever 1937–45, 111–14; Heller 1976:14, 138; Dronke 1979; Wolf 1994:736.
[15] On the author's handling of the love story, see Sävborg 2002.

The greatest enrichment accrues from the imposition of a second mythic pattern, the legend of Brynhild and Sigurd, which is developed in extraordinary depth in a dozen Eddic poems. This is the central myth of the Norse heroic tradition; it was reworked elaborately in *Gísla saga* and echoed incidentally in *Ljósvetninga saga*. It is not so much the story of an erotic triangle, as in the skald sagas, as a tale of mismatches crisscrossing the destinies of two couples. The paramount hero, Sigurd, is betrothed to the incomparable Brynhild, but a potion of forgetfulness erases his memory and opens the way for him to marry Gudrún, the daughter of King Gjúki. The matter is further aggravated when Sigurd disguises himself as Gudrún's brother (and his own blood brother) Gunnar, leaps over the flame wall that shelters Brynhild from all but the right man, and wins her hand for the wrong man, the quite secondary Gunnar. Thus Sigurd has not only abandoned her but also played her into the hands of an inferior. The truth emerges in a quarrel between the queens (Brynhild and Gudrún), and Brynhild is consumed by grief and vengefulness. She fabricates the claim that Sigurd, disguised as Gunnar, slept with her and thus persuades Gunnar and his brothers to contrive his murder.

Laxdœla saga plays off this legend in ways too numerous to tabulate, but here are some primary parallels:

1. A betrothal, explicit or tacit, is broken (Brynhild to Sigurd, Gudrún to Kjartan).
2. The greater hero is redomesticated with the wrong woman (Sigurd with Gudrún, Kjartan with Hrefna).
3. The best woman gets the second-best husband (Brynhild gets Gunnar, Gudrún gets Bolli).
4. A fateful love token gets into the wrong hands and betrays the misalliance (the ring that Sigurd takes from Brynhild and gives to Gudrún, the headdress that Kjartan gets for Gudrún but gives to Hrefna).
5. There is a pervasive atmosphere of suspicion and distrust.
6. There is a futile effort to suppress the mischief that threatens to undermine both marriages.
7. There is social contention between the leading women that culminates in open enmity.
8. The peaceable husbands (Gunnar and Bolli) are incited against a blood brother (or a foster brother) by implacable wives who use the threat of marital alienation.

9. The chief hero (Sigurd, Kjartan) is killed when almost defenseless.
10. He is avenged.[16]

The contrast between the unsuspecting idyll in the early part of *Laxdœla saga* and the cataclysm in the story of Gudrún and Kjartan is so stark that it prompts questions. Is the author deliberately constructing a mirage of peace and prosperity only to confound it with the harsh reality of passion and betrayal? Is this a story of lost illusions? Or is it rather the story of a lost paradise, a story in which a falsification is injected into an otherwise stable community, with the inevitable consequence of disintegration? Are Kjartan's dilatoriness, Bolli's less than perfect loyalty, and Gudrún's less than perfect constancy subtle signs of moral decay? Does too much good fortune carry the seed of its own destruction? Or is misfortune simply an endemic factor that is bound to emerge sooner or later?[17]

The saga does not provide the tools with which to resolve these questions, but it does pose them, and that is in itself a revolutionary advance over earlier sagas. *Laxdœla saga* is more historically probing, more abstract, more suggestive of large issues than the politically oriented *Saga of King Magnús and King Harald, Egils saga,* and *Ljósvetninga saga.*

The death of Kjartan seems clearly to be the dramatic high point, but another 40 percent of the story remains to be told. Part of it is devoted to the vengeance phases following Kjartan's death. In the first phase, he is avenged in three separate sequences, culminating in an attack on Bolli himself. Olaf Peacock tries to protect Bolli (his foster son) and at first succeeds in diverting the revenge onto others who participated in the assault on Kjartan. But after Olaf's death the momentum for more direct vengeance cannot be arrested. Kjartan's mother Thorgerd incites her other sons against Bolli in vivid terms. They gather forces and surprise Bolli in a summer shieling, where a certain Helgi Hardbeinsson inflicts the actual death blow.

---

[16] On the exploitation of the Brynhild legend, see van Ham 1932, 134–43; Bouman 1962b, 133–47; Beck 1976; Heller 1976:13; Zimmermann 1982, 92–141. A further (in some sense) "mythic" background predicated on Kjartan's status as an outsider is offered in Sayers 1988, esp. 98–99.

[17] Cf. esp. Wolf 1994, 748.

In a memorable aftermath to this killing, Bolli's widow Gudrún makes an exact mental tally of the participants in the attack in preparation for reprisals. These reprisals constitute the second act in the vengeance phase. Gudrún allies herself with her friend and adviser Snorri the Chieftain in an elaborate plan to avenge Bolli's death. The plan requires the recruitment of a man powerful enough to organize and lead the revenge party, and the chosen leader is won over with a crassly deceitful promise of marriage to Gudrún when the deed is accomplished, a promise that is never fulfilled. The targets of the revenge are not Thorgerd's sons, who mounted the expedition, but the actual killer, Helgi Hardbeinsson, who, like Bolli, is surprised and slain in a summer hut. The case is then ultimately settled by Snorri.

This revenge narration is remarkable in several ways. It is developed with unparalleled ingenuity and projected in some of the most vivid scenes to be found anywhere in the sagas. The author's dramatic flair may, again, come as something of a surprise to the reader who has become accustomed to an ornamental style rich in display but poor in action. The transition from decorative canvas to intense drama, beginning with the ambushing of Kjartan, is quite unmediated, and it poses further questions. We might think once more in terms of the transition from golden age to iron age, the latter being traditionally associated with armed conflict and war. Or we might think more narrowly in terms of the Norse heroic tradition so consciously exploited in Kjartan's tragedy. It is the gist of that tradition that a community is suddenly overtaken by an irrational calamity, followed by bloody reprisals that are put to rest only with time. Perhaps the revenge in *Laxdœla saga* answers to the literary expectations generated by the heroic tradition: it is simply a continuation of Kjartan's tragedy. However we construe the antecedents, we must take note of how the author adroitly switches from a somewhat rococco palette to hard epic action.

The argument I offer here is that the structure of *Laxdœla saga* is generational or historical and that the early generations are the beneficiaries of spontaneous and almost magical success, whereas Kjartan's generation is overwhelmed by an equally autonomous doom. It must be conceded, however, that not everything in the saga fits smoothly into this reading, and much that has been written about the saga runs counter to such a thrifty narrative flow. The burden of early studies was that *Laxdœla saga* is to be understood rather as a concatenation of district traditions strung together without much central thrust.[18] We have seen that this form of composition is by no means unprecedented and can be clearly identified in the early sagas about Olaf Tryggvason and Olaf Haraldsson as well as several of the early sagas about Icelanders. It can therefore reasonably be argued that a good deal of episodic and incompletely integrated district tradition persists in *Laxdœla saga*. Not everything seems immediately pertinent to the transition from golden age to iron age. For example, after Melkorka gives birth to Olaf Peacock in Iceland, there is a detailed story about a quarrel between two farmers, Hall and Thórólf, which culminates when a certain Vigdís takes Thórólf's part and divorces her pusillanimous husband Thórd goddi (chapters 14–16; ÍF 5:28–39).[19] At first blush this story would seem to have little connection with the main thread of the story. But since Thórd goddi seeks help from Hǫskuld and offers to foster his son Olaf Peacock, the story attaches to both Hǫskuld and Olaf and serves to explain some of Olaf's subsequent wealth, inasmuch as he inherits from a rich foster father. The reader can debate whether the story needed to be told in such detail, but it is clearly the author's style to narrate in breadth and not merely to summarize.

Immediately after this episode we are told that Hǫskuld deals with the revenant of a certain Hrapp, who has already been introduced some twenty pages earlier (in chapter 10). This too has no real bearing on the central action, but it appears to be what the author knew about Hǫskuld's district activities. Once more there is a preference for inclusiveness.

A considerably more substantial recording of tradition focuses on the figure of Hrút Herjólfsson, Hǫskuld's half-brother, who comes of age in Norway before settling in Iceland. Hrút is closely tied to Hǫskuld because they quarrel over their inheritance, but he is also a great man in his own right. Still, we may wonder whether the author needed to tell at such length how, for example, Hrút killed a certain Eldgrím (chapter 37; ÍF 5:102–5). That this was a local tale is empha-

[18] Bååth [1885]; van Ham 1932; Kersbergen 1933. Schildknecht-Burri (1945, 29) offered a more balanced assessment: "Die Laxd. ist beides, Chronik und Roman. Sie ist Chronik der Leute aus dem Lachswassertal. Als Roman ist sie die Geschichte der Gudhrún und des Kjartan." (*Laxdœla saga* is both chronicle and novel. It is the chronicle of the people of Laxárdale; as a novel it is the story of Gudrún and Kjartan.)
[19] On this sequence, see Davíð Erlingsson 1988 and Meulengracht Sørensen 1993, 250–57. The former treats the story as a microcosm of ethical values in the saga as a whole, the latter as a microcosm of social strains.

sized by the place name Eldgrímsholt, where Hrút buried Eldgrím's corpse. The story could certainly have been omitted, but even though the author was primarily concerned with the larger tale of Kjartan's death and avenging, there appears to be a secondary imperative to record as much family lore as possible. The same may be said of the following episode, in which Hrút and Olaf Peacock kill a pack of sorcerers, giving rise to the place name Skrattavardi (sorcerers' cairn).[20]

Another episode that raises the issue of relevance is the story of the Norwegian Geirmund's marriage to and abandonment of Olaf Peacock's daughter Thúríd. Once again the episode is not essential and could have been omitted, but it is neatly tied to the central story by Geirmund's prize possession, the sword Fótbít. When Geirmund abandons his wife, she possesses herself of the sword, and he retaliates by putting a curse on it "This sword will be the death of the man in your family who is least expendable and the least deserving of it" (chapter 30; ÍF 5:82). The sword ends up in the hands of Bolli, who uses it to kill Kjartan. Geirmund thus belongs to the prehistory of Kjartan's demise. At a somewhat higher level of abstraction the story of Geirmund's failed marriage anticipates the blighted marriages that preface Kjartan's death.

Another such ill-starred marriage is the one contracted for Gudrún Ósvífrsdóttir with Thorvald Halldórsson. Gudrún rids herself of this unwanted husband with the collusion of Thórd Ingunnarson, who then divorces his wife in order to marry Gudrún. His spurned wife Aud rides out to exact a dramatic and nocturnal vengeance against him. Once more this digression takes us quite far out onto the periphery of the action. Indeed, we could argue that the full information on Gudrún's four successive marriages is hardly essential to the core theme of her thwarted love for Kjartan. Yet, as Gudrún is the preeminent figure in the saga, it is difficult to maintain that any narrative pertaining to her lies beyond the scope of the plot. We are perhaps justified only in saying that the author drew concentric boundaries of the saga generously—far more so, for example, than the authors of *Egils saga* or *Ljósvetninga saga*.

If we inquire why the author adopted this course, we might simply suppose that it was in response to a larger epic vision, a new impulse

---

[20] I treat these matters as residues of local tradition, but it should be noted that Heller (1976, 135) viewed them as authorial fictions. See also Heller 1974, 91, 123n.76.

to delve farther back in time and expand the genealogical coverage beyond the immediate requirements of the story. The rippling genealogical details in the opening chapters convey an almost incantatory spell. Inclusiveness, both vertical and horizontal, was part of the author's program. It may reflect a literary disposition, but it may also have been conditioned by the growing dimensions of saga writing by midcentury. The saga holdings, quite modest around 1200 and even as late as 1220, by 1250 would have included the compendious kings' lives in *Morkinskinna, Fagrskinna,* and *Heimskringla,* along with a growing library of sagas about early Icelanders. Perhaps the narrative ambition that gave rise to the kings' saga compendia carried over to the native sagas and inspired expansions in chronology and rhythm.

The billowing dimensions of *Laxdœla saga* do not, however, compromise the thrust of the narrative: the displacement of a prehistorical idyll by a Saga Age tragedy tinged by heroic legend. That trajectory is quite clear. But Kjartan's fall and the sanguinary aftermath are not the end of the story; they are merely preliminary to a third act in the drama, an act that is recuperative. The recuperation is realized in the persons of Gudrún's two sons, Thorleik and Bolli Bollason, who reenact the lives and retrieve the grandeur of their most illustrious ancestors. Thorleik sails to Norway and is received with open arms into the service of King Olaf Haraldsson. Bolli comes of age and sues for the hand of Thórdís, daughter of Snorri the Chieftain. His suit is granted, and the marriage is celebrated at a brilliant wedding feast, thus restoring the traditions of royal reception and crowning marriage. Although the loss of their father still rankles the brothers, and they secretly plot ongoing revenge, Snorri intervenes to arrange a final settlement and call a halt to the protracted feud.

The saga could well conclude here, but there are still greater heights to scale. Bolli sets out with Thorleik on a new expedition, landing first in Norway, where he immediately becomes preeminent:

> It was soon apparent that Bolli was ambitious and wished to outstrip other men. He succeeded, for he was a munificent man. He soon gained a great reputation in Norway. He maintained a following in Trondheim during the winter, and wherever he attended drinking parties, it was obvious that his men were better dressed and better armed than the other townsmen. He also footed the bill for his followers alone at these parties.

That was typical of his liberality and high distinction. (Chapter 73; ÍF 5:212–13)

When the two brothers appear at the royal court, King Olaf is immediately struck by Bolli's appearance and soon esteems him even more highly than Thorleik. Accordingly he offers him a distinguished place in his retinue, but Bolli is intent on his travels, provoking the following response from the king:

> Your travels are up to you, for you Icelanders mostly know what you want, but I will make no secret of my opinion that you, Bolli, are the most distinguished man who has come from Iceland in my time. (Chapter 73; ÍF 5:214)

We are back in the world of display and appearance, the world of instantaneous recognition granted without question and without tests, the world of Olaf Peacock.[21] It is also a world of escalating stakes. Bolli is not content with the highest honor at the Norwegian court and travels on to Constantinople, where he joins the Varangian Guard: "He was always among the most distinguished, and the Varangians esteemed Bolli highly as long as he was in Constantinople" (chapter 73; ÍF 5:214–15).

The final epiphany is reserved for Iceland, where one day Bolli arrives home in brilliant panoply:

> Bolli had great wealth and many precious objects that men in high places had given him. Bolli was so ostentatious when he returned from this expedition that he would wear nothing but the finest woollen and silken clothes, and all his weapons were ornamented with gold. He was called Bolli the Magnificent.
>
> Bolli rode from his ship with eleven men. Bolli's followers were all dressed in fine woollen garments and were mounted on golden saddles. They were all stately men, but Bolli was preeminent. He wore a silken attire that the emperor had given him, covered with a scarlet woollen

---

[21] Van Ham 1932, 90 took a decidedly negative view of Bolli as a vacuously idealized figure. See also Schildknecht-Burri 1945, 49, 51; and Kolbrún Bergþórsdóttir 1989, 21.

cape. He wore the sword Fótbít by his side, and the hilt and handle were worked in gold. On his head he had a golden helmet and on his arm a red shield on which was depicted a knight in gold. He carried a blade in his hand, as is customary in foreign lands, and wherever they stopped, the women could not take their eyes off Bolli and the magnificence displayed by him and his companions. (Chapter 77; ÍF 5:224–25)

Bolli thus reembodies the chivalric vision of Olaf Peacock in Ireland and in his role as Thorgerd's suitor—if possible in an even higher potency. Not only is the tragedy of Kjartan laid to rest, but there emerges a still more brilliant chapter in the history of the family. Bolli's service in Byzantium surpasses and relativizes earlier allegiances to the Norwegian court. The Laxdœlir are once more supereminent by comparison with others, perhaps even with the Mýramenn, whose last fully delineated scion in *Egils saga*, Thorstein Egilsson, remains a local landowner standing somewhat in his father's shadow. The dramatic line of *Laxdœla saga* thus proceeds from quasi-royal distinction in the settlement period through tragic but temporary eclipse, only to reemerge in the brilliant light of imperial auspices. The saga ends as a tale of rebirth.

The larger story line may also be predicated on a mythic model, the core of Norse mythology found in the Eddic poem "Vǫluspá" (the sybil's prophecy), which tells the cosmic story of generation from a vacuum, the twilight of the gods, and the ultimate rebirth of a new golden age. The model has been applied to *Njáls saga* but may be more appropriate to *Laxdœla saga*, which, despite the lugubrious central legend, concludes on an exalted note.[22] The points of comparison between "Vǫluspá" and *Laxdœla saga* are quite persistent. The settlement of Iceland is in some sense a creation from a void and reminiscent of the Norse cosmogony. The gods are also settlers and builders in a new world:

> The Æsir met   on Idavellir,
> Altars and temples   they timbered aloft;
> They framed hearths   and forged treasures,
> Shaped fittings   and fashioned tools.[23]

[22] Allen 1971, 130–31; Lönnroth 1976, 148n.63.
[23] *Edda*, ed. Neckel/Kuhn, 2. The translations from the *Edda* are my own.

Like the original settlers of Laxárdale the gods are strangely carefree and affluent:

> They gamed in the yard   in good cheer,
> Where nothing failed   fashioned from gold.[24]

Most of the poem, however, is given over to dire forebodings of disaster, auditory and visionary. Foreboding comes to dominate the texture of *Laxdœla saga* as well. Gest Oddleifsson foresees the strife between the foster brothers Kjartan and Bolli and forecasts the fatal outcome of Gudrún's four marriages. Geirmund curses the sword destined to inflict Kjartan's death. The long central plot of the saga is enveloped in a sense of gathering doom. The specific calamity, also foreshadowed in the legend of Brynhild and Sigurd, is the antagonism of foster brothers and the dissolution of a preeminent family. That fate haunts "Vǫluspá" as well, in which the falling out of kin is one of the final doomsday omens:

> Brothers will battle,   banes to each other,
> Close relations   cling in adultery;
> Harsh is the world,   great whoredom,
> Ax age, sword age,   shields cloven,
> Wind age, wolf age   ere the world falls;
> No man is destined   another to spare.[25]

But the destruction of the gods is not final, and the sybil foresees a rebirth:

> She sees arise   a second time
> Earth from the sea   ever green.[26]

This new world will retrieve the golden attributes of the first creation:

> Once again   wondrously wrought
> Will be found in the grass   golden game tables
> Possessed by the gods   in bygone days.

---

[24] Ibid.

[25] Ibid., 10–11. The stanza is also cited by Conroy and Langen (1988, 128) in line with their view of the deterioration they see in the saga.

[26] *Edda*, ed. Neckel and Kuhn, 14.

> A hall she sees standing fairer than the sun,
> Roofed with gold in Gimlé.[27]

The persistent gold trimmings of *Laxdœla saga* look like a reflex of the golden rebirth of the gods.

The author of the saga thus combines the most melancholy of heroic myths (Brynhild and Sigurd) with the most hopeful of divine myths, the promise of a new world. Of particular interest is the way in which the two myths are joined. The promise of a new world is wrapped around the dark myth of heroic despair, in effect subsuming and bracketing it. The analogies in heroic legend have received more attention and are at the center of our understanding of *Laxdœla saga*, but this descent into mythic gloom is not the last word. The view seems rather to be that secular bleakness is dispelled by a glorious recrudescence. The emphasis is not on a past calamity but on future resplendence. We are left with an optimistic vision.[28]

It seems clear that *Laxdœla saga*, to some extent like *The Saga of King Magnús and King Harald* and to a fuller extent like *Egils saga* and *Ljósvetninga saga*, is about Iceland. Since the saga seems to have been written in the closing years of the Icelandic commonwealth, with the looming prospect of subjugation to Norway (1262–64), the question of the author's political outlook has often been raised.[29] Is the last glimpse of a golden age in the Icelandic settlement period a nostalgic farewell to political independence? Or is it rather a vision of what is prospective and capable of resurrection?

Links with the Norwegian court are ever present in the saga and are clearly not subject to the queries raised in *Egils saga*. The associations with Norway are always positive. Even the archsorceress Gunnhild, who is roundly condemned in *Egils saga*, is not subjected to the slightest detraction. It is difficult to see an antiroyalist in this author and much easier to surmise a writer who would have welcomed continuing and perhaps even closer ties to Norway.

Whatever the political orientation of the saga may be, the literary advance is noteworthy. The author draws on both highly ornamental and grimly epic resources. These larger dimensions are achieved not only by greater genealogical, chronological, and regional coverage but also

---

[27] Ibid., 14–15.
[28] Wolf 1994, 748–49; Ármann Jakobsson 1998, 362; Bjarni Guðnason 1999, 19.
[29] Wolf 1994, 740–41, 745; Ármann Jakobsson 1998, 380; Bjarni Guðnason 1999, 19.

by the bold introduction of mythic patterning. The author of *Laxdœla saga* thinks in more universal terms about national trajectory and historical alternatives than do earlier saga writers. At this stage in the development of the saga form the author succeeds in harnessing in prose epic the two great expressions of Icelandic myth: heroic legend and the history of the gods.

CHAPTER EIGHT

Two Views of Icelandic History

Eyrbyggja saga and *Vatnsdœla saga*

Eyrbyggja saga

Laxdœla saga and *Eyrbyggja saga* are linked, but the relationship between them is notoriously difficult to disentangle. The difficulty may
perhaps be of our own making, because toward the end of *Eyrbyggja
saga* the text refers in so many words to *Laxdœla saga* and *Heiðarvíga
saga*. The editor Einar Ólafur Sveinsson took the latter reference at face
value but was more doubtful about the author's knowledge of *Laxdœla
saga*.[1] In addition, it seems quite clear that the author knew *Gísla saga*,
even though there is a discrepancy in the chronology of Thórdís's divorce from Bǫrk.[2] The verbal echoes are nonetheless so close that the
author must have known a written version of *Gísla saga*.

My discussion here proceeds from the assumption that the author
knew not only *Gísla saga* but also *Heiðarvíga saga* and *Laxdœla saga,* all
in written form. The contrary assumption, that the reference to *Heiðarvíga saga* is authentic but the reference to *Laxdœla saga* spurious,
seems arbitrary. Einar Ólafur Sveinsson agonized over the problem
chiefly because, of the two, *Eyrbyggja saga* seems older in form and
style, whereas *Laxdœla saga* exhibits a taste for a more decorative style.
The difference can be accounted for, however, by the differing tastes of
two individual authors: one a modernist enchanted by the splendor of
foreign courts and eager to stake out a share in such splendor for Ice-

[1] ÍF 4:XX and XLVI–LII.
[2] ÍF 4:XXII.

land; the other a local historian with a taste for old ways and even old superstitions. The latter may even have taken a somewhat sardonic view of the gold and glitter in *Laxdœla saga*.

Moreover, the supposition that the author of *Eyrbyggja saga* knew and reflected on *Laxdœla saga* is encouraged by a similarity in focus. Both begin with an account of the colonization of a region in Iceland; indeed, some of the same colonists play a part in both sagas. Both rehearse the dealings of early colonists, although the author of *Laxdœla saga* displays a penchant for marriage history, whereas the author of *Eyrbyggja saga* prefers to relive the armed encounters of the settlers. The relationship between these two sagas may in fact be quite similar to the relationship between *Víga-Glúms saga* and *Reykdœla saga*. I suggested in Chapter 3 that the author of the latter knew the former but also had a pool of regional lore with which to supplement it. *Reykdœla saga* thus became an extension of *Víga-Glúms saga*, including new information about the people who lived somewhat to the east of Eyjafjord. The author of *Eyrbyggja saga*, if he had read *Laxdœla saga*, was in an analogous position. There was more information available, this time about the people living somewhat to the west on Snæfellsnes. *Eyrbyggja saga* could therefore have been a regional response to *Laxdœla saga*, much as *Laxdœla saga* looks like a regional response to *Egils saga* and the glorification of the Mýramenn in that text.

There is, however, a striking difference. Whereas *Laxdœla saga* gives the impression that the home district fostered the greatest men and women of Iceland and proceeded from glory to glory, with one tragic interlude, the author of *Eyrbyggja saga* had a darker view of the early history in the neighboring district, a view more in keeping with what we found in *Reykdœla saga*. It is a bleak view that profiles family dissensions and wanton or aggressive behavior, a tone set by the ancestor of the Álptfirðingar, Thórólf bægifótr, who acquires his land by challenging the rightful owner to a duel and killing him. He is described as "a most inequitable man" (chapter 8; ÍF 4:14), and (Víga-)Styr, whom we met in *Heiðarvíga saga*, is described similarly as "a very arrogant man and thoroughly inequitable" (chapter 12; ÍF 4:21). That the author is interested in the interactions of these difficult characters is summed up in the concluding words: "Here ends the saga of the Thórsnesingar, the Eyrbyggjar, and the Álptfirðingar" (chapter 65; ÍF 4:184).

That the focus is clearly regional has made this saga more difficult to read and classify than most. There are many characters with somewhat interchangeable roles and none projected in high relief. Such diffusion is a marked departure from most of the earlier sagas, not just *Egils saga* and *Laxdæla saga*, in which the central protagonist is conspicuous and memorable. We may think of figures such Víga-Glúm, Víga-Skúta, Thorgeir, Thormód, Bardi, and Gísli. Indeed, the project in the early sagas seems to have been to shape larger-than-life personalities distinguished by prowess, guile, or (in Gísli's case) a particular ideology. This feature is missing in *Eyrbyggja saga*, despite the fact that the leading character is none other than Snorri the Chieftain, perhaps the most ubiquitous and politically astute character in all the sagas.

Snorri is introduced with a master stroke that bids fair to put him in the top rank of of saga tricksters. Having traveled abroad and acquired considerable wealth, he returns home and affects poverty. He proposes to divide his patrimony with his uncle Bǫrk, who, believing that Snorri is short of money, puts a low valuation on the homestead, hoping thereby to minimize the cash settlement that he will have to pay out in order to keep it. Snorri, however, produces the necessary payment with no hesitation, retains the homestead, and drives Bǫrk off the property. *Eyrbyggja saga* also reports Snorri's trick to rid Víga-Styr of troublesome berserks, as in *Heiðarvíga saga*, but there are no further contrivances worthy of a Víga-Glúm Eyjólfsson or a Thormód Bersason.

This lack of profile is quite in line with the full characterization given Snorri by the author: "He was normally of a quiet disposition. It was hard to tell whether he was well- or ill-disposed. He was a prudent man and good at foreseeing the future, given to harboring grudges and vengeful by nature. He gave good counsel to his friends, but his enemies found that his counsels were rather cold" (chapter 15; ÍF 4:26). It is no doubt Snorri's very inscrutability that makes him hard to characterize. He does not tip his hand, nor does he say much. To the extent that characterization depends on flamboyant gestures or unusual eloquence, there is not much to work with. His career is summed up at the end of the saga but again more in political than in personal terms: "When Snorri began to age, his popularity began to grow. It was a contributing factor that his enemies started to thin out. It also contributed to his popularity that he formed family ties with the greatest men in Breidafjord and many other places" (chapter 65; ÍF 4:180).

By and large, the saga is an account of political maneuvering, and as in most political narratives the fortunes are mixed. In his first case, involving sorcery, Snorri actually loses and harvests only dishonor. In a second case he is successful, but in a third he must settle for what he can get. He kills an antagonist named Vigfús Bjarnarson but must eventually pay heavy damages. In a seduction case involving his sister Thuríd, Snorri can reach only an indecisive accommodation with the seducer. And in a protracted dispute with the great chieftain Arnkel Thórólfsson, Snorri emerges victorious only because there are no powerful men to prosecute the case for Arnkel's killing. Further hostilities are likewise inconclusive. Only in a final action against a force of brigands holed up in a fortress does Snorri manage a clear-cut victory. About all that can be said to summarize these encounters is that Snorri holds his own. He outlasts his opponents and does not get himself killed, but he does not cut a remarkable figure. He displays no special warrior-like qualities, nor does he demonstrate the leadership qualities we observed in a Bardi Gudmundarson. He is always cautious, sometimes even tentative, but like many another successful politician he limits his losses and avoids critical mistakes.

As a result of Snorri's low profile, *Eyrbyggja saga* is a somewhat faceless story. The protagonist does not hold the narrative together or guide the action; he merely reacts to events. There are none of the vivid scenes that occur in all the sagas discussed so far. There is no sharp dialogue, as in *Fóstbrœðra* saga; no melancholy exchanges, as in *Gísla saga;* no really sustained narrative as in Thormód Bersason's vengeance for Thorgeir or Bardi Gudmundarson's protracted revenge for his brother. There are no dramatic moments with which to organize the action and commit it to memory. The editor of the standard edition prints it in long paragraphs because the story is not incisively articulated. As a result, the narrative does not flow easily and is less compelling to read than almost any other saga.

How do we account for this lifeless style in a period that produced so much eminently readable prose? To say that the author was a poor storyteller does not get us very far. It may be more helpful to suggest that the author opted for an alternative style in preference to the dramatic tradition. If we assign *Eyrbyggja saga* to the middle of the century or a little later, there were in fact narrative alternatives, particularly in the writing of sagas about contemporary events. The earliest of these seem to have been *Sturlu saga* and *Guðmundar saga dýra,* presumably from the first decades of the thirteenth century. They are fashioned in very much the same way as *Eyrbyggja saga:* that is, as a sequence of a chieftain's encounters with his rivals, sometimes successful and some-times not. These sagas also lack the focusing moments of dialogue and drama found in the early native sagas.

Another source of relatively unarticulated narrative may be the royal chronicles that grew out of the earliest royal biographies. The first of these was *Morkinskinna,* which we sampled in Chapter 4. This compilation is eminently unsuitable for comparison because it com-bines the chronicle form with all the most notable attributes of saga style—well defined character, dialogue, honed repartee, lively anec-dote, vivid scenes, and cultivated drama—but *Morkinskinna* was the exception. Both *Fagrskinna* and *Heimskringla* curtail the dramatic ef-fects in favor of a more measured narrative. This impulse may stem from some suspicion that anecdotal narrative with high-profile heroes and high drama was not likely to mirror history faithfully. We might even imagine a nostalgia for the bare bones of history, such as could be found in the spare pages of Ari Thorgilsson.

Perhaps the author of *Eyrbyggja saga,* then, imagined that it would be possible to disguise the early days on Snæfellsnes as history by shedding what was historically suspect—the heroic figures, the re-joinders that people devise only in fiction, the rising drama found only in good storytelling, and the idea that the past was greater than the present. Perhaps the author had documentary aspirations and the con-viction that history could be restored by presenting it in realistic terms. This idea was once entertained by modern scholars who thought that Snorri Sturluson was closer to the truth than his predecessors because he was less hagiographic and more "realistic."[3] The author of *Eyr-byggja saga* may also have thought that peeling away the most obvious exaggerations would produce something more like history, and read-ers—rather than feeling bored or esthetically cheated—would be drawn into a world not adorned by overstatement but recognizable as the world in which they actually lived.

Vatnsdœla saga

Vatnsdœla saga has little in common with *Eyrbyggja saga* except that it too trails in the broad wake left by *Laxdœla saga.* Although it does not

[3] Sigurður Nordal 1953, 220.

refer directly to *Laxdæla saga*, it betrays some of the same taste for style and grandeur.[4] This tendency is apparent from the very outset, which relates the Norwegian prehistory of the Vatnsdœlir in something approaching fairytale terms.[5] Ketil raumr, a great chieftain in the province of Raumsdale (Romsdalen), chides his son Thorstein for not living up to the high aspirations and accomplishments of his ancestors. Thorstein takes the reproach much to heart and heads for the wilderness in which a notorious outlaw has been raiding unhindered.

Like Jack in the beanstalk tale, he finds an empty house and lies in wait for the return of the malefactor, who searches the house in vain for an intruder. But this malefactor is no barbarous, man-eating ogre: "The man was very tall and had blond hair that fell on his shoulders in fair locks. He seemed to Thorstein to be very handsome." His utensils and provisions are of the finest quality: "Altogether this man's bearing seemed to Thorstein to be very courtly." (chapter 3; ÍF 8.7). Soon the outlaw falls asleep, and although Thorstein thinks it is a pity to harm such a man, he is mindful of his father's reproaches and delivers what will prove to be a fatal thrust with his sword while the man lies defenseless in his gold-embroidered shirt. It turns out, however, that the man is even finer in character than in appearance. Though far stronger than his assailant and capable of instant revenge, he spares Thorstein and tells his story. He reveals that he is the son of a jarl named Ingimund but has somehow gone wrong, as he freely admits. He was about to abandon his evil ways, however, and having turned over a new leaf, he now counsels Thorstein to take the news of his death to his father and to ask for the hand of his sister in marriage. This is a fairy realm indeed.

But first Thorstein returns home to a hero's welcome and his father's contrition. His father reasonably counsels against a visit to Jarl Ingimund, but Thorstein, having given his word, is determined to make it good. On his arrival the jarl is out hunting, "as is the custom of great men," and Thorstein is able to make his appeal to the jarl's wife. Quite magically, it succeeds, because there is something persuasive in Thorstein's look: "You bear the mark of good fortune." Not only is his life spared, but his suit for the hand of his victim's sister succeeds. The jarl agrees with his wife's judgment: "I will not refuse because it may turn

[4] ÍF 8:XXI.
[5] On fairytale patterns in the sagas, see Ármann Jakobsson 2004.

out to the good fortune of my family line" (chapter 5; ÍF 8:13–16). Thorstein clearly has good fortune written on his features, and that is destined to become the hallmark of his family.

The wedding is celebrated with no less grandeur than we saw in *Laxdœla saga,* and when Ingimund is on his deathbed, he calls Thorstein to his bedside and bids farewell with the conferral of great wealth. When a son is born to Thorstein and his wife, Thorstein takes one look and says, "This boy will be named Ingimund after his grandfather, and I expect that the name will bring good fortune to him." Indeed, when Thorstein's friend Ingjald looks at the child, he confirms the impression: "You look like a lucky boy, and because of the friendship between your father and me I will invite you home to partake of the best fosterage I know how to give" (chapter 7; ÍF 8:17–18).

As Ingimund grows up, he shows none of the hesitation that characterized Thorstein's early youth but becomes an accomplished raider: "It was soon revealed that Ingimund was bold on the attack and a good fellow, reliable in arms and valor, devoted to his friends and good-hearted, trusty in dealings with his friends, as only the best chieftains were in the days of the old faith" (chapter 7; ÍF 8:19). To be sure, Ingimund is a raider, because that is how young men were imagined to have made their fortunes and reputations in the old days, but a remarkable feature sets Ingimund apart: it turns out that his raids are directed against robbers and plunderers who waylay farmers and traders. He is in effect a "good" viking.

This is symptomatic of the Vatnsdœlir throughout the saga. They seem to anticipate the gentler dispensation of Christianity, and Ingimund's son Thorstein is destined to call on "him who created the sun because I believe him to be the most powerful" (chapter 37; ÍF 8:97). At the end of the saga the last in the line of the Vatnsdale chieftains, Thorkel krafla, declines to convert and wants to abide by the religion practiced by Thorstein and his brother Thórir: "They believed in him who created the sun and governs all things." A bishop reassures him that he recommends the same religion with the understanding that it means "to believe in one God the Father, the Son, and the Holy Ghost, and to be baptized in water in His name" (chapter 46; ÍF 8:125). It is thus revealed that the Vatnsdœlir are not only good vikings but noble heathens to boot.

Ingimund confirms his good fortune by making the right political choices. When King Harald Fairhair goes about unifying the whole of

Norway, the threatened chieftains and petty kings must decide which way to lean. As we know from *Egils saga*, some dissidents resist, and some of Ingimund's companions are among them, but Ingimund himself knows better. He joins Harald's cause and consequently enjoys great favor. Harald magnificently rewards his service at the great Battle of Hafrsfjord but does not stop at that; he also marries him to a jarl's daughter, and the marriage feast is again celebrated in a style worthy of *Laxdæla saga.*

This Norwegian prelude is by any measure a strange and exotic twist on those that we find in so many sagas. It is far removed from the hard political realities entailed by Harald's rise to power in *Egils saga* and much closer to the great ancestral romance that prefaces *Laxdæla saga.* Like the Laxdœlir, the people of *Eyrbyggja saga* descend from a known genealogical quantity, the famed forefather Ketil flatnefr, so that however inflated the story may be, it has a certain historical plausibility about it. But Ketil raumr—though he is mentioned in a few other sagas[6]—is not anchored in any known history, and his son Thorstein lives only in a fairytale twilight. Why is the prelude to *Vatnsdæla saga* not more firmly rooted in history, as the preludes are in many other sagas? It is tempting to think that because the dynasty of the Vatnsdœlir chieftains broke off at an early period, allowing power to pass to other families, the recollection of the original family dimmed and became a more legendary tradition before the story was committed to writing.

The function of the prelude is nonetheless clear enough. Just as in *Laxdæla saga*, the Norwegian prehistory redounds to the credit of the Icelandic descendants and provides them with glorious antecedents, which they can and do aspire to emulate. The aspirations in *Laxdæla saga* are overtly royal, whereas *Vatnsdæla saga* is content to link its protagonists with Norwegian jarls: both Thorstein and Ingimund marry the daughters of jarls and carry that distinction forward. Ingimund, however, moves into the royal orbit as well by performing distinguished service for King Harald Fairhair. It is indeed King Harald who gives him the hand of a jarl's daughter, as well as conferring no less munificent royal rewards than we are accustomed to from *Laxdæla saga.*

Not only the prelude but also the transition from Norway to Iceland

6 ÍF 8:3 n. 1.

has something of the folktale about it. In *Laxdœla saga*, the great matri-arch Unn the Deepminded ruled Laxárdale like a queen and therefore cast it in the luster of a royal enclave. In *Vatnsdœla saga*, Ingimund has no intention of abandoning Norway for Iceland. When a prophetess predicts that he will nonetheless end up in Iceland, he blurts out an ironic rejoinder: "That's quite a prophecy given the fact that I have re-solved never to go to that place; it would be a bad trade indeed if I were to sell all my excellent ancestral lands and move to those desolate set-tlements" (chapter 10; ÍF 8:29). Here the exalting of the family prehis-tory becomes a backhanded dismissal of the Icelandic future.

But destiny cannot be averted. The prophetess declares that a certain token has disappeared from Ingimund's purse and is now buried at the spot where he is fated to settle. Ingimund continues to mock the notion, but there is much talk about the inescapability of destiny, and Ingimund does indeed wind up in Iceland after dispatching two Lapps on a psychic exploration to find the location of his token. This is not what he intended, but King Harald has informed Ingimund that he will be held in high esteem wherever he goes.

One can only imagine what a Norwegian jarl's daughter might think of moving to the "desolate settlements" of Iceland, but on that point the saga does not comment. On the eve of their departure she gives birth to a boy, whom Ingimund names with a view to continuity: "This boy has an intelligent look about him and there is no need to look for a name; his name will be Thorstein, and I trust good fortune will fol-low" (chapter 13; ÍF 8:36–37). Though the residence changes, the tra-dition of good fortune does not. Ingimund is not quite the regal presence that Unn the Deepminded was, but he immediately puts his stamp on the new district, most conspicuously by assigning place names (chapters 14–15; ÍF 8:39–42). He also revisits King Harald, pre-sents him with the most magnificent of traditional gifts, a polar bear, and gets the customary splendid reception and gifts before finally set-tling down in his new-found home.

As Ingimund grows older, the author provides a particularly signif-icant piece of information about him: "There is no report of his being involved in court cases or major disputes with other men, because he was in agreement with almost everyone and was not aggressive" (chapter 17; ÍF 8:47). This is a new orientation. The early sagas were predominantly about assembly litigation and great disputes: *Víga-Glúms saga, Reykdœla saga, Fóstbrœðra saga, Heiðarvíga saga, Ljósvetninga* saga, and *Eyrbyggja saga*. This author chooses to attribute the absence of such disputes to Ingimund's peaceable nature, but there may be a further implication. In *Laxdœla saga* there is also a notable absence of public litigation, but the explanation seems to be that the chieftains are conceived of as being in such a dominant and unchallenged position that there is no opportunity for dissension. It may be the implied case in *Vatnsdœla saga* too that no one is strong enough to contest the authority of the chieftains, who thus have the same sort of quasi-royal authority as do those in *Laxdœla saga*.

The function of the Vatnsdale chieftains is not to dispute but to maintain order. That too is very much in the royal tradition: both the skaldic panegyrics and the kings' sagas make it clear that one of the king's foremost duties is to suppress malefactors, and that is also the role of the Vatnsdœlir. The first such malefactor is a certain Hrolleif, who is the nephew of Ingimund's foster brother Sæmund. He is the prototypical troublemaker: "Hrolleif was a very strong man and used his strength against lesser men with ill effects; he was provocative and aggressive and reciprocated good with evil, with the counsel of his mother" (chapter 18; ÍF 8:50). Hrolleif makes his mark by seducing the daughter of a farmer named Uni, then killing Uni's son Odd when he seeks to intervene. Hrolleif is consequently exiled from the district, but his uncle, Sæmund, appeals to his foster brother Ingimund to take the scoundrel in. Ingimund proceeds to bear out his accommodating reputation by acceding to the request and relocating Hrolleif and his mother in a place called Ás.

At this point, Ingimund's grown sons (Thorstein, Jǫkul, Thórir, and Hǫgni) begin to take part in the action. They quarrel with Hrolleif over priority at a fishing site, and during one such confrontation Hrolleif casts a spear at Ingimund himself. Like Áskel in *Reykdœla saga*, Ingimund conceals his state and returns home, fatally wounded. Such is his standing in the district that two of his friends, on hearing the news, commit suicide. His sons take revenge by killing both Hrolleif and his mother Ljót.

The following episodes are also cases of egregious villainy involving the thief Thórólf sleggja, the malicious adviser Thorgrím skinnhúfa, and the sorcerer Thórólf heljarskinn: Thórólf sleggja succumbs in a swamp; Thorgrím skinnhúfa is exiled; and Thórólf heljarskinn is dispatched by Jǫkul. Only at this point does the focus shift from a righteous contest against supernatural evil to a regional dispute on a human scale. The arrogant Berg inn rakki appears to challenge the precedence of Ingimund's sons and engages in provocative behavior. In the course of several incidents, in which Thorstein in particular demonstrates model conciliatoriness, Berg and his uncle, Finnbogi, are discountenanced in the most humiliating way.

After the demise of two more sorceresses, the action passes to the next generation, notably Thorstein's son Ingólf. Here the unbroken record of good fortune and the unchallenged rectitude of the family line fails: Ingólf persists in the seduction of a certain Valgerd, daughter of Óttar; he eludes the attempts of two assassins sent against him by Óttar but loses his brother in the process. After an intrepid attack on a nest of robbers he ultimately succumbs to the wounds incurred during the battle.

The chieftainship now passes out of the family of the Vatnsdœlir and, in an unusual elective procedure, is transferred to one Thorkel krafla. After a distinguished career, Thorkel dies and earns a remarkable eulogy: "After that he died and was a sore loss to his followers and everyone in the district, for he was rightly deemed to be a very great district chieftain and a man of great good fortune, very much in the tradition of the earlier Vatnsdœlir such as Thorstein and Ingimund, though Thorkel had the advantage of the true faith, loved God, and prepared for death in a very Christian manner. Here we conclude *Vatnsdœla saga*" (chapter 47; ÍF 8:131).

Vatnsdœla saga is comparable to *Eyrbyggja saga* in the sense that it is a little longer than average and extends from the Norwegian prehistory to the colonization and governance of a district. But the perspective on governance could hardly be more different. *Eyrbyggja saga* projects a realistic vision bordering on cynicism: Snorri the Chieftain is guided only by a practical assessment of what is most likely to succeed. Although his success rate is no doubt better than average, it is by no means consistent; thus, the saga is about the vagaries of political life. The perspective offered in *Vatnsdœla saga* is symmetrically opposed. It is the story of unmitigated success, determined, we are given to understand, by moral correctness. It underscores the unfailing success of the Vatnsdale chieftains partly with the mystical notion of good fortune, partly by pitting them against manifest villains rather than honorable antagonists, and partly by endowing them with some anticipatory consciousness of a better religion.

The discrimination of personalities is minimal; Thorstein is the wise and moderate brother and Jǫkul the redoubtable warrior, but Thórir (who is afflicted by berserk seizures that are mentioned but not enacted) and Hǫgni have no detectable attributes. Even the amorous Ingólf is exempt from explicit criticism and dies a hero's death. The narrative suffers from a facile opposition of generalized virtue and generalized villainy. Since the saga is also about governance, this opposition may also seem politically naive and too inclined to credit an unchallenged leader. If the saga was written around or somewhat after the time of the Norwegian king's annexation of Iceland, we might suspect a royalist sensibility underlying this simplification, just as in the case of *Laxdœla saga.* And yet it may have been written at more or less the same time as the three sagas of the next chapter, notable for their appreciation of political complexities and the problem of political morality.

CHAPTER NINE

Pondering Justice

Hœnsa-Þóris saga, Bandamanna saga, and *Hrafnkels saga*

The three sagas under study in this chapter are among the most elegant of the shorter texts. They are generally dated in the middle or late thirteenth century, although the criteria are, as usual, tenuous.[1] To the extent that we see saga writing as having evolved and improved over time, we may be tempted to think that the sharp contours and narrative economy of these sagas reinforce the likelihood that they are late and represent the culmination of the short form. It might also be argued that they share a new skepticism about governance, specifically about the reliability of chieftains, since all three focus on the demise of chieftains. In this respect they run counter to the tenor of *Vatnsdœla saga,* which is uniformly uncritical of the leading men and portrays them in an almost legendary light.

Hœnsa-Þóris saga

The theme of a chieftain's demise is perhaps less emphatic in *Hœnsa-Þóris saga* than in the others because the action is more evenly distributed over a variety of characters, ranging from the idealized Blund-

---

[1] Sigurður Nordal (ÍF 3:XXVIII–XXXI) places *Hœnsa-Þóris saga* between 1250 and 1270. Guðni Jónsson (ÍF 7:XCI–XCII) places *Bandamanna saga* around the middle of the thirteenth century. Jón Jóhannesson (ÍF 11:LV–LVI) places *Hrafnkels saga* closer to 1300. The fact that all three are so clearly issue-oriented, in contrast to the earlier character-oriented and history-oriented sagas, suggests to me that they belong together, perhaps around 1280.

Ketil to the villainous Hen-Thórir. It is therefore easy to lose sight of the central role alloted to the chieftain Tungu-Odd Ǫnundarson, who has the highest standing among the characters and the most precipitous fall. He is introduced first and has the most extended genealogy, reaching back five generations. He is also ushered in with the ominous words "he was not reputed to be an equitable man" (chapter 1; ÍF 3:3–4). He bears out this reputation by attempting to dictate the price of the goods put up for sale by Norwegian merchants and then prohibiting all trade.[2] The portrait is not altogether one-sided, however. Odd wisely refrains from further action when Blund-Ketil intervenes to help the Norwegian traders. Furthermore, when Odd's reckless son Thorvald returns and proposes to take the part of the scoundrel Hen-Thórir, Odd does what he can to discourage such an ill-advised alliance.

Despite this apparent moderation, he finally allows himself to be drawn into the subsequent antagonism, which brings about the burning of Blund-Ketil's house and those within it. When Blund-Ketil's son Herstein appeals to him, he cold-bloodedly confiscates the burnt-out house site and rides off without a word. In the large-scale litigation and armed conflict that follow, Odd is bested, and when he seeks to renew the conflict, he is outwitted and foiled by his own son Thórodd. Ultimately, he loses both sons and is left a sick and melancholy old man: "Odd now began to age in earnest. When he learned that neither of his sons would come back, he succumbed to a serious illness, and when it began to oppress him, he told his friends that they should move his body up to Skáneyjarfell when he was dead, and he said that from there he would look out over the whole river valley. And so it came to pass" (chapter 17; ÍF 3:46–47).

If we consider Tungu-Odd to be a failed chieftain, the story appears to be political, but in one respect it seems rather less political than we might expect. About 150 years earlier, Ari Thorgilsson had written about the conflict at the assemblies, in which several men lost their lives; according to Ari the resulting legal reform was calculated to prevent the recurrence of such bloodshed. The author of *Hænsa-Þóris saga* makes no mention of this legal reform. The critique is therefore not so much institutional as personal. The saga is about the personalities en-

<hr>

[2] On price-setting by chieftains, see Helgi Þorláksson 1992, 241–42; and Norseng 2000, 174.

gaged in the hostilities, not about deficiencies in the law, and that orientation is in the spirit of the earlier sagas.

Odd's character defects are underscored in no uncertain terms by contrasting him with perhaps the most idealized figure in the sagas, Blund-Ketil. The author echoes the prescient religious sense of the heathen Vatnsdœlir by introducing Blund-Ketil as "the most upstanding man in the time of the old religion" and "the most popular man in the district" (chapter 1; ÍF 3:5). He treats the Norwegian merchants with exemplary generosity, and when his son warns of hostile consequences, Blund-Ketil responds with an explicit contrast to Odd's conduct and an expression of perfect confidence in justice: "If our case is no worse than Odd's, it may be that it will proceed smoothly" (chapter 3; ÍF 3:10).

Not only is Blund-Ketil benevolent; he is also a prudent planner with a steady eye on his responsibilities. During a hay shortage he plans ahead by determining the number of livestock his tenants should maintain and how many they should slaughter. Unfortunately, they do not all heed his advice; as the winter progresses, they begin to run short of hay and make special appeals to him. He helps out the first petitioner from his own supplies, at the same time urging him not to tell others, but the man is so overwhelmed with gratitude that he soon spreads the word that Blund-Ketil "is like no other man" (chapter 4; ÍF 3:12). When two other tenants run low on hay, he helps them too, even at the expense of slaughtering forty horses in his own herd. A third appeal made by two more tenants is more than he can manage, but he advises them to apply to the wealthy upstart Hen-Thórir, who is known to have surplus hay. They ask him to join the appeal, and he agrees.

Hen-Thórir is the perfect model of meanness. Although he has ample supplies, he refuses to sell any hay out of pure malice. Blund-Ketil tries to overcome his resistance with a series of offers, one more generous than the last. Finally, when no offer will avail, he takes the hay that he calculates to be in surplus and leaves appropriate payment. This seizure, which is dealt with in Icelandic law and figures in the dating of the saga, becomes the engine for the ensuing action.[3]

Hen-Thórir is disgruntled but makes no headway in his representations to the still cautious Tungu-Odd. This reticence gives way when

[3] On the legal question see Ebel 1982, 30; Ebel 1989, 54–55 (with the text of the much-debated provision in *Jónsbók*); Miller 1990, 98–99.

Odd's much less cautious son Thorvald returns from abroad, takes an interest in Hen-Thórir, and decides to support him, against the explicit advice of Arngrím the Chieftain. He apparently intervenes for no better reason then to assert himself. Despite his eagerness, Thorvald is at least inclined to consult before he acts, but Thórir insists on issuing an instant summons against Blund-Ketil. When Blund-Ketil's neighbors catch sight of the advancing summons party, they demonstrate their loyalty by spontaneously assembling to protect him, since the delivery of a summons can be a moment of high tension and danger.

On this occasion, however, Blund-Ketil's response is to repeat his generous offers of compensation, in effect giving Thorvald self-judgment. That would seem to blunt the summons, and Thorvald is momentarily speechless, but, goaded on by Hen-Thórir, he collects himself and delivers a famous non sequitur: "It seems to me that there is no choice but to summon"(chapter 8; ÍF 3:22).[4] The summons is formulated in the most injurious terms, and Blund-Ketil's Norwegian guest Qrn is so indignant on his host's behalf that he shoots an arrow into the crowd of summoners. The arrow strikes Helgi, the young son of Arngrím the Chieftain and Hen-Thórir's foster son. Hen-Thórir rushes to Helgi's side, ostensibly to catch his last words, but it is clear that Helgi is already dead and that Hen-Thórir fabricates his dying words, to the effect that Blund-Ketil should be burned in his house. Accordingly, the summoners withdraw until night has come on and the solicitous neighbors have dispersed. Then they return to carry out the burning.

A dominant theme in this story is righteousness; nowhere in the sagas is there a more unrighteous villain than Hen-Thórir, who finally manufactures the motivation for killing, and nowhere is there a more righteous leader than Blund-Ketil, who is prepared to submit to any humiliation rather than to put himself in the wrong or leave his tenants unprovided for.[5] But a second, rather less conspicuous theme has

[4] Ebel 1989, 32–33.

[5] Since the mid-1980s there has grown up an interesting special literature on the commercial implications of *Hænsa-Þóris saga*. The drift of these studies has been to use Hen-Thórir as a key to Icelandic attitudes toward small-time, internal trade (or "peddling") in the late thirteenth century. Ebel 1982 (e.g., 33, 43) analyzes the contrasting portraiture of Hen-Thórir and Blund-Ketil as a displacement of a strictly legal discourse in favor of a moral discourse. Baumgartner (1987) takes the opposed view and argues that it is not Hen-Thórir's moral deficiencies that condemn him but rather his status as a social upstart in an aristocratic society. Durrenberger, Durrenberger, and

to do with the baleful influence of money. Some characters have both standing and wealth. Blund-Ketil and Thorkel trefil (whom we will meet presently) are introduced as very wealthy men. Arngrím the Chieftain, on the other hand, is pointedly not credited with wealth. As a result, when Hen-Thórir approaches him with the offer to foster his son Helgi in exchange for a bequest of half his wealth, Arngrím has an inkling that he should not make such a bargain with the devil—"It seems to me that there is little honor to be had from this fosterage"— changes his tune when the money is offered, and succumbs to the temptation: "I think the best thing to do is not to refuse such a good offer" (chapter 2; ÍF 3:7). He therefore enters an agreement that is manifestly unwise, given the character of his associate.

This is the first of two occasions on which money intrudes into human affairs with disastrous consequences. The second is when Thórir wins the political support of Thorvald by again offering half his money. It is not clear whether this is the same half promised to Arngrím (now withdrawn because Arngrím has offered no support) or whether it is the second half. It has the same effect on Thorvald, a young man who has no significant stake yet and cannot resist easy money.

There is clearly a contrast between old money and new money: Blund-Ketil has old money and uses it benevolently; Hen-Thórir has new money acquired "in trade" and uses it to make mischief. It can hardly be happenstance that old money is associated with virtue and new money with malice. The outlook seems aristocratic, although that hardly comports with the sharp criticism leveled against the traditional chieftain, Tungu-Odd. Perhaps we should consider the corrup-

---

Ástráður Eysteinsson (1987–88) and Durrenberger and Wilcox (1992, 65–74) argue that the disfavor heaped on Hen-Thórir derives from his attempt to substitute commerical exchange for traditional social networking. Ebel 1989 is a critique of Baumgartner, arguing that the saga is not a picture of social disruption pointing toward the advisability of kingship but rather an index of Icelandic resistance to Norwegian hierarchization and an object lesson in how traditional institutions in Iceland can mend themselves. Miller 1990, 93–105 (esp. 97) suggests that Hen-Thórir refuses to sell hay to Blund-Ketil—in a situation that is potentially hostile because sale was a problematical mode of exchange—in order to lure him into litigation. Helgi Þorláksson (1992, 243–44) argues that Hen-Thórir is disparaged because his activity runs counter to "a prevailing opinion that people should have an income befitting their rank and status," whereas Blund-Ketil's protection of the Norwegian trader Ǫrn may be viewed in the context of a growing acceptance of free trade beginning in Norway and spreading to Iceland. Norseng 2000 emphasizes the distinction between high-status long-distance trade and low-status local trade.

tion of Odd's son Thorvald with new money to be part and parcel of the criticism aimed at chieftains. The message would seem to be that chieftains should be not only temperate and devoted to their followers but also financially independent and above venal temptation. However we want to formulate the exact gist of the saga, it clearly has much to do with the conduct of chieftains and their exercise of authority.

The second part of the saga seems at first glance less focused on the problem of character and conduct and more concerned with the outcome of the narrative. It details the aftermath of the burning with some rather mysterious, even magical, effects and an exploitation of well-calculated deceit that does not seem quite in keeping with the high-minded principles advocated in the first part. The action centers on Blund-Ketil's son Herstein, who happens to be away from home with his foster father Thorbjǫrn at the time of the burning. Thorbjǫrn has a monitory dream, which is soon confirmed when they see the house in ashes. Thorbjǫrn, like the wise foster fathers in *Heiðarvíga saga* and *Ljósvetninga saga*, immediately conceives a plan to help Herstein, but it is presented in rather elliptical form.

Thorbjǫrn's first recommendation is to seek help from Tungu-Odd. This seems like a most unlikely remedy, since Tungu-Odd is the father of the chief burner, and Herstein accordingly expresses doubts. These doubts are borne out when Tungu-Odd provides no help and merely confiscates the house site in his own name. The sequel, however, leads us to believe that this is the first step in a deep-seated plan to pit the chieftains Tungu-Odd and Thórd gellir against each other in such a way as to benefit Herstein. It appears that the two chieftains have already been in contention, and Thorbjǫrn proposes the drive the wedge deeper.

Thorbjǫrn's second act is pure magic: he vanishes in the twinkling of an eye and, all invisible, gathers the livestock and the remaining property, telling Herstein to hold his peace whatever he may see. When he reappears, they drive the livestock to the home of Thorkel trefil, who is destined to be the first pawn in Thorbjǫrn's game. He receives them warmly and offers right away to graze the animals, presumably motivated by his high regard for Blund-Ketil. Only after they have accepted Thorkel's hospitality do they reveal the killing of Blund-Ketil. Thorkel is not sure that he would have been so quick with his hospitality if he had known the news beforehand, but he does not want to renege on his offer. It is clear that he begins to ruminate immediately, and it is indeed Thorkel who plans the next move—although it was doubtlessly foreseen by Thorbjǫrn.

All three of them now ride off to visit Gunnar Hlífarson, who is married to the daughter of Thórd gellir. They call him out in the middle of the night and, in a most implausible sequence, pressure him to betroth his daughter to Herstein on the spot. Against all odds he does so, and only after the betrothal is contracted do they tell him of the burning. He is now caught in the same toils as Thorkel and falls silent.

The next morning they approach Thórd gellir, and Gunnar persuades him to lend his authority to the betrothal and hold the wedding feast at his farm. Only then do they reveal the burning of Blund-Ketil, and Thórd sees that he too has been deceived. Gunnar notes that Thórd has long been at odds with Tungu-Odd and that the time has come to make the final test of strength. At the wedding feast Herstein makes a solemn vow to outlaw Arngrím the Chieftain, and Gunnar makes the same vow to the detriment of Thorvald Oddsson, but Thórd is too wise to commit himself against Tungu-Odd.

The result of these preparations is a large-scale recruitment of men on both sides, told very briefly. In the first encounter at the district assembly, Thórd gellir comes off second best and resolves to bring the case to the Allthing. But between the first and second clash there is an interlude in which Herstein is able to ferret out an ambush laid for him by Hen-Thórir, capture the culprits, and put them to the sword, thereby gaining great credit. In the meantime, Tungu-Odd must yield at the Allthing and allow a settlement that prescribes full outlawry for Arngrím and lesser outlawry for Thorvald. Thus the conclusion provides justice for the villain and the ill-advised chieftains of the first part, whereas Thorkel, Gunnar, and Thórd maintain their status, and Herstein emerges well married and in high repute.

The moralizing is palpable, but we may ask how the second part supplements the first part in moral terms. After all, the magic and deception of the revenge sequence is not altogether edifying. The point may be ironic. What failed the chieftains in the first part was not only moderation and financial disinterest but also foresight and an ability to calculate the consequences. These are precisely the qualities demonstrated, in almost parodistic terms, by Thorbjǫrn, Thorkel, and Gunnar in the second part. The sequel is a story of how keen analysis triumphs over momentary impulse. Intelligence, planning, and precise calculation provide the winning combination, just as they did in *Fóstbrœðra saga* and *Heiðarvíga saga*. The approval of wisdom is still unreserved, but we will see in Chapter 10, on *Njáls saga*, that wisdom too has its limitations.

Bandamanna saga

Whereas *Hœnsa-Þóris saga* may be understood as a serious critique of chieftainly conduct, *Bandamanna saga* is generally appreciated as a comedy or an outright lampoon of the chieftains as a class.[6] The author pits a sly old man against an alliance of eight chieftains (the "banded men" of the title), whom he not only outwits but also derides in a thoroughly demeaning way. These chieftains are portrayed as hard-up, small-minded, self-absorbed, and easily deceived men. Once the old man has fragmented their alliance, they turn on each other and continue to expose one another's personal foibles in the same shameless style put to effective use by their wily antagonist. Thus the final stages of the action are characterized by a rather breathless stream of charge and countercharge that leaves the chieftains' reputations in shambles. They attack one another not with oratory, of which we will see flashes in *Njáls saga*, but with pointed barbs and jibes that delight the reader's taste for the inventiveness and destructiveness of language. The art of the well-turned and damaging phrase is as old as the earliest Norse poetry, but nowhere is it used with such tireless ingenuity as in *Bandamanna saga*. The fact that it is devised by a low-status and ostensibly helpless old man against a group of high-status chieftains has inevitably suggested that the saga is a social satire at the expense of the aristocracy.

That the point is something other than the historical panorama unfolded in Chapters 7 and 8 is confirmed by the preface. *Laxdœla saga* and *Eyrbyggja saga* in particular deploy an unsurveyable wealth of genealogy, but *Hœnsa-Þóris saga* introduces no more than three personages directly involved in the plot (only the key chieftain Tungu-Odd merits a real genealogy), and *Bandamanna saga* is even more economical. It provides only the genealogy of the wily old man Ófeig and his

---

[6] On the mechanisms of satire in *Bandamanna saga*, see Durrenberger and Wilcox 1992.

son Odd, informing us that they are the descendants of the impressive chieftain Ófeig Járngerdarson, with whom we became acquainted in *Ljósvetninga saga*. Thus the reader does not survey an epic canvas but is presented with a minimal cast of characters and a narrow issue. The point seems to be to shed the traditional complexities of the earlier sagas and to isolate the central issue with the greatest possible efficiency.

Ófeig is by no means a resurrected counterpart of his illustrious great-grandfather, Ófeig Járngerdarson. He has extensive lands and is described as a very wise and resourceful man, but he appears to be cash-poor. He and his son Odd are not on the best of terms, for reasons that are not revealed, and when Odd asks for a stake to get started in life, Ófeig is not forthcoming. The following day, Odd simply takes what he needs and sets out on his own. Father and son will not see each other again for a number of years, long enough that Odd appears not to recognize his father when they do meet.

In the meantime, Odd prospers. He starts as a menial fisherman, but he is hard-working and a good companion, and he soon makes his fortune. He is in fact so well off that he is said to be richer than the three next richest men in Iceland. He is of good lineage, but he is also a self-made man like Hen-Thórir, though without any of the disagreeable qualities that set Hen-Thórir apart. Thus the role of money is central in both sagas. Odd's affluence even allows him to procure a chieftaincy and advance to the forefront of Icelandic society.

But the forefront has its perils. Yielding to a special appeal, Odd takes in a man named Óspak Glúmsson. Although Óspak has an unsavory reputation, he works hard for Odd and behaves so well that when Odd decides to go abroad, he turns over not only his household but his chieftaincy to Óspak for safekeeping. While Odd is away, Óspak sets up a household with a woman named Svala, and when Odd returns, it appears that Óspak has discharged all his duties faithfully and skillfully. The only problem is that he seems reluctant to relinquish the chieftaincy, so that Odd must finally force him to do so. That leads to a marked chill in the relationship, and Óspak moves away to his wife's farm.

At the next roundup, forty of Odd's geldings are missing, and people in the neighborhood suspect that Óspak is responsible. Odd's good friend Váli offers to get to the bottom of the mystery and is able to conclude that Óspak is indeed the culprit. He offers to spare Óspak if he will only make a clean breast of his theft, but Óspak refuses, with the result that Odd mounts an expedition against him. Váli rides ahead, but as he enters the house, Óspak mistakes him for Odd and delivers a fatal sword stroke. Váli, still solicitous of Óspak's welfare, sends word back to Odd to the effect that a settlement has been reached. Then he succumbs to his wound. For his part, Óspak disappears and is nowhere to be found.

Despite the entertaining thrust and parry of the dialogue in this saga, the author works with a palette that is no less black and white than that of *Hænsa-Þóris saga*. Odd is not quite so idealized as Blund-Ketil, but he has the same engaging, and misplaced, trust. Óspak is no less a villain than Hen-Thórir, perhaps more so by dint of his hypocrisy and a series of bloody deeds: he not only kills his would-be benefactor Váli, but, after his disappearance and his wife's remarriage, he kills the new husband and wantonly slaughters animals on Odd's farm. Having suffered a wound in the first of these encounters, he is later found dead in a cave in rather lugubrious surroundings. Like *Hænsa-Þóris saga,* this tale tends to emphasize the extremes of admirable and despicable behavior. Both develop a moralizing outlook reminiscent of *Reykdæla saga* and *Vatnsdæla saga* but largely missing in the other sagas.

The second part of the story perhaps moralizes no less but does so in a different vein. It is a comedy of duplicity and dupes. In the aftermath of Óspak's depredations, Odd brings a case against him for the theft of his sheep and Váli's killing. The case seems clear enough, and Odd's success would seem to be a foregone conclusion until two chieftains, Styrmir and Thórarin, apparently envious of Odd's preeminence, find a way to block the litigation. As Odd leaves the assembly grounds in defeat, he is approached by an old man who rallies him gently and then promises to right the wrong if he is provided with a bag of silver. The old man of course turns out to be his long-lost father Ófeig, who now goes before the stymied jurors and quizzes them about the nature of justice. This is a question raised repeatedly in *Njáls saga* but never with the same explicitness that Ófeig brings to it:

Ófeig asked: "Has my son Odd's case been judged?" "Whatever judging can be done has been done," they said. "How can that be?" asked Ófeig. "Was the case against Óspak wrongly brought? Did he not kill Váli, an innocent man? Was the problem that the case was unclear?" They replied: "A defect was found in the case, and it was disqualified." "What sort of a defect?" asked Ófeig. He was told.

He said: "Does it really seem to you in any way just to pay heed to things of no importance and not condemn the worst sort of man to outlawry, a thief and a killer? Is it not a terrible burden of responsibility to find for a man who deserves death and thus judge contrary to justice?" They said that they did not think it right, but that was how it was put to them.

"That may be so," said Ófeig, "but did you swear an oath?" "Of course," they said. "That will have been the case," he said, "but what was the wording? Wasn't it to the effect that you would judge according to what you know to be most just and lawful?" They acknowledged that. Then Ófeig said: "And what could be juster than to condemn the worst sort of man to outlawry, free for the killing and forfeit of all assistance, a man who is guilty of theft and of killing an innocent man, Váli? Now the third part of the oath [pertaining to the law] might be called somewhat flexible. Consider what is more important, the two words having to do with 'truth and justice,' or the one word referring to the 'laws.' You will conclude, as you should, by grasping that it is a greater burden of responsibility to free a man who deserves death although you have sworn oaths that you would judge according to what you know to be most just." (Chapter 6; ÍF 7:322)

As Ófeig delivers these tricky but powerful words, he dangles his purse of silver up and down to give the jurors a clear view of it. When the visual lure has done its work, he offers each juror an ounce of silver, but those to whom it falls to sum up the case are offered a more generous half-mark, if they will only do what is, after all, the right and proper thing. Óspak is duly outlawed, and Odd emerges victorious at a very moderate cost.

When Styrmir and Thórarin learn what has happened, they feel mightily disgraced, but they surmise that a case for judicial bribery may be brought against Odd. They therefore form an alliance with six other chieftains, all agreeing under oath to stick together until they get either outlawry or self-judgment. The odds appear to be overwhelming, and in due course they summon Odd for bribery. Ófeig, with whom Odd is once again on close terms, advises his son to gather all his movable property and load it onto a ship in preparation for departure. Ófeig then proceeds to the assembly and his next round of chicanery.

Walking about in a decrepit posture to suggest helplessness, he first approaches the chieftain Egil Skúlason under the guise of sociable conversation, gradually bringing the discussion around to the fact that Egil is short of money but has high hopes of getting rich at Odd's expense. He then reveals that Odd has all his movable property in safekeeping and that the only property subject to confiscation is his land. Since half the land will go to the men of the district, Egil stands to gain only one sixteenth of the farm after sharing with his coconspirators. This is indeed a disappointing prospect. At the same time, Ófeig expresses great goodwill toward Egil in particular and renews his sight gag with another large bag of silver, eventually counting out two hundred ounces to show his favor if Egil will withdraw from the alliance.

Egil is at first indignant at the supposition that he might contravene his oath and betray his companions, but Ófeig delicately reminds him that he swore only to get self-judgment and that self-judgment might, under the right circumstances, be left up to him. Egil still hesitates to open himself to the anger of his seven associates, but Ófeig suggests the possibility of a second defection, leaving Egil a free choice in designating the candidate. The choice falls on Gellir Thorkelsson, and the comedy begins anew. This time, however, Ófeig adds the additional incentive that Odd will marry Gellir's daughter. Unable to resist the thought of marrying into so much money, Gellir succumbs and joins the plot.

When everyone convenes for the legal hearing the next day, Ófeig uses his verbal dexterity to get an agreement that the chieftains will settle for self-judgment rather than outlawry. He then pleads the unfairness involved in having one poor old man submit to the self-judgment of eight powerful opponents. The chieftains acquiesce and allow him to designate just two of their number. The process of choosing gives Ófeig the welcome opportunity to disqualify the other six with ringing denunciations of their flawed characters. He completes the round with mock distress at being left with only the dregs, Egil and Gellir. These two are dismayed at the prospect of incurring the wrath of their associates, but they agree between themselves that Gellir will announce the settlement and Egil will counter the objections.

Gellir duly announces the risible payment of thirteen ounces, to be turned over in the lowest quality silver. At first the chieftains think that they have not heard correctly; then they are both incredulous and furious. As they object, one after the other, Egil silences them with unsavory details or threats of revelations from their private lives. The chieftains are thus discountenanced and discredited, while Odd celebrates a grand marriage to Gellir's daughter and ends the story, like Herstein in *Hœnsa-Þóris saga*, well married, rich, and in high spirits.

Bandamanna saga occupies such a unique position because of its satirical edge that it is seldom compared with other sagas, yet it has not a little in common with *Hœnsa-Þóris saga*. Although it is even more explicitly about chieftains, it has less to say about the relationship between great men and little men. There is only one specific indication, a particularly pointed moment in the series of rebukes dealt out by Odd as he disqualifies six chieftains, including his own: "There you are, Styrmir, and people will think it strange that I don't include you in the business at hand, because I am your constituent, and it is to you I should look for help, but you have received many good gifts from me and given an ill reward for all of them" (chapter 10; ÍF 7:347). This is the only comment on the behavior of chieftains toward their followers in *Bandamanna saga*, but it fits in well with the general disparagement of the chieftain class.

Money has a large part to play in both sagas discussed so far in this chapter. It is a problem that some people have money and others not. It is also a problem that some people make prudent use of their money and others not. In *Hœnsa-Þóris saga*, Hen-Thórir is awash in money but is the soul of meanness. Arngrím the Chieftain has rather less money and therefore allows himself to be seduced by Thórir's wealth. Thorvald has not come into his inheritance and similarly succumbs to Thórir's pecuniary blandishments. In *Bandamanna saga*, Odd and his father Ófeig have a falling-out over money. Odd becomes incomparably rich but learns that money by itself has limited success. Some of the chieftains, for want of money, become easy marks for Ófeig's maneuvers.

What gives money its power is prudence and foresight. Odd has already demonstrated that he is lacking in these qualities when he takes in the hypocrite Óspak. In the proceedings against Óspak he confirms his failing by making a procedural error and jeopardizing his case. Fortunately, superior knowledge is at hand in the person of his father, Ófeig. Thus the story presents a complementary pattern: Odd has deep pockets but limited knowledge; Ófeig has limited resources but a profound knowledge of the law and human nature. When the two are joined, they carry all before them. *Hœnsa-Þóris saga* suggests a similar mechanism. The orphaned Herstein is a young man with little experience of the law or the world, but when he works with his resourceful (and supernaturally gifted) foster father, Thorbjǫrn, they succeed. Both sagas contrive the perfect marriage of sagacity and resources.

Since *Bandamanna saga* is so engaging at the level of comic diversion, it has prompted little analysis of larger issues, but it might be read to mean that naked power, in the case of the chieftains, and naked money, in the case of Odd, are naked indeed. Power and money need to be wed with intelligence to be effective. The chieftains fail because they lack the necessary intelligence, and Odd succeeds because he can call on the extraordinary mental and rhetorical powers of his old father.

Hrafnkels saga

Hrafnkels saga, like *Bandamanna saga*, occupies a singular position in the history of saga writing. Although it is even shorter than the two texts discussed above—thirty-five pages in the standard edition—it has been the subject of more commentary than any other saga, most recently in a 330-page book by Tommy Danielsson, which includes a full review of scholarly opinion.[7] Given the availability of that compendious treatment, I refer only occasionally to the critical literature.

The gist of the literature has been not to locate *Hrafnkels saga* in the context of other sagas but rather to isolate it as a special case. The central problem is that it appears to invite interpretation more overtly than any other saga in the corpus, but an interpretive consensus seems particularly elusive. The focal point is the character of the chieftain Hrafnkel, who rises to a position of unchallenged dominance in his East Fjord district. Like Tungu-Odd in *Hœnsa-Þóris saga,* he is introduced as an "inequitable man": "He forced the men in Jǫkulsdale to become his followers; he was gentle and kind to his own men but harsh and unyielding toward the Jǫkulsdalers, so that they got no fair treatment from him. Hrafnkel was much given to duels and paid no compensation for any man [whom he killed], for no one got any compensation from him no matter what he did" (chapter 2; ÍF 11:99). There

---

[7] Danielsson 2002a. There is also a full review of the problems in Müller 2005.

is thus a certain contradiction in Hrafnkel from the very outset; he is at once an extraordinarily successful man and a man with a defective sense of justice. How then are we to judge him?

The action proper begins with an example of Hrafnkel's questionable conduct. His poor neighbor Thorbjǫrn finds himself so hard pressed that he cannot maintain his eldest son Einar at home and is obliged to send him away to look for work elsewhere. Hrafnkel hires him as a shepherd, with the strict injunction not to ride his favorite stallion Freyfaxi, so named because Hrafnkel has declared that the heathen god Frey has half ownership in the horse. But Einar contravenes this proviso while searching for lost sheep: Freyfaxi is the only horse that will allow himself to be caught and ridden, and Einar thinks it will do no harm under these special circumstances. When Hrafnkel learns of the infraction, he kills Einar on the spot, believing that a man must honor his oath.

The old man Thorbjǫrn duly appeals for monetary compensation. Hrafnkel reminds him that it is not his custom to pay compensation but admits that the killing of Einar is not among his more praiseworthy deeds and that he should not have adhered so blindly to his vow. He therefore offers to provide for Thorbjǫrn as long as he remains on his farm, to arrange good marriages for his other sons and daughters and to give Thorbjǫrn whatever he needs within reason. He may remain on his farm as long as he wishes, and when he becomes too old, Hrafnkel will take him in and care for him until his dying day. Thorbjǫrn declines and asks for an arbitration commission, but Hrafnkel refuses on the ground that such an arrangement would imply that they are equals.

This particularly interesting passage anticipates some of the interpretive complexities. Thorbjǫrn would presumably have settled for two hundred ounces of silver, and Hrafnkel offers him a settlement worth many times that amount, though he declines to call it compensation. Yet Thorbjǫrn refuses and insists on something that he will be allowed to classify as compensation. What is at stake here is not money but self-esteem. Hrafnkel, in contrast to Blund-Ketil in *Hœnsa-Þóris saga*, will not enter into any agreement that appears to infringe on his social preeminence. In a similar situation Blund-Ketil demonstrated humility, and it is clear that the author admires that quality. In the case of *Hrafnkels saga*, however, what the author thinks of Hrafnkel is so unclear that critics are divided on whether he is portrayed as arrogant or merely zealous in the maintenance of his status.

Thorbjǫrn's position is even more puzzling. He has very little status but nonetheless turns down an extraordinarily magnanimous offer. It is easy to treat him as a fool, and his brother Bjarni does just that. But for Thorbjǫrn it is not merely a question of money; he has a robust sense of self and a deep sense of injury. He has, after all, lost his oldest son, a son he cherished. When he is forced to send Einar away to look for work, he assures him that it is for no lack of love but only because he is so impoverished. No doubt Thorbjǫrn feels guilty for having thrust Einar onto the open job market and thus indirectly bringing about his death.

Perhaps Hrafnkel's exaggerated evaluation of his chieftainly status is forgivable, and perhaps Thorbjǫrn's exaggerated evaluation of his loss is no less forgivable. In any event, the encounter between the two men will be perceived by the reader as a nontrivial moment in terms of both psychology and social dynamics. Both are jeopardized by their self-esteem, and what follows is the tale of their vulnerabilities.

Thorbjǫrn is not prepared to forgo what he sees as his due. After he has been dismissed with little sympathy by his brother Bjarni, he appeals to his nephew Sám, who has been introduced earlier as a promising young man, self-assertive and skilled in the law. He is at first cautious and suggests that they explore whether Hrafnkel might still be willing to abide by his earlier offer, but Thorbjǫrn dismisses this option out of hand and taunts Sám mercilessly for his dismal lack of initiative. Sám continues to be doubtful but finally agrees, against his better judgment, to take over responsibility for the case. He is a character analogous to Thorvald Tungu-Oddsson, though a little more guarded; both are young men eager to make their mark and therefore not averse to taking chances.

Hrafnkel hears of the project and finds it laughable, but Sám duly delivers the legal summons and gathers men to back him in the dispute. Having arrived at the Allthing (annual assembly), he appeals to every chieftain he can find for help, but none is prepared to join his cause; on the one hand, none of the chieftains is in Sám's debt, and on the other hand, they all consider Hrafnkel to be a far too intimidating opponent. The prospects for success seem so dim that at one point Thorbjǫrn breaks down in tears.

What follows is among the most mysterious passages in the sagas and certainly the most mysterious in *Hrafnkels saga*. One morning Thorbjǫrn's party catches sight of a group of five men on the other side of the river and learns that their leader is not himself a chieftain but that his brother is indeed a chieftain from the West Fjord district. One part of the mystery is that these brothers are not known from other sources and that the chieftaincies in the West Fjords during this period (the end of the tenth century) are otherwise accounted for.[8] Whoever these mysterious strangers may be, Sám makes his customary appeal for help. The brother thus addressed—his name is Thorkel—refers Sám to his brother, the chieftain Thorgeir, but he advises the suppliants to proceed in a particular way. It turns out that Thorgeir is lying in his booth recovering from a painful boil on his foot, which has recently burst. Thorkel advises that the old man, Thorbjǫrn, should enter the booth first, stumble about clumsily, and wrench the sore toe. This does not strike Sám as good advice, but Thorkel tells him to follow his directions or expect no help.

Sám and Thorbjǫrn now do as they are told and fall all over Thorgeir, who is appropriately indignant. Sám and Thorbjǫrn remain speechless, but Thorkel enters at the crucial moment and draws a somewhat strained analogy for his brother: Thorgeir may well feel the pain in his sore foot, but he may imagine that old Thorbjǫrn feels no less pain at the loss of his son and the refusal of compensation. After some further negotiation this contrived metaphor somehow convinces Thorgeir to join Thorbjǫrn's cause. His agreement only compounds the mystery. After all, these brothers stand in no relationship to Thorbjǫrn or Sám; they are under no obligation; and they have absolutely nothing to gain from the alliance. Are we to believe that the power of compassion is greater than the fundamentals of self-interest?

Despite the weak motivation, Thorkel takes great pains to inveigle Thorgeir's help. This is one of the characteristic saga sequences in which a prudent man gives advice with an exact foreknowledge of how the advice will bring about a desired end, no matter how counterinstinctive it may appear to be. Thorkel knows exactly how susceptible his brother will be and is on the spot to clinch the outcome. Like other saga advisers, he does not share any hint of his foreknowledge with his clients, who remain in the dark. The situation is in fact reminiscent of the sequence in *Hœnsa-Þóris saga* in which Herstein's foster father initiates a series of unlikely moves without revealing what will happen. Both sagas suggest a quasi-magical prescience.

[8] Sigurður Nordal 1940/1958, 7–13.

Both sequences also underscore not only the psychological acuity of the adviser but also a certain lack of perspicacity on the part of the man who unwittingly benefits from the advice, Herstein in *Hœnsa-Þóris saga* and Sám in *Hrafnkels saga*. To these figures can be added Odd in *Bandamanna saga*, who finds himself in a similar position. Herstein is a young man with a serious case on his hands (his father's killing); Odd has lost a case he had every expectation of winning; and Sám has seemingly exhausted every resource without gaining support for his cause. Herstein's foster father intervenes with a plan too ingenious to be credible; Odd's father comes to his assistance with a plan that strains credence no less; while Sám is rescued from despair by a complete stranger whose very existence is historically doubtful.

In the first two instances there is a clear issue of a wrong to be righted; both Herstein and Odd are entitled to win their cases. In Sám's case the issue is less clear-cut. Is he wise to proceed against Hrafnkel? Is he serving his own interests more than Thorbjǫrn's, since he is an ambitious and self-assertive man? To be sure, a wrong has been committed, but are the reparations offered by Hrafnkel not adequate? However we wish to allocate the merits of this last case, the issues seem quite similar: the weak find themselves aligned against the powerful and are the beneficiaries of an unexpected and almost supernatural salvation. It is as if the authors imagine, or wish for, some sort of cosmic justice that operates to protect the weak.

The mysterious brothers from the West Fjords also have mysterious resources. They are popular men and are able to gather a large body of allies in support of their cause. It had been Hrafnkel's intention "to teach men of no account wishing to oppose him a lesson" (chapter 4; ÍF 11:117), but the West Fjord contingent assembles in such force that they block the court and prevent Hrafnkel from gaining access. As a result, he is duly outlawed, to the satisfaction of many people who have suffered inequitable treatment at his hands. Sám is quite beside himself with delight and struts about in a show of self-satisfaction. But the judgment of outlawry against Hrafnkel is only the first step, and Thorgeir reminds Sám that he must next execute the confiscation of Hrafnkel's property prescribed by law—a most unlikely prospect, given Hrafnkel's unassailable position in his own district.

As if the West Fjord brothers had not done enough for Sám already, they now volunteer to accompany him across the breadth of Iceland to assist in the confiscation. They are able to catch Hrafnkel and his household off guard early one morning and capture all the residents. Hrafnkel takes the prospect of being killed calmly but asks to be spared indignities. Sám replies that he has not been sparing of his enemies and that it is only just that he suffer the consequences. Accordingly, they suspend Hrafnkel and seven of his men by their pierced heels while they conduct the confiscation. Then Sám offers Hrafnkel the choice between death and the surrender of self-judgment, in effect leaving the decision up to his antagonists. Hrafnkel chooses life chiefly because of his young sons, and Sám exiles him with precious little property, despite Thorgeir's advice that it is not wise to let him live. The judgment of the district is not favorable to Hrafnkel: "People talked a lot about how his arrogance had suffered a fall and many of them were reminded of the old proverb that immoderation is short-lived" (chapter 5; ÍF 11:122). Hrafnkel goes into exile in a new district, where he quickly rises to preeminence once again.

In the meantime, Sám holds a great celebratory feast, takes over the chieftaincy, kills the ill-starred horse Freyfaxi, burns the temple dedicated to Frey, bestows handsome gifts on the West Fjord brothers, and becomes a popular chieftain. Hrafnkel also thrives in his new surroundings and acquires a new character to match: "A change had now come over his disposition.[9] The man was much more popular than before. He had the same attitude with respect to industry and outlay, but he was much more popular and restrained and accommodating in every respect than before" (chapter 7; ÍF 11:125). When Hrafnkel and Sám occasionally meet, there are no recriminations. This apparent truce lasts for six years, but it is illusory.

At the expiration of the six years, Sám's brother Eyvind—mentioned only at the very outset, as being in the service of the emperor in Constantinople—returns to Iceland. He has become a great man and is promptly invited home by Sám. Hrafnkel gets wind of the fact that Eyvind is on his way and, goaded by a scolding washerwoman, sets out instantly with a company of eighteen men in all. They overtake Eyvind and kill him and his four companions, albeit with a disproportionate loss of life among their own men.

This is the last great crux in the saga. Given such a cold-blooded killing of a man who is in no way implicated in the previous hostili-

---

[9] The manuscript reading for the word translated here as "disposition" is actually *land* (land), but that reading makes so little sense that the printed editions conjecture *lund* (disposition).

ties, can we say that Hrafnkel is truly reformed? The answer is provided by the West Fjord brothers, who seem to represent not only a miraculous intercession but also a sort of commenting chorus. After the reemergent Hrafnkel has repossessed his former chieftaincy and driven Sám back to his old home, Sám once more appeals to the West Fjord brothers for help, but this time they quite reasonably refuse. It is Thorgeir who speaks for them:

> We thought we had arranged things very well for you before we departed, so that it would be easy for you to maintain your position. But what I expected came to pass when you granted Hrafnkel his life, although I told you that you would regret it greatly. We urged you to kill Hrafnkel, but you wanted to be in charge. Now it is easy to see the difference in intelligence between the two of you; he let you sit in peace and made his attempt only when he was able to dispatch the man whom he judged to be more formidable than you. We will take no part in your misfortune. (Chapter 10; ÍF 11:132–33)

The central debate in the critical literature has been between those who think that Hrafnkel is a defective chieftain who is punished and reformed and those who think that he is a consummate politician who has a setback but rallies to recover his losses. The debate is in effect between those who construe the story morally and those who construe it politically.[10] The problem for the moralists is that Hrafnkel kills Eyvind *after* his apparent change of heart. The problem for the political interpreters is that Hrafnkel in fact miscalculates, is disgraced, and spends six years in exile.

[10] Fredrik Heinemann (1975a and b) and Peter Hallberg (1975a and b) engaged in single combat over related issues in 1975. Hallberg accused Heinemann of being too moralistic, but since Heinemann thought that Eyvind provoked his own killing and Hallberg thought that he was innocent, moral categories can be detected in both arguments. More recently, von See (1979/1981a, 486–95) took a clear position on the political wisdom of Eyvind's killing, arguing that the saga advocates the aristocratic status quo. Miller (1990, 198–202) followed suit with a similar argument to the effect that Eyvind is the appropriate target for Hrafnkel's revenge. Fulk (1986) seeks to alter the terms of the discussion by proposing that the choice is not between a moral and a political outlook but between an ideological outlook (e.g., the oath-inspired killing of Einar) and a pragmatic outlook (e.g., the killing of Eyvind). This interpretation does not quite account for the explicit comments on good and bad conduct and Hrafnkel's improved disposition. In Andersson 1988b I argue for a moralizing viewpoint, a stance not foreign to such sagas as *Reykdœla saga*, *The Saga of King Magnús and King Harald*, *Vatnsdœla saga*, and *Hœnsa-Þóris saga*.

Perhaps we have focused too exclusively on Hrafnkel. It might be more satisfactory to argue that the saga is about two characters, Hrafnkel and Sám. *Hœnsa-Þóris saga* is centrally about one defective chieftain, Tungu-Odd. *Bandamanna saga* is about an unfinished chieftain, Odd, who needs the special intervention of his father to achieve complete success. *Hrafnkels saga* is about two chieftains, both of them unfinished, each defective in his own way. The advocates of a political reading cannot argue that Hrafnkel is the complete chieftain, because the text makes it clear both that he is an "inequitable man" and that he does not reform fully. The moralists cannot argue that Sám is a perfect replacement for Hrafnkel, because he is given to swagger and heedlessness; he succeeds only to the extent that he depends on the West Fjord brothers, and he fails because he does not listen to them carefully enough. In *Bandamanna saga* the qualities exhibited by Odd and Ófeig may be understood as complementary: the sum of their qualities are prerequisite for a chieftain. The same cannot be said for the unreformed Hrafnkel and Sám: taken together they add up only to a complex of shortcomings.

It is not only a modern readership that would find Hrafnkel's killing of Eyvind repugnant. Readers of *Reykdœla saga* and *Heiðarvíga saga* in the thirteenth century would have had the same impulse. There is no moral precedent for preemptive killing. The killing of Hrafnkel would have been legally acceptable because he was outlawed, and his death would have been considered vengeance for Einar, but there is no such justification for the killing of Eyvind. Thorgeir's approval of this strategy can only be regarded as deeply disillusioned. If the saga tells us that the best chieftain is in effect the most preemptive chieftain, that must surely reflect negatively on the nature of a chieftain. *Hœnsa-Þóris saga* and *Bandamanna saga* might be regarded as positive blueprints for the design of a successful and admirable chieftain—that is, an optimistic vision of what a chieftain might be—but *Hrafnkels saga* seems not to share that vision. Whether we look at it through a moral lens or a political lens, it appears to offer only an array of the deficiencies that afflict the Icelandic chieftaincy.

CHAPTER TEN

Demythologizing the Tradition

Njáls saga

By common agreement, *Njáls saga* occupies a transcendent place in the Icelandic tradition as the greatest, if not quite the latest, of the classical sagas.[1] It represents such a pinnacle of style, range, and drama that it tends to overshadow the earlier sagas and relegate them to the status of preliminary attempts at a form that matures only in *Njáls saga*.[2] My approach departs from this perspective. Rather than viewing *Njáls saga* as the crowning achievement, I suggest that it consciously subverts the narrative positions constructed in the earlier sagas. I consider the author less as the master architect perfecting inherited forms than as the satirist and caricaturist who holds these forms up to a searching gaze, revealing what is doubtful and even fraudulent about the older conventions. This reversal is accomplished by isolating patterns in the inherited narratives and inverting them in such a way as to reveal quite different perspectives.[3]

We may note first of all that *Njáls saga* dispenses with a historical prelude recounting the settlement in Iceland of an ancestral clan.[4] This sort of prelude had been devised in elaborate form for *Egils saga* and no less stylishly for *Laxdœla saga*. By the time *Njáls saga* was written, the historical prelude was so ubiquitous in the classical sagas that it was virtually *de rigueur*. Such preludes focused on the discovery of a

---

[1] Wolf 1982, 62.

[2] On the distinctive style of *Njáls saga,* see Heusler 1922; Einar Ólafur Sveinsson 1971, 61; Clover 1974, 65.

[3] Allen 1971, xvi.

[4] Lönnroth 1976, 209–10; Wolf 1982, 64.

new land and the creation of a new polity; they may be considered mythological in the sense of being originary stories. They share a certain excitement about origins, new institutions, a new independence, a new assertion of self. There is a prevailing nostalgia about the founding moment when Iceland, like the earth in the cosmogony of "Vǫlu-spá," seemed to rise out of the sea as the scene of a new experiment.

But *Njáls saga* is a story with no prehistory, no focus on the first phases of a new state and a new ideology. How are we to construe this absence of an almost paradigmatic feature in the saga form? On the one hand, it could reflect a new maturity at the end of the thirteenth century, a rejection of nostalgia and patriotic lore. Perhaps the author no longer felt the need to dwell on Iceland's sense of connection with or separation from Norway. On the other hand, the omission could reflect growing doubts about the golden age of national foundation. Whatever the explanation, *Njáls saga* shifts away from Iceland's part in the larger history of the North to focus on one brief moment in its internal history around 1000 CE, a moment that becomes peculiarly burdened in the absence of a fuller context.

Just how burdened the moment will be is revealed in the most memorable opening scene to be found in any saga. Hǫskuld Dala-Kollsson (whose notable credentials were presented at leisure in *Laxdæla saga*) shows off his beautiful girl child Hallgerd to his half-brother Hrút, but Hrút unaccountably demurs, observing that she is fair enough but that he does not know how thief's eyes got into their family.[5] This is the first of many ominous premonitions in the saga and nothing short of an explosive revelation.[6] It instantly transforms the proudest lineage of *Laxdæla saga* into a sinister brood, for thievishness is as unsavory an accusation as can be leveled in the sagas: it is associated with cowardice, sorcery, and sexual perversion in men and with nymphomania in women.[7]

This last association comes to haunt Hallgerd as the saga unfolds. We never learn all there is to know about her intimate life, but there are suggestive hints. She has an oddly close relationship with her villainous foster father, Thjóstólf. She uses a certain Sigmund Lambason in her feud against Njál's wife, Bergthóra, and "was no less subservient

[5] On this scene, see esp. A. Heinrichs 1994, 333.
[6] On the system of premonitions in the saga, see Zimmermann 1984.
[7] Helga Kress 1977, 310.

to him than to her own husband" (chapter 41; ÍF 12:106). Further, she is suspected of having an affair with the scoundrel Hrapp: "Some people said that he was involved with Hallgerd and was seducing her, but others denied it" (chapter 88; ÍF 12:220). It is therefore not entirely groundless when Njál's son Skarphedin accuses her of being "either a castoff or a whore" (chapter 91; ÍF 12:228).

The most unambiguous charge against her is disloyalty to her heroic husband, Gunnar, when she abandons him to his fate by refusing to give him a strand of her luxuriant hair with which to restring his bow. Gunnar responds with one of the celebrated laconisms of the sagas: "Everyone has her own claim to fame," he says (chapter 77; ÍF 12:189), and then succumbs. But that is already the midpoint of the saga and the climax of an extended narrative.

The Story of Hallgerd

Despite Hallgerd's portentous thief's eyes, she has become something of an icon in Iceland and in feminist readings of the text.[8] The view that there is something more to Hallgerd than meets the eye goes back in earnest to a famous essay by the Norwegian writer Hans E. Kinck, first published in 1916.[9] Its title, "A Few Remarks on the Family Saga: Characters It Didn't Understand," suggested that there was some historical reality underlying the fictional personality, and Kinck has been duly criticized for such a naive assumption.[10] In fact, Kinck argued only that the author knew a more sympathetic version of the fiction and compromised it merely to accommodate a hostile audience eager to derogate Hallgerd.[11] The essay as a whole is a covert attack on the lowbrow readership of Kinck's own day. A negative view of Hallgerd is in any case not a product of antifeminist bias, because a similarly negative

---

[8] On the older view of Hallgerd see the passage from P. A. Suhm's evaluation from 1781 quoted by Lönnroth (1976, 3): "One may justly call this saga an *Iliad* in prose, since all the incidents are the result of a female's viciousness, just as in the case of Helen." See also Hallberg 1966, 141. For more positive views, see Kinck 1916/1982; Einar Ólafur Sveinsson 1971, 49, 88, 117–37, 207–8; Mundt 1976; Helga Kress 1977, 1979; A. Heinrichs 1994.

[9] Kinck 1982.

[10] Lönnroth 1976, 12.

[11] Kinck 1916/1982, esp. 192.

view can be taken of most of the characters in *Njáls saga*, men and women alike.[12] We shall see that Hallgerd's heroic husband, Gunnar, has his foibles as well.

It is not with Gunnar, or even Hallgerd, that the saga begins, but rather with her uncle, Hrút. Some of his story is familiar from *Laxdœla saga*, in which he has a quite subsidiary role in relation to his half-brother Hǫskuld, but in *Njáls saga* he emerges as a key figure who sets the tone for the narrative as a whole. No sooner has he been introduced than he decides to marry and addresses his suit to a certain Unn, daughter of Mǫrd gígja (fiddle), on the advice of Hǫskuld. In *Laxdœla saga*, marriage was likely to be the culminating moment after a period of successful adventures abroad; in *Njáls saga*, the pattern is reversed, and the marriage suit precedes the adventures. Hǫskuld points Unn out to Hrút and asks what he thinks of her. Hrút's reaction is positive, but he immediately reverts to the premonitory mode of the first scene by adding, "I'm not sure we are destined to be lucky together" (chapter 2; ÍF 12:8). Foreseen is foregone, and we can be in little doubt about the outcome. Whereas *Laxdœla saga* begins with grand and successful marriages, *Njáls saga* specializes in doomed marriages, notably those of Hallgerd.[13]

Hrút's marriage must be deferred when he learns that he has fallen heir to considerable wealth in Norway. He therefore requests and obtains a three-year delay of the marriage to allow him to collect his Norwegian inheritance. The delay is in itself foreboding because we know from the skald sagas, from the little story of Ívar Ingimundarson in *Morkinskinna*, and not least of all from Kjartan's experience in *Laxdœla saga* that a betrothal prolonged by a voyage abroad can only lead to disaster.[14] The literary pattern is hardly less predictive than prophecy. The sequel to the delay is normally that the bride left behind is stolen or married off to some other suitor, with melancholy consequences, but *Njáls saga* offers a variant of this stereotype.

Once arrived in Norway, Hrút presents himself at the court of King Harald Graycloak, where he is granted special favor by the queen

[12] See Heusler 1922, 8; Einar Ólafur Sveinsson 1950, 8.

[13] It has been generally assumed that the author of *Njáls saga* knew *Laxdœla saga*, although there is no conclusive evidence. See Kersbergen 1927, 90–94; Einar Ólafur Sveinsson 1933, 106–20, and 1950, esp. 14; Heimir Pálsson 1967.

[14] For "Ívars þáttr," see *Morkinskinna*, trans. Andersson and Gade, 326–28. On the skald sagas in general, see Clunies Ross 2001, 25–49. On the motif of the prolonged betrothal see Kersbergen 1927, 109–10.

mother (nicknamed "kings' mother"), Gunnhild.[15] This is indeed the same Gunnhild we know as an adept of witchcraft and as Egil Skalla-grímsson's sworn enemy in *Egils saga*. In *Njáls saga* she is a more benign figure because she sponsors Hrút, but she, anticipating Hallgerd, is an exponent of *ergi* (perversion) and requires sexual favors in return. When Hrút has secured his inheritance and is ready to set sail for Iceland, Gunnhild poses the undoubtedly jealous question of whether he has a woman in Iceland. Sensing the jealousy, he promptly denies having such a woman, but she easily penetrates the deception, reverts to her witchcraft, and places a disabling sexual curse on Hrút that will prevent him from consummating his marriage with Unn.

In the traditional story of failed betrothal in the skald sagas it is the woman who is disqualified because she is married to someone else. In *Njáls saga,* it is the man who suffers disqualification because the curse makes it impossible for him to consummate the marriage. In the traditional story the intended marriage is foreclosed, but in *Njáls saga* it is in fact contracted. Because it remains unconsummated, however, it ends in divorce, although Hrút faces down his father-in-law, Mǫrd, and remains in possession of the community property. This is the first intimation in *Njáls saga* of an institution that breaks down, but it is only the first of several.

Not only does the marriage institution fail, but it becomes an object of ridicule. Two little boys and a little girl are at play in the presence of Hrút and Hǫskuld and decide to reenact the drama: "One of the boys said: 'I'll play Mǫrd's part and divorce your wife from you on the grounds that you haven't screwed her.' The other answered: 'I'll play the part of Hrút and dispossess you because you don't dare fight me'" (chapter 8; ÍF 12:29). The little play naturally provokes much mirth and makes the calamity more notorious than ever. This moment of marital travesty could scarcely be further removed from the high-status marriages of *Laxdœla saga,* but, setting the marriage aside, we can detect other parodistic tonalities in Hrút's story.

When he arrives in Norway, he presents himself before the king with exquisite diplomacy. Asked what his business is, he alleges a desire to view the king's magnificence. Only as an afterthought does he mention that he has an inheritance to collect. He then requests, like so many

---

[15] On Gunnhild, see Kersbergen 1927, 120–26; Sigurður Nordal 1965; Allen 1971, 84; Dronke 1981, 6.

another distinguished Icelander (though born in Norway, Hrút identifies himself as an Icelander), to be accepted into King Harald Graycloak's court as a retainer. King Harald gives him free access to the law to obtain his legacy, reminding us that Egil Skallagrímsson had made the same request with less diplomacy and less success some years earlier. But the king hesitates over the request for membership in the court and grants it only out of deference to his mother's representations. Traditionally, Icelanders earned their way at the Norwegian court with service in arms and were rewarded accordingly. Hrút earns his way in a rather different sense, by rendering sexual services, and the reader may feel that this author takes a more cynical view of political realities than some of his predecessors.

An Icelander's adventures abroad include, almost routinely, one or more confrontations with vikings. Hrút's experience is no exception. He learns that a certain Sóti, a name reserved for disreputable scofflaws, is in possession of his inheritance and has gone south to Denmark. Hrút sets out after him and wins a notable victory over another band of vikings, but he can make no contact with Sóti, who has doubled back to Norway. Gunnhild organizes an expedition to kill Sóti and seize the inheritance, which she duly bestows on Hrút when he returns. Once again Hrút turns out to be less his own master than Gunnhild's thrall, the very opposite of Egil Skallagrímsson, whose pertinacity had vanquished Gunnhild. Hrút's subservience continues, psychologically, in Iceland; Egil had returned home in triumph, but Hrút returns under a debilitating curse.

The story of Hrút subverts a series of literary myths. One such myth describes an Icelander who goes abroad and has a notable affair with a great lady: for example, Kjartan and Ingibjǫrg in *Laxdœla saga*. Hrút goes abroad and has an affair with a notorious witch who controls him at every turn. Another form of the myth is that an Icelander goes abroad and loses his betrothed to a rival. Hrút goes abroad and keeps his betrothed but would have done better to lose her. Or should we say that he loses her in a particularly humiliating way?

A third variant of the myth takes an Icelander abroad, where he incurs difficulties at the Norwegian court but demonstrates his innate superiority and returns a great man. Hrút ingratiates himself at court, becomes the queen mother's creature, and returns to an unenviable fate. Yet a fourth variant involves an Icelander who earns fame and fortune abroad, then returns home to make a splendid marriage and settle down in grand style and high repute for the remainder of his life. Hrút earns little fame and fortune and returns to an ill-fated marriage that culminates in public mockery. In effect Hrút turns the introductory phases of the typical saga upside down. If he emerges as such a caricature of the traditional heroic Icelander, we can hardly have high expectations for Hallgerd, who now moves to the center of the stage.

Hallgerd, like Gudrún Ósvífrsdóttir, is a woman of many marriages, but by no means does she share Gudrún's status as the greatest woman in Iceland. Gudrún loses four husbands; Hallgerd loses one and contrives the death of two others. This too is a foretold tale. When her first husband, Thorvald, looks in her direction, his father warns him against such a match. It is arranged notwithstanding, but Hallgerd feels unconsulted. Her foster father, Thjóstólf, offers her the cold consolation that this will not be her only marriage, and Hrút reinforces the omen by stating that there will be no luck in it for either partner. By contrast to the great marriage festivities of *Laxdœla saga,* the wedding feast is here disposed of in four words—"the feast went well" (chapter 10; ÍF 12:32–33)—but even so, Hrút predicts that the attendant costs will not be the least of the outlays occasioned by Hallgerd. In this sequence the prophetic utterances are incessant.

We may well ask how it is that Hallgerd communicates such an unmistakable sense of trouble. It is as if she displays some outward mark that signals impending doom. That is in fact the tonality of the saga as a whole, which captivates the reader with intimations of catastrophe.[16] The denouement of Hallgerd's first marriage is that she provokes her husband with her extravagance and willfulness and harvests the first in a series of three marital slaps. That is construed by her zealous—or jealous?[17]—foster father, Thjóstólf, as a call for action, and he wastes no time in burying his ax in Thorvald's skull.

We will see that the author traces Hallgerd's career in insistent threefold repetitions. Her second marriage, to Glúm Óleifsson, follows hard on the heels of the first, though the auspices are more promising: she is formally consulted and agrees to the match. But once again, trouble flares, and she quarrels with her husband over Thjóstólf's presence, provoking a second slap. This time, however, she is grieved rather than angered, and she forbids Thjóstólf to avenge the blow. Nothing

---

[16] Einar Ólafur Sveinsson 1950, 27, and 1971, 56–57.
[17] Kersbergen 1927, 93.

daunted, he takes matters into his own hands and kills the offending husband on his own account. She arranges prompt retribution, but the damage is done. The second marriage should have worked; the right feelings were in place and the right forms scrupulously observed. But there is no arresting the inevitable calamity. It seems not to matter whether the auspices are favorable or portentous—the outcome is the same.

Hallgerd's third marriage is introduced more deliberately, as befits the third act of an epic triad. It will unite her with the most legendary hero of the Icelandic sagas, Gunnar Hámundarson of Hlídarendi. At first there is no intimation that he is the destined third husband; rather, he enters the action in his capacity as a distant relation of Unn, who approaches him with the request that he retrieve the property she lost at the time of her divorce from Hrút. Gunnar obliges, with the aid of an ingenious stratagem devised by Njál, who is now introduced as the unrivaled expert in the law. On the strength of Njál's advice, Gunnar approaches Hrút disguised as a vagrant peddler and induces him to pronounce the legal formula that will reactivate the case of the forfeited property. Ultimately, Gunnar regains the property by challenging Hrút to a duel, since Hrút is no more equal to this challenge than Mǫrd was equal to the challenge issued by Hrút. We must return to the curiosity that Gunnar and Njál, the celebrated protagonists of the saga, are both introduced in the context of a highly questionable legal trick.[18]

In the meantime, Gunnar authenticates himself as a figure of truly mythic proportions by steering the true course of those foreign adventures that turned out so erratically for Hrút. He fights two epic actions against vikings, presents himself first at the Danish court and subsequently at the Norwegian court (now under the rule of Jarl Hákon Sigurdarson), distinguishes himself in athletic events like a latter-day Odysseus in Phaeacia, receives precious gifts, falls in love with the jarl's relation Bergljót, and (we are told) could have married her for the asking, just as Odysseus could have married Nausicaa.[19]

Thus far the myths of foreign adventure are intact, but on his return to Iceland, Gunnar, if anything, exceeds the mythic measure. Njál warns him of envious people, but he responds with pious right-mind-

---

[18] Hauch 1855, 424–25, 456; Lehmann and Schnorr von Carolsfeld 1883, 44–49; Einar Ólafur Sveinsson 1933, 206–15, and 1950, 21, and 1971, 164; Gottzmann 1982, 160; Vésteinn Ólason 1998, 139.

[19] Kersbergen 1927, 127–28.

edness: "I want to be on good terms with everyone." Admonished that he will need to defend himself, he adds, "Then it would be important that I have a just cause" (chapter 32; ÍF 12:84). What are we to make of these declarations of rectitude in the light of Gunnar's hoodwinking of Hrút? The saga avoids the issue and passes on to the next phase of Gunnar's legend, the distinguished marriage that any practiced saga reader will foresee as the culmination of his other conquests. But here the expectation is sadly misplaced.

Once back in Iceland, Gunnar attends an assembly and falls into conversation with a well-dressed woman who turns out to be Hallgerd. The situation is quite reminiscent of the meeting between Olaf Peacock and Thorgerd in *Laxdœla saga*, the two most magnificent people at the assembly where their betrothal is concluded. Gunnar wastes no time in proposing, and the match is agreed on, despite warnings that are very soon reinforced by Njál. The marriage feast is staged with the same sort of splendor we have learned to associate with *Laxdœla saga*, but the feast is disturbed by ill omens. In the first place, it is disrupted by a peculiarly tasteless divorce and precipitate rebetrothal in the midst of the festivities.[20] In the second place, a quarrel over seating precedence breaks out between Gunnar's wife Hallgerd and Njál's wife Bergthóra. Thus the wedding feast fails to usher in a period of eminence and tranquility, as in the case of Olaf the Peacock and Thorgerd; rather, it opens the way for a full-fledged feud.

The feud between Hallgerd and Bergthóra is related in elaborate and symmetrical detail; it is self-consciously constructed to the point of being comic.[21] Each woman foments killings in the other's household in precise alternation and with ever increasing stakes. The first two victims are slaves, the next two are free men, and the last two are men of importance. The feud might be expected to drive a sharp wedge between the households, but Gunnar and Njál are imperturbably loyal to their friendship. They settle each killing amicably, compensating for the slaves with twelve ounces of silver, the free men with a hundred ounces, and the men of importance with two hundred ounces. Their friendship survives the test, but this test, which has the dimensions of a self-contained story, raises fundamental issues concerning character and the institution of the feud. Hallgerd is irrepressibly aggressive;

[20] Maxwell 1957–59, 29; A. Heinrichs 1994, 339.
[21] Kersbergen 1927, 66–68; Allen 1971, 125.

Bergthóra is unyielding; and their husbands are implacably patient. The husbands seem to be portrayed as paragons, but they do nothing to forestall the violence, which takes on an uncontrollable life of its own.

The core issue in this strangely mannered feud story is perhaps the institution of feud itself. The cultivated formality of the quarrel is abstracted from the feud structure that is ubiquitous in the sagas, a structure in which tensions lead to minor aggressions, then to major aggressions, and ultimately to lawsuits, killings, and self-perpetuating violence. The almost parodistic simplification of the feud between Hallgerd and Bergthóra makes not only the formalism but also the irrationality of the practice transparent. Both women and men are caught up in a mechanism that overwhelms them. To some extent it is the feud world turned upside down, with the feud controlling the characters rather than vice versa.[22] The traditional roles are also reversed: the women are assigned the active roles and the men the passive roles. The law too seems abject, offering no remedies and providing no mechanisms to contain the outbreak of violence. The moral of the feud seems to be that although it is initially shaped by the personalities of the participants, it soon reduces them to the status of helpless victims carried off in the tide of hostility.

The Story of Gunnar Hámundarson

Although the friendship of Gunnar and Njál suffers no attenuation as a result of their wives' quarrel, they will both succumb in the aftermath. When Gunnar returned from Norway, Njál warned him that he would become an object of envy. This envy is visited on him in two narrative sequences shaped so quintessentially as saga disputes that they stand in for the overall feud pattern hardly less paradigmatically than the quarrel of Hallgerd and Bergthóra.

The first sequence is set in motion by a refusal to sell Gunnar hay, a motif also found at the center of *Hœnsa-Þóris saga*.[23] The second sequence involves a contest between fighting stallions, a motif found in *Bjarnar saga Hítdœlakappa, Grettis saga, Víga-Glúms saga,* and "Þorsteins

[22] Vésteinn Ólason 1998, 201.
[23] Kersbergen 1927, 72; Miller 1990, 85–104.

þáttr stangarhǫggs." The underlying motivation is the envy of a certain Mǫrd, the son of Hrút's divorced wife, Unn, and her later husband, Valgard the Gray. The envy is not specifically explained (chapter 46; ÍF 12:119), but envy seems to be the peril of distinguished men, as Olaf Tryggvason and Harald Sigurdarson learned in their youthful years at the Russian court.

It is one Otkel Skarfsson who refuses to sell Gunnar hay, which he needs to help his neighbors in a time of famine, but he does sell him a slave of very questionable character named Melkólf. It is unclear why Gunnar would purchase a slave with nothing to recommend him when he is apparently in no need of one, but it is one of Gunnar's characteristics that he makes repeated mistakes.[24] Hallgerd avails herself of the defective slave by sending him on a mission to Otkel's farm to steal two horse loads of food and then burn down the storage shed to obliterate the traces. This too seems strangely gratuitous, but there is a certain spontaneous quality to the evil impulses in *Njáls saga.*

When Hallgerd's theft is later revealed, Gunnar responds by administering the third marital slap in the epic sequence. She vows revenge. Gunnar also tries to settle her crime on generous terms, but Otkel, together with his villainous henchman Skammkel and abetted by the advice of Mǫrd Valgardsson, continues to make deliberate difficulties. The provocations escalate to the point that Gunnar finally kills both Otkel and Skammkel, along with six others. With considerable public support and some tactical use of the law, Gunnar is able to achieve a settlement of the case, but Njál warns him that he must not kill twice in the same family and must never break a proper legal settlement (chapter 55; ÍF 12:139).

In this sequence, Gunnar seems besieged by malice in the persons of the troublemaker Otkel, the liar Skammkel, the envious schemer Mǫrd, the thievish Melkólf, and, not least of all, his mischief-making wife, Hallgerd. Up to this point the saga is largely about defects: defects in character, defects in judgment, defects in marriage choices, defects in the selection of friends, and the first inkling of deficiencies in the law. Gunnar has become entangled in a web of deceived expectations.

The second act in Gunnar's demise begins no more auspiciously with the introduction of two new characters, Starkad Barkarson and

---

[24] Sigurður Guðmundsson 1918, 238; Einar Ólafur Sveinsson 1950, 27; Fries 1981, 41; A. Heinrichs 1994, 346–47; Sayers 1997, 49.

his brother-in-law Egil Kolsson. Each has three sons, all equally unprepossessing. Starkad's sons are described as "very arrogant, intransigent, and quarrelsome—they treated other men in a domineering way" (chapter 57; ÍF 12:146). Egil's sons get no better press: "Egil's sons were big men, contentious, and very inequitable" (chapter 58; ÍF 12:146). These men are all in league with each other. Starkad has a fighting stallion, and they are on the lookout for a match. When they learn that Gunnar also has a good stallion, they issue a rather belligerent challenge. Gunnar makes yet another mistake by accepting the challenge. The match ends, as most such matches in the sagas do, in violence—in this case with the discomfiture of the challengers.[25] No settlement is reached, and a year later Starkad ambushes Gunnar with a large force. Gunnar prevails against insuperable odds, killing fourteen men, and this time, major litigation ensues. But Njál outwits Mǫrd Valgardsson and engineers a settlement favorable to Gunnar. Nonetheless, the legal recourse seems increasingly strained and Gunnar's circumstances increasingly perilous.

Starkad's party is far from satisfied, and he appeals to Mǫrd for some deep scheme to undo Gunnar. Mǫrd, who has wind of the prohibition against Gunnar's killing twice in the same family, proposes to maneuver him into the position of killing Thorgeir Otkelsson, thus contravening the prohibition. After one failed attempt Mǫrd organizes a renewed ambush, and Gunnar does indeed kill Thorgeir Otkelsson. At this point Njál can only achieve a legal settlement stipulating Gunnar's exile for three years. There follows a famous scene in which Gunnar sets out, stumbles, looks back at the hillside, and cannot bring himself to leave his farm.[26] He therefore ignores the second prohibition, against failing to carry out the terms of a proper agreement.

There is no need to rehearse the equally famous narrative of Gunnar's death. Trapped in his house, he is able to stave off his attackers as long as he has the use of his celebrated bow, but when the bowstring is severed and Hallgerd, ever mindful of the slap administered at the time of her theft, refuses a strand of hair to restring the bow, he finally succumbs. The scene is so dramatic that not even the absurdity of using human hair for a bowstring detracts from the effect.[27]

[25] Lehmann and Schnorr von Carolsfeld 1883, 64; Kersbergen 1927, 73.
[26] Sigurður Guðmundsson 1918, 230–32; Lie 1937, 14–15; Einar Ólafur Sveinsson 1971, 88; Hallberg 1973, 62–63; Lönnroth 1976, 150–60; Gottzmann 1982, 112–29.
[27] Sigurður Guðmundsson 1918, 85–86; Einar Ólafur Sveinsson 1971, 122–23.

Gunnar's story is the story of his indeterminate moral status. He is at once the unsurpassed hero victimized by ubiquitous malice and a man whose instincts, despite his own protestations, are open to question. He is a party to legal trickery. He bullies Hrút to recover a dowry. He marries a notorious wife despite ample warnings. He buys a villainous slave and accepts a horse match with challengers whose ill will is plain for all to see. And, finally, he contravenes the terms of his exile with no attempt at explanation. It therefore seems difficult to believe that Gunnar is not a partner, voluntary or involuntary, in his own undoing.

The Story of Njál and His Sons

For a long time it was believed that *Njáls saga* was a rather artificial amalgamation of two separate sagas, one about Gunnar and one about Njál. A residue of that theory is the view that the central chapters falling between Gunnar's death and avenging and the onset of Njál's story proper (chapters 82–90) are a sort of interlude loosely joining the two parts of the saga.[28] This "interlude" may, however, also be viewed as a prelude to the story of Njál and his sons.[29] It functions just as the story of Hrút functioned as a prelude to the tale of Gunnar. In both cases the prelude is somewhat oblique, focusing on a character who is peripheral to the main action but who sets it in motion.

The peripheral character in Njál's story is a certain Thráin Sigfússon, the man who precipitated an unceremonious divorce in the midst of the wedding feast for Gunnar and Hallgerd. Just as Hrút initiated the original action by undertaking a visit to the Norwegian court, a visit with dire consequences, so too does Thráin sail to Norway, now ruled by Jarl Hákon Sigurdarson, with consequences that are no less fateful. Hrút's Norwegian adventure had the unforeseen effect of bringing him into conflict with Gunnar, and Gunnar in turn with others. Thráin's Norwegian adventure brings him into direct conflict with Njál's sons, who have also gone to Norway to test their mettle. Whereas Njál's sons form a close friendship with the redoubtable Kári Sǫlmundarson, who is destined to have a distinguished role in the saga, Thráin falls in with the scoundrel Hrapp.

[28] Clover 1982, 28–33.
[29] Lönnroth 1976, 27–28; Clover 1982, 29.

Hrapp operates in the worst tradition of the villains who stud this saga. He defrauds the ship owner with whom he takes passage to Norway of his passage money. Once in Norway, he seduces the daughter of the ubiquitous but mysterious chieftain Dala-Gudbrand, whom we have already met in *The Legendary Saga of Saint Olaf.*[30] He subsequently kills the steward whom Dala-Gudbrand has charged to protect his daughter, and as a result, Jarl Hákon outlaws and pursues him, but Hrapp escapes. In the process he plunders and incinerates the jarl's temple and kills several pursuers, including Gudbrand's son. This collision of Icelander and Norwegian ruler is superficially reminiscent of Egil Skallagrímsson's dealings with Erik Bloodax, but Hrapp has no claim to defend and seems motivated by the purest malice. The encounter casts no shadow on the ruler, only on the Icelander. This renewed inversion of an established pattern may be understood once again to illustrate the disillusionment that underlies the saga as a whole.

Hrapp ultimately makes good his escape on Thráin Sigfússon's ship and returns to Iceland, where he is rumored to seduce Hallgerd. In Norway, meanwhile, the suspicion of having harbored Hrapp falls on Njál's sons Grím and Helgi, whom Jarl Hákon puts in fetters and who are barely saved by the intervention of Kári Sǫlmundarson. All return to Iceland, where Kári marries Njál's daughter Helga and where Grím and Helgi nurse their resentment against Thráin for being at the root of their disastrous experience in Norway.

Their sojourn in Norway in search of fame and fortune is in the tradition of the grand figures in *Laxdœla saga,* but the outcome is quite different. Instead of returning to Iceland as richly dowered heroes, they return with little credit; even the gifts they receive at court remain unspecified (chaper 90; ÍF 12:225). Instead of the traditional gallant love affair with royalty, there is only the sordid tale of Hrapp's seduction. Instead of basking in a royal reception, the Icelanders become the victims of disreputable countrymen and a ruler of mixed repute, as we remember from Odd Snorrason's *Saga of Olaf Tryggvason.* The hero of the adventure is in fact not an Icelander but the Hebridean Kári. Finally, Grím and Helgi return to Iceland not with international recognition but with a serious grievance against Thráin that will play a part in the downfall of the family.[31] Their voyage abroad results not in enhanced distinction but in a ruinous feud.

[30] Lehmann and Schnorr von Carolsfeld 1883, 169; Hermann Pálsson 1984, 91–96.
[31] See Miller 1983, 323–24.

The first phase of the feud is brought about when Njál's sons deliberately provoke insults in order to have a pretext for attacking Thráin and Hrapp. They avail themselves of the pretext to kill both. A legal settlement is reached, and Njál tries to solidify it by taking Thráin's son Hǫskuld as his foster son. The ultimate effect of this arrangement is not to forestall the feud but to bring the tension into the very heart of the family.[32] Thráin's killer, Njál's eldest son Skarphedin, has now become, if not technically the foster brother, at least the housemate of Thráin's son.[33] The question is whether such a volatile and contradictory situation can remain stable.

The second phase of the feud between Njál's sons and Thráin's family has a quite separate point of departure, in a different part of the country. A group of Easterners are introduced into the mix and will have an important part in the subsequent action. Njál, still focused on securing his family, attempts to win the hand of Hildigunn, the niece of the eastern chieftain Flosi Thórdarson, for his foster son, Hǫskuld Thráinsson. But Hildigunn is a proud woman and represents to her uncle that he has promised her no less than a chieftain in marriage; Njál must therefore procure a chieftainship for Hǫskuld in order to bring about the match, though no chieftainship is available.

To realize his plan Njál resorts to a deeply deceitful maneuver. He departs from his traditional practice of offering helpful advice and promotes deadlock so as to bring legal business almost to a standstill. Then, availing himself of the artificially induced crisis, he proposes a constitutional amendment, the establishment of a Fifth Court (over and above the four courts already in operation). The reform, once accepted, opens up additional chieftainships, one of which goes to Njál's foster son Hǫskuld and thus makes possible his marriage to Hildigunn.[34]

On the heels of this apparent coup comes the next stage in the fatal feud, almost as if it were in reprisal for Njál's legal chicanery. Thráin's brother-in-law, the unsavory Lýting, rather suddenly becomes aware that he has received no share in the blood money for Thráin and compensates himself by killing Njál's illegitimate son (also named Hǫskuld) on the spur of the moment. Njál's sons take immediate re-

[32] On the legal problem involved in Njál's assuming fosterage, see Lehmann and Schnorr von Carolsfeld 1883, 92; and Miller 1983, 325.

[33] Miller 1983, 319.

[34] Allen 1971, 137; Lönnroth 1976, 191, 194; Ordower 1991; Ziolkowski 1997, 55, 61.

venge by killing two of Lýting's brothers, though Lýting himself escapes with only a wound. Njál and his foster son, Hǫskuld, arrange a settlement, but the feud has clearly been reactivated.

What follows is a story that we already know from Odd Snorrason's biography of Olaf Tryggvason and from *Laxdœla saga*, the story of how Iceland was converted. Perhaps it is positioned here only because the following episode requires us to know that Iceland is now a Christian land, but because it seems overly protracted for that purpose, it has more frequently been understood as a watershed in the moral trajectory of the saga.[35] Whatever the explanation, the next episode is in fact a Christian miracle. The illegitimate son of the slain Hǫskuld, the blind Ámundi, regains his sight just long enough to kill Lýting, then relapses into blindness. That we are indeed to understand this as a miracle is suggested by Ámundi's exclamation at the moment when he regains his vision: "Praise be to my Lord God! It is evident what He wants" (chapter 106; ÍF 12:273).[36]

We may be prompted to ask what sort of miracle it is that is wrought to facilitate a killing. Is it a miracle or the mockery of a miracle? Since it serves only the purpose of giving Njál's party the satisfaction of revenge, now it appears that like the legal system, which has already been bent to accommodate Njál's wishes, the religious system is being bent as well.

After this episode the action seems to come to a resting point. Ámundi's killing is settled, and we might be encouraged to believe that the feud has run its course—until Mǫrd's father Valgard arrives back from abroad and reinflames the conflict, advising Mǫrd to sow discord between Njál's sons and Hǫskuld Thráinsson. Once more, contrary to expectation or any reasonable assessment of character, Mǫrd succeeds with his campaign of slander, detaches the sons from Hǫskuld, and persuades them to kill him.[37] On the one hand, this slaying is a product of consummate wickedness, but on the other hand, it is not a totally unforeseeable consequence of Njál's ill-advised decision to bring his sons' natural enemy under his roof and into daily contact

---

[35] Hauch 1855, 435–36; Allen 1971, 117; Einar Ólafur Sveinsson 1950, 28–30, and 1971, 177–80; Hallberg 1973; Gottzmann 1982, 334, 339; McTurk 1990, 44; Jesch 1992, 77–81.

[36] Bååth [1885], 145; Einar Ólafur Sveinsson 1933, 52–53; Maxwell 1957–59, 38; Lönnroth 1976, 145; Gottzmann 1982, 329; Hamer 1992.

[37] Kersbergen 1927, 50.

with them. For the moment, the slain Hǫskuld's wife, Hildigunn, preserves her husband's bloody cloak for future use and bides her time.

Chapters 95–96 saw the introduction of several prominent men from the Eastern Quarter. In chapters 113–14 the author introduces the greatest chieftain from the Northern Quarter, Gudmund the Powerful, and the equally distinguished chieftain from the Western Quarter, Snorri the Chieftain. This is a radical departure from earlier practice, for the classical sagas are almost by definition regional sagas. *Egils saga* and *Laxdæla saga* are specifically western, and *Ljósvetninga saga* is specifically northern. *Njáls saga* is initially southern but comes to envelop East, North, and West in addition. Njál's introduction of the Fifth Court affects a national institution, and the Christian conversion is a national event as well. Finally, the feud, in which Njál's family is the center, expands to engulf the other quarters in a kind of maelstrom effect. *Njáls saga* is the first and only one of the classical sagas to embrace these national horizons.[38]

The contending parties thus recruit support from the country as a whole. Flosi gathers forces in the East, while Njál's party gains the adherence of Gudmund the Powerful in the North and, rather more indirectly, Snorri the Chieftain in the West. The initial legal maneuvering at the Allthing produces a mediation commission and a huge settlement for Hǫskuld's death, but at the last moment, and for reasons that are somewhat opaque, Flosi rejects the arbitrated settlement. The lack of clarity may well have been intended by the author and may be understood to mean that the burden of antagonism has become so great as to overwhelm the legal machinery. No amount of goodwill and no marshaling of legal redress are adequate to control a dispute that has brought the whole nation under arms. Instead, Flosi and his party march on Njál's house amid dire portents; Njál makes the imprudent decision to retreat into the house; and after some inconclusive fighting, the house is put to the torch.[39] Njál, Bergthóra, and their three sons succumb; only Kári Sǫlmundarson makes good his escape.

The ensuing litigation at the Allthing, which pits Kári's party against Flosi's and goes on for sixty pages, is an epic of quibble and counterquibble. New readers will find the legal complexities and formalities strained, but they will also appreciate the quality of courtroom

---

[38] Bååth [1885], 90; Maxwell 1957–59, 20, 24; Vésteinn Ólason 1998, 199.
[39] Einar Ólafur Sveinsson 1971, 173–75; Nanna Ólafsdóttir 1977.

drama, in which the mental jousting is more riveting than any battle-field action.[40] They will also have little difficulty in recognizing the author's ongoing preoccupation with the theme of the law's inadequacy to deal with civil mischief.[41] A settlement is eventually reached and goes largely against the burners, but Kári exempts himself from the settlement and carries out a protracted and bloody vengeance of his own, with the help of a most unlikely ally: the cowardly but self-glorifying Bjǫrn the White.[42] It is not the least of the author's ironies that the final act of the great Icelandic epic is played out by a Hebridean and a buffoon.

The last act is followed by an epilogue. That too is a saga tradition, but the epilogue to *Njáls saga* is by far the most sanguinary. Many of those involved in the burning of Njál and his family go abroad, and fifteen of the burners fall in the great Battle of Clontarf (1014), in which the Irish king Brian Boru and an attacking viking army destroy each other. The battle is prefaced by visions and portents—including the eeriest of the Norse poems, "Darraðarljóð," and it ends in indiscriminate slaughter. The Battle of Clontarf seems to have so little to do with the saga that it has sometimes been viewed as an interpolation, but it does serve to reinforce and universalize the apocalyptic tone of Njál's burning.

Conclusion

The argument offered here is that *Njáls saga* persistently subverts a series of traditional narrative patterns and the authorial perspectives they imply. The Icelandic experience is lifted out of the historical context in which most of the sagas are embedded, with the result that Iceland is isolated and focused more sharply than elsewhere. It is no longer seen as emerging from a colonial period and maintaining ongoing ties and ongoing issues with the mother country, as was still the unspoken assumption in *The Saga of King Magnús and King Harald, Egils saga*, and, to a lesser extent, *Laxdœla saga*. In *Njáls saga*, Iceland has acquired more independence, toward the end even something ap-

[40] Lehmann and Schnorr von Carolsfeld 1883, 4; Maxwell 1957–59, 24; Einar Ólafur Sveinsson 1971, 34.

[41] Allen 1971, 137.

[42] Ker 1897/1957, 228–29; Sigurður Nordal 1919.

proaching a national perspective. The Icelandic system comes into its own, but at the same time the saga exposes the vulnerabilities of the system.

These vulnerabilities are not only systemic but personal. Many sagas make use of the occasional villain to incite trouble, but *Njáls saga* has an unparalleled gallery of evildoers. The opening scene sets the tone with the recognition of Hallgerd's thief's eyes, and she goes on to demonize much of the action. She also has a genius for keeping bad company: the satellites in her feud with Bergthóra, her foster father Thjóstólf, the thief Melkólf, and her alleged seducer Hrapp. Gunnar's antagonists are men of oddly uniform ill will: Otkel Skarfsson and his prevaricating friend Skammkel, Starkad Barkarson and Egil Kolsson, with three aggressive sons apiece. The later narrative dedicated to Njál is also dogged by characters of unexampled meanness. The series is initiated by the implacable Thráin Sigfússon and the evil genius Hrapp, continues with Hǫskuld Njálsson's killer Lýting and his equally wicked brothers, then culminates in the perpetual malefactor Mǫrd Valgardsson.

The author of *Njáls saga* is much preoccupied with the problem of character. We have come a long way from the early Olaf sagas, in which character played virtually no part at all. The problematizing of character was left to the early northern sagas and *Egils saga,* but that model did not find favor with the author of *Laxdœla saga,* for whom character was suffused with and obscured by nostalgia. The author of *Njáls saga* reacted against nostalgia and focused almost exclusively on defects of character. Norwegian royalty, in the persons of Gunnhild and Jarl Hákon, fare no better than the Icelandic cast. This severity embraces not only the villains of the piece but the high-minded protagonists as well.[43] Gunnar may be the incomparable athlete and warrior and the soul of reliability in his dealings with Njál, but he seems beset by misjudgment, notably in his marriage to Hallgerd. Njál is the quintessence of wisdom, but he is capable of misusing it, and it fails him at the critical moment when he elects to retreat into his house. The author appears to question both supreme valor and supreme wisdom, the twin qualities widely credited in earlier sagas.[44]

The author's critical stance extends to institutions as well as charac-

[43] Vésteinn Ólason 1998, 198.
[44] Wolf 1982, 65.

ters. The foreign adventures so spectacularly chronicled in the older sagas end in grief in *Njáls saga*. The splendid marriages of *Laxdœla saga* become ill-starred misadventures in *Njáls saga*. The sacrosanct bonds of kinship, much emphasized in other sagas, loosen when Njál intro- duces a potential feud antagonist into his own home. The gendered tradition promoting the admiration of heroic men collapses in favor of dynamic women.[45] Abstract morality is open to question in Gunnar's naive assertion of right-mindedness and the Christian sponsorship of Ámundi's killing. Common decency, which prevented the burning of Gunnar in his house, is reduced to ashes in the conflagration that en- gulfs Njál and his family. Nor does the law hold up well under scrutiny but is subject to repeated perversions, including those of Gunnar and Njál. Feud no longer figures as a temporary upheaval, as in earlier sagas, but as an endemic state that is not so much rectified as it is ex- hausted in bloodshed. The trajectory of the plot leads not to peace and tranquility but rather to a haunting disillusionment.[46]

The study of high-profile characters also guides the total composi- tion of the saga. Even in *Laxdœla saga* there were still telltale signs of an author collecting local tradition, although, beginning with *The Saga of King Magnús and King Harald,* there was a growing trend toward im- posing an overall idea as a framework for tradition. Curiously, there is a long tradition of considering *Njáls saga* a paramount example of the gathering of traditions.[47] My argument takes an opposed view. The plot of *Njáls saga* is not so much a concatenation of separate actions as a sequence of personal stories in which the characters are meticulously connected.[48] The opening scene, in which Hrút identifies Hallgerd's thief's eyes, establishes the parameters for half the saga. Hrút's story comes first and establishes a connection with Gunnar. Hallgerd's ini- tial marriages follow and likewise point toward Gunnar. That prepares the way for Gunnar's tale, and his demise in part at Hallgerd's hands. At no point does the narrative veer into folkloristic compilation.

The narrative on the fate of Njál and his family is more complicated, burdened with more characters and details, but it is no less tightly structured. The meeting of Njál's sons with Thráin Sigfússon and

---

[45] Allen 1971, 82; O'Donoghue 1992.
[46] Vésteinn Ólason 1998, 204.
[47] Bååth [1885] and Lönnroth 1976, in different centuries and with differing em- phases, represent this viewpoint.
[48] Kersbergen 1927, 8.

Hrapp in Norway unleashes a feud that proceeds from the killing of Thráin's son Hǫskuld to the burning of Njál and, finally, to the protracted vengeance sequence played out between Kári and Flosi. Whereas *Egils saga, Ljósvetninga saga,* and *Laxdœla saga* were largely organized as a succession of generations, the author of *Njáls saga* abandons the generational structure completely, opting instead for a thematic principle. That principle is failure: failed characters, failed institutions, the failed values of valor and wisdom, and, not least, the failed literary conventions of the saga, which are shown to be hollow or perverse.

EPILOGUE

It should come as no surprise that the Icelandic sagas are centrally about Iceland, more particularly about stages in Icelandic self-consciousness. The first sagas appear at the end of the twelfth century, a century literarily dominated by the appropriation of Christian writings. They capitalize on that tradition by exalting the conversion kings, first in Latin and then in the vernacular. The hypothesis advanced in this book is that Olaf Tryggvason had priority because, according to both Ari and Odd, he brought Christianity to Iceland and thus initiated the integration of Iceland into the Christian world. Though ostensibly about a Norwegian king, Odd's saga is surreptitiously about Iceland's place in the larger historical scheme: hence the space devoted to the retelling of the Icelandic conversion and the conversion of individual Icelanders both at home and at the Norwegian court.

Odd's saga also stakes an Icelandic literary claim: in effect, it copyrights the biography of Olaf Tryggvason. The first part may be dependent on a Norwegian source, but I am more inclined to believe that it derives from the fathers of Icelandic (and Norwegian) history, Sæmund and Ari. The second part codifies anecdotal material ultimately of Norwegian provenance but transmitted by Icelandic informants. The third part presumably goes back to Icelandic participants at the Battle of Svǫld and has passed through the transforming filter of Icelandic oral tradition. Thus the saga as a whole bears a distinctively Icelandic stamp. It asserts Icelandic literary authority.

That the lesser Olaf took literary precedence perhaps made it inevitable that the greater Olaf would eventually receive similar attention. But even in the surviving versions of the saga about the Norwegian candidate for sainthood, it is remarkable how little evidence there is of Norwegian sources. The curious tale of Olaf's birth must be ultimately Norwegian, but the confused transmission may suggest that the tradition was quite fragile. The rest of the saga relies on the transmissions of Olaf's Icelandic skalds, sometimes in the form of quite trivial anecdotes. These skalds are inclined to overshadow Olaf, as Hjalti Skeggjason does on the diplomatic front and Thormód Kolbrúnarskáld does again at Stiklarstadir. The "legendary" redaction of the saga adds in a fine conversion story from Norway, but the narrative style suggests that it was written by an Icelander. It also adds a long series of miracles, which are no more than an appendix and do not participate in saga style. The author of *The Oldest Saga of Saint Olaf* was surely an Icelander, resolutely reinforcing the literary proprietorship already asserted by Odd Snorrason.

Some twenty years later, after the Icelanders had already begun to record their own Saga Age traditions, the author of *The Saga of King Magnús and King Harald* embraced the Icelandic cause more explicitly. The Icelandic adventurers who people the semi-independent tales are a counterweight to King Harald Sigurdarson, notably the unflinching warrior Halldór Snorrason. These figures often serve not so much to profile the king as to relativize him. Harald no longer enjoys the exemption of quasi-sanctity, as the Olafs did, but is fair game for political commentary. That emerges with great clarity in the contrast to King Magnús and the polarity established by their views on foreign policy. This author is no longer an Icelander merely by dint of commanding a specifically Icelandic tradition but has become a free agent with a broad perspective and an analytical bent. *The Saga of King Magnús and King Harald* marked a new emancipation and a new level of authorial self-possession. The author was not content simply to recount but also makes judicious judgments on courses of action.

The author of *The Saga of King Magnús and King Harald* made important strides in the art of characterization, as well. Olaf Tryggvason and Olaf Haraldsson were largely faceless figureheads, but Magnús Óláfsson, though perhaps a trifle too saintly for our taste, has a certain depth to his saintliness; his character has specific as well as admirable dimensions. King Harald, in contrast, is problematical to a degree that has made it difficult for modern students to agree on the exact shading.[1] As we saw, his ingenuity verges on deceitfulness, and his self-assertiveness is less than principled, but it is this very indeterminacy that makes him a memorable personality.

We can surmise that Harald's portraitist was not the first to contrive such complexities. At some point, presumably between 1200 and 1220, Icelanders had begun to develop a strong interest in their own native traditions, and this interest emerges in the first sagas about their Saga Age ancestors. These ancestors were a mixed group, including the arch-trickster Víga-Glúm, the hardly less resourceful Víga-Skúta, the steely Thorgeir Hávarsson, the sentimental Thormód Bersason, and the self-contained and iron-willed Bardi Gudmundarson. The author of *The Saga of King Magnús and King Harald* could have learned much from this slightly caricatural art, perhaps most from the characterization of Víga-Glúm. The duality of the saintly Magnús and the machinating Harald may even have owed something to the contrasting figures of Áskel Eyvindarson and Vémund kǫgurr Thórisson in *Reykdœla saga* or, for that matter, the contrast between Thorgeir and Thormód in *Fóstbrœðra saga.* It is in any event clear that the fashioning of character became a dominant technique in the early sagas set in Iceland and could have enriched the kings' sagas after about 1220.

The royal policies of King Magnús and King Harald are viewed at arm's length and somewhat obliquely, but the author of *Egils saga* brings the political issues much closer to home. The action shifts from Norway to Iceland and focuses unabashedly on a celebrated Icelander. In some sense the Icelanders are no longer measured against Norwegian kings; rather, the kings are measured against an Icelandic protagonist. This shift requires a temporizing diplomacy for a double readership in Norway and Iceland in order to ease the transition from Norwegian to Icelandic primacy. The diplomacy appears in the form of an ironizing ambiguity in Egil's character which results in a more complex portraiture than was practiced in the early sagas. Such complexity appears first in the portrait of King Harald, but it takes on new vigor and humor in the figure of Egil. Characterization is destined to become one of the chief distinctions of Icelandic saga writing, and we may wish to weigh the possibility that it was born of the political

---

[1] Ármann Jakobsson's book of 2002 takes a much more positive view of King Harald, which is clearly opposed to my own view in this book.

strains between Norway and Iceland. These strains fostered the development of literary subterfuge as well as the increasingly overt self-assertiveness in the Icelandic sagas.

Growing self-confidence soon gave rise to sagas with an exclusive Icelandic focus and no sign of deference to the Norwegian court. *Ljósvetninga saga* is one such, whatever its exact date may be. It displays a strong interest in Icelandic history and Icelandic politics as legitimate subject matters and marks a well-defined stage in what we think of as the classical sagas about early Icelanders. The culmination of this introspection may be found in *Laxdœla saga,* in which not only is the focus trained on Iceland but early Iceland is invested with a quasi-royal grandeur. In place of Icelanders paying deference to Norwegian monarchs, as in *The Saga of King Magnús and King Harald,* we find Norwegian monarchs paying rather inexplicable deference to Icelandic visitors. The Icelandic past is suddenly suffused with a glow of bygone greatness not only comparable with but seemingly exceeding the splendor of the Norwegian court that had been a magnet for Icelanders in the earlier sagas. In *Laxdœla saga,* Icelanders travel to the Norwegian court for an opportunity to display their own accomplishments.

It is quite conceivable that *Laxdœla saga,* a popular saga as attested by a relatively large number of manuscripts, established something akin to a school of saga writing, best represented by *Eyrbyggja saga* and *Vatnsdœla saga.* Both have in common with *Laxdœla saga* that they are longer than average and have a special focus on the period of colonization. They unfold a broad historical canvas and convey a sense of dynasty, albeit with emphatically different emphases. *Eyrbyggja saga* takes a rather cynical view of the past, whereas *Vatnsdœla saga* shares the glorifying perspective of *Laxdœla saga* and imagines a past of unequaled splendor. All three texts seem to be motivated by a desire to resurrect regional history.

These sagas yield to, or perhaps run parallel with, a more issue-oriented and analytical school of saga writing represented by *Hœnsa-Þóris saga, Bandamanna saga,* and *Hrafnkels saga.* The latter abandon historical breadth in favor of pinpointing civil and political probems. They aspire not to retrieve past history but to identify failings in the civil system, notably in the role of chieftains. If they were written after the incorporation of Iceland under the Norwegian crown, perhaps they were calculated to offer an explanation for the failure of the Icelandic Commonwealth in general. Or perhaps they should be read as critiques of current or recently existing mechanisms and the ease with which such mechanisms can be corrupted. They share a sense of human and institutional fragility.

The tone of these short sagas is satirical, sometimes even comical, but by the time the author of *Njáls saga* went to work, the Icelandic past had become seriously problematical. The glittering vision of the past was extinguished, and the great historical figures had become not only ironically but genuinely ambiguous. Tragedy had become more interesting than triumph. Marriage patterns, the feud system, and legal processes were open to question. Many of the sequences read like parodies of traditional narrative conventions, and the optimism of *Laxdœla saga* looks almost comical by comparison. The total effect of *Njáls saga* is to problematize the whole tradition of saga writing during the preceding century. It is at once the best and bleakest of the sagas. It is the bleakest because the author had evolved a jaundiced vision of Icelandic institutions and the underlying assumptions. It is the best because this same author profited from a century of experimentation with the long narrative form.

The first experiments with the two Olafs were quite awkward because the authors saw themselves primarily as collectors of tradition. Their collections were roughly chronological, but the authors did not impose a definite narrative structure. Their sources remain separable and for the most part identifiable. The compositional procedure is additive rather than dramatic. *The Saga of King Magnús and King Harald* revolutionizes the style but not the structure. The composition is still episodic—although the episodes are brilliantly contrived—and the narrative skeleton remains biographical. The biographical form persists also in the first sagas about early Icelanders, the skald sagas, *Víga-Glúms saga, Reykdœla saga, Fóstbrœðra saga, Heiðarvíga saga, Gísla saga, Egils saga,* and *Ljósvetninga saga.* In these texts the individual episode continues to be the basic building block, although *Ljósvetninga saga* develops an impressive dramatic line in the section on Gudmund the Powerful's revenge, and *Gísla saga* offers an impressive study of psychology and values.

It is not until the writing of *Laxdœla saga* that we witness a real break with the episodic and biographical traditions. The unknown author surveys an unfolding of Icelandic history from the colonial period down to the eleventh century. It is a history subject to the fluctuations of fortune, but it suggests a strong continuity that subsumes the momentary catastrophes and promises a future equal to the past. The author, under the influence of heroic lay and elegy, also displays a flair for dramatic construction in fashioning the tragedy of Gudrún and Kjartan. Their destinies unwind from birth to death, but the focus is no longer biographical. The selection of narrative matter is governed by their fateful relationship: that is, by a dramatic principle.

Margrit Schildknecht-Burri pointed out that *Laxdœla saga* is both novel and chronicle—chronicle presumably in the sense that it records local traditions not always relevant to the tragic tale.[2] They are a residue of the older episodic composition, but the incidental traditions are so subordinate to the central focus on the tragic romance that they no longer obtrude or compete with the dramatic thrust of the narrative. They are more likely to be seen as narrative breadth than as inapposite digressions.

The final stage in this compositional progress is *Njáls saga*. Scholars have singled out a few episodes as digressive, but the arguments in favor of their being integral seem equally good if not better. The saga certainly does not seem burdened by what W. P. Ker referred to as "the difficulties of reluctant subject-matter and of the manifold deliverances of tradition."[3] The dramatic line leading to the demise of the protagonists Gunnar and Njál is steady and uninterrupted. The question of chronicle (local tradition) or novel, of biography or drama, is resolved in favor of drama. This choice of options has been at the center of the saga debate for a long time. In the first century or so of modern saga research, judgment was rendered in favor of tradition, but it was the mission of the Icelandic school, most particularly Sigurður Nordal, to make the novelistic alternative plausible. The position I take in this book, quite in line with the recent studies of Tommy Danielsson and Gísli Sigurðsson, is that after the ungainly beginning in the Olaf biographies, the sagas consistently combine tradition with novel writing, but the proportions shift over time. The role of tradition diminishes, and the formative role of the authors grows. The Olaf sagas are predominantly records of tradition, but it is perhaps not too much to say that *Njáls saga* is predominantly a novel.

Implicit in this view is the assumption that the sagas under study, although always founded on oral traditions, nonetheless evolve in a

[2] Schildknecht-Burri 1945, 29.
[3] Ker 1897/1957, 199.

literary framework. As Carol Clover argues, the saga authors knew and read each other.[4] It is hard to believe that the author of *Laxdœla saga* did not know *Egils saga* and did not engage in an almost polemical debate with the earlier text on matters of regional and ancestral preeminence. It is equally hard to believe that the author of *Njáls saga* did not know *Laxdœla saga* and did not view the dream world of that text with a skepticism bordering on disdain. The matter of the sagas is surely traditional, but the authors' overall perspective on the structuring and understanding of that matter is largely literary.

[4] Clover 1982, 200–201.

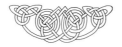

BIBLIOGRAPHY

Texts and Translations

Ágrip af Nóregskonungasǫgum: A Twelfth-Century Synoptic History of the Kings of Norway. Ed. and trans. M. [Matthew] J. Driscoll. London: Viking Society for Northern Research, 1995.

Biskupa sögur, gefnar út af Hinu Íslenzka Bókmenntafèlagi. 2 vols. Copenhagen: S. L. Møller, 1858.

The Complete Sagas of Icelanders including 49 Tales. 5 vols. Ed. Viðar Hreinsson. Reykjavik: Leifur Eiríksson, 1997.

The Disciplina Clericalis of Petrus Alphonsi. Trans. and ed. Eberhard Hermes; English trans. P. R. Quarrie. Berkeley: University of California Press, 1977.

Edda. Die Lieder des Codex Regius nebst verwandten Denkmälern. Ed. Gustav Neckel, rev. Hans Kuhn. 4th ed. Heidelberg: Winter, 1962.

Egil's Saga. Trans. Hermann Pálsson and Paul Edwards. London: Penguin, 1976.

Historia Norwegie. Ed. Inger Ekrem † and Lars Boye Mortensen, trans. Peter Fisher. Copenhagen: Museum Tusculanum Press, 2003.

A History of Norway and The Passion and Miracles of Blessed Óláfr. Ed. and trans. Carl Phelpstead and Devra Kunin. Viking Society for Northern Research, Text Series 13. London: University College; Viking Society for Northern Research, 2001.

Islandske annaler indtil 1578. Ed. Gustav Storm. Christiania: Grøndahl, 1888.

Íslenzk fornrit. Reykjavik: Hið Íslenzka Fornritafélag, 1933–91.

Vol. 1 (pts. 1 and 2): *Íslendingabók; Landnámabók.* Ed. Jakob Benediktsson. 1968.

Vol. 2: *Egils saga Skalla-Grímssonar.* Ed. Sigurður Nordal. 1933.

Vol. 3: *Borgfirðinga sǫgur.* Ed. Sigurður Nordal and Guðni Jónsson. 1938.

Vol. 4: *Eyrbyggja saga.* Ed. Einar Ól. Sveinsson and Matthías Þórðarson. 1935.

Vol. 5: *Laxdœla saga*. Ed. Einar Ól. Sveinsson. 1934.

Vol. 6: *Vestfirðinga sǫgur*. Ed. Björn K. Þórólfsson and Guðni Jónsson. 1943.

Vol. 7: *Grettis saga Ásmundarsonar*. Ed. Guðni Jónsson. 1936.

Vol. 8: *Vatnsdœla saga*. Ed. Einar Ól. Sveinsson. 1939.

Vol. 9: *Eyfirðinga sǫgur*. Ed. Jónas Kristjánsson. 1956.

Vol. 10: *Ljósvetninga saga*. Ed. Björn Sigfússon. 1940.

Vol. 11: *Austfirðinga sǫgur*. Ed. Jón Jóhannesson. 1950.

Vol. 12: *Brennu-Njáls saga*. Ed. Einar Ól. Sveinsson. 1954.

Vol. 13: *Harðar saga*. Ed. Þórhallur Vilmundarson and T. Bjarni Vilhjálms-
son. 1991.

Konunga sögur, vol. 3: *Hákonar saga gamla*. Ed. Guðni Jónsson. [Reykjavik]:
Íslendingasagnaútgáfan, 1957.

*Monumenta Historica Norvegiae: Latinske kildeskrifter til Norges historie i Middel-
alderen*. Ed. Gustav Storm. Christiania: A. W. Brøgger, 1880; rpt. Oslo: Aas
& Wahl, 1973.

Morkinskinna. Ed. Finnur Jónsson. STUAGNL 53. Copenhagen: J. Jørgensen,
1932.

*Morkinskinna: The Earliest Icelandic Chronicle of the Norwegian Kings (1030–
1157)*. Trans. Theodore M. Andersson and Kari Ellen Gade. Islandica 51.
Ithaca: Cornell University Press, 2000.

Njal's Saga. Trans. Magnus Magnusson and Hermann Pálsson. London: Penguin, 1960.

Njal's Saga. Trans. Robert Cook. London: Penguin, n.d. [1997].

Den norsk-islandske skjaldedigtning. Vols. IA–IIA, *Tekst efter håndskrifterne;* vols.
IB–IIB, *Rettet tekst*. Ed. Finnur Jónsson. Copenhagen: Gyldendal, 1908–15;
rpt. Copenhagen: Rosenkilde & Bagger, 1967–73.

*Olafs saga hins helga. Die "Legendarische Saga" über Olaf den Heiligen (Hs. Dela-
gard. saml. nr. 8^{II})*. Ed. and trans. Anne Heinrichs, Doris Janshen, Elke
Radicke, and Hartmut Röhn. Heidelberg: Winter, 1982.

*Olafs saga hins helga efter pergamenthaandskrift i Uppsala Universitetsbibliotek,
Delagardieske samling nr. 8^{II}*. Ed. Oscar Albert Johnsen. Christiania: Jacob
Dybwad, 1922.

Óláfs saga Tryggvasonar en mesta. Ed. Ólafur Halldórsson. 3 vols. Editiones Ar-
namagnaeanae, series A. Copenhagen: Ejnar Munksgaard, 1958–61 (vols.
1–2); Copenhagen: Reitzel, 2000 (vol. 3).

Otte brudstykker af Den ældste saga om Olav den hellige. Ed. Gustav Storm.
Christiania: Grøndahl, 1893.

Saga Óláfs Tryggvasonar af Oddr Snorrason munk. Ed. Finnur Jónsson. Copenhagen: Gad, 1932.

The Saga of Olaf Tryggvason by Oddr Snorrason. Trans. Theodore M. Andersson. Islandica 52. Ithaca: Cornell University Press, 2003.

The Saga of the Volsungs. Ed. and trans. R. G. Finch. London: Nelson, 1965.

Sturlunga saga. Ed. Örnólfur Thorsson et al. 3 vols. Reykjavik: Svart á hvítu,
1988.

Theodoricus Monachus. *Historia de Antiquitate Regum Norwagiensium; An Account of the Ancient History of the Norwegian Kings.* Translated and annotated by David and Ian McDougall; intro. Peter Foote. Viking Society for Northern Research, Text Series 11. London: University College London; Viking Society for Northern Research, 1998.

Víga-Glúms saga. Ed. G. Turville-Petre. Oxford: Oxford University Press, 1940.

Viga-Glums Saga with the Tales of Ogmund Bash and Thorvald Chatterbox. Trans. John McKinnell. [Edinburgh]: Canongate, 1987.

Critical Studies

Allen, Richard F. 1971. *Fire and Iron: Critical Approaches to Njáls saga.* Pittsburgh, Pa.: University of Pittsburgh Press.

Andersson, Theodore M. 1964. *The Problem of Icelandic Saga Origins: A Historical Survey.* New Haven: Yale University Press.

——. 1966. "The Textual Evidence of an Oral Family Saga." *ANF* 81:1–23.

——. 1968. "Some Ambiguities in *Gísla saga:* A Balance Sheet." *BONIS*, 7–41.

——. 1985. "Kings' Sagas." In *ONIL*, 197–238.

——. 1988a. "Lore and Literature in a Scandinavian Conversion Episode." In *Idee, Gestalt, Geschichte: Festschrift Klaus von See. Studien zur europäischen Kulturtradition,* ed. Gerd Wolfgang Weber, 261–84. Odense: Odense University Press.

——. 1988b. "Ethics and Politics in *Hrafnkels saga.*" *SS* 60:293–309.

——. 1998. "The Continuation of *Hlaðajarla saga.*" *JEGP* 97:155–67.

——. 2000. "Character and Caricature in the Family Sagas." In *Studien zur Isländersaga,* 1–10.

——. 2002. "The Long Prose Form in Medieval Iceland." *JEGP* 101:380–411.

——. 2004a. "The First Icelandic King's Saga: Oddr Snorrason's *Óláfs saga Tryggvasonar* or *The Oldest Saga of Saint Olaf?*" *JEGP* 103:139–55.

——. 2004b. "Five Saga Books for a New Century." *JEGP* 103:505–27.

Andersson, Theodore M., and William Ian Miller. 1989. *Law and Literature in Medieval Iceland: Ljósvetninga saga and Valla-Ljóts saga.* Stanford, Calif.: Stanford University Press.

Ármann Jakobsson. 1997. *Í leit að konungi. Konungsmynd íslenzkra konungasagna.* Reykjavik: Háskólaútgáfan.

——. 1998. "Konungasagan Laxdæla." *Skírnir* 172:357–83.

——. 2002. *Staður í nýjum heimi. Konungasagan Morkinskinna.* Reykjavik: Háskólaútgáfan.

——. 2004. "The Hunted Children of Kings: A Theme in the Old Icelandic Sagas." *Scandinavica* 43:5–27.

Auður Magnúsdóttir. 2001. *Frillor och fruar. Politik och samlevnad på Island 1120–1400.* Gothenburg: Historiska Institutionen.

Bååth, A. U. [Albert Ulrik]. [1885]. *Studier öfver kompositionen i några isländska ättsagor.* Lund: Berling.

Baetke, Walter. 1956. *Über die Entstehung der Isländersagas.* Berichte über die Verhandlungen der Sächsischen Akademie der Wissenschaften zu Leipzig, Philol.-hist. Kl., vol. 102:1–108. Berlin: Akademie-Verlag.

Baldur Hafstað. 1995. *Die Egils saga und ihr Verhältnis zu anderen Werken des nordischen Mittelalters.* Reykjavik: Rannsóknarstofnun Kennaraháskóla Íslands.

Bandle, Oskar. 1972. "Strukturprobleme in der *Njáls saga.*" In *Festschrift für Siegfried Gutenbrunner: Zum 65. Geburtstag am 12. Mai 1971.* Ed. Oskar Bandle, Heinz Klingenberg, and Friedrich Maurer, 1–14. Heidelberg: Winter.

Bang, A. Chr. 1897. "Om Dale-Gudbrand." In *Skrifter udgivne af Videnskabsselskabet i Christiania,* hist.-filos. kl., no. 2:3–11. Christiania: Jacob Dybwad.

Baumgartner, Walter. 1987. "Sozio-logisches Erzählen in der Hœnsa-Þóris saga." In *Applikationen. Analysen skandinavischer Erzähltexte,* ed. Walter Baumgartner, 17–93. Frankfurt am Main: Peter Lang.

Beck, Heinrich. 1973. "Erzählhaltung und Quellenberufung in der *Egils saga.*" *Skandinavistik* 3:89–102.

———. 1976. "Brynhilddichtung und Laxdæla saga." In *Festgabe für Otto Höfler zum 75. Geburtstag,* ed. Helmut Birkhan, 1–14. Vienna: Wilhelm Braumüller.

———. 1977. "Laxdæla saga—A Structural Approach." *SBVS* 19:383–402.

Berman, Melissa. 1982. "*Egils saga* and *Heimskringla.*" *SS* 54:21–50.

Bjarni Aðalbjarnarson. 1937. *Om de norske kongers sagaer.* NVAOS II, hist.-filos. kl., 1936, no. 4. Oslo: Jacob Dybwad.

Bjarni Einarsson. 1975. *Litterære forudsætninger for Egils saga.* Reykjavik: Stofnun Árna Magnússonar.

———. 1977. "Fólgið fé á Mosfelli." In *Sjötíu ritgerðir.* 1:100–106.

Bjarni Guðnason. 1993. *Túlkun Heiðarvígasögu.* Studia Islandica 50. Reykjavik: Bókmenntafræðistofnun Háskóla Íslands.

———. 1994. "Aldur og einkenni *Bjarnarsögu Hítdœlakappa.*" In *Sagnaþing helgað Jónasi Kristjánssyni sjötugum 10. apríl 1994,* 2 vols., ed. Gísli Sigurðsson, Guðrún Kvaran, and Sigurgeir Steingrímsson, 1:69–85. Reykjavik: Hið Íslenzka Bókmenntafélag.

———. 1999. "Guðrún Ósvífrsdóttir och Laxdæla saga." *SI* 50:9–30.

Björn Sigfússon. 1934. "Veldi Guðmundar ríka." *Skírnir* 108:191–98.

———. 1937. *Um Ljósvetninga sögu.* Studia Islandica 3. Reykjavik: Ísafoldarprentsmiðja H. F.

Bley, André. 1909. *Eigla-Studien.* Ghent: Van Gothem.

Borggreve, Cecilia. 1970. "Der Handlungsaufbau in den zwei Versionen der Ljósvetninga saga." *ANF* 85:238–46.

Bouman, A. C. [Arie Cornelis]. 1962a. "Literature and Myth: The Picture of Hallgerðr Hǫskuld's Daughter." In *Patterns in Old English and Old Icelandic Literature,* by A. C. Bouman, 3–13. Leyden: Universitaire Pers.

——. 1962b. "Patterns in the Laxdoela Saga." Ibid., pp. 109–59.

Böðvar Guðmundsson, Sverrir Tómasson, Torfi H. Tulinius, and Vésteinn Ólason. 1993. *Íslensk bókmenntasaga,* vol. 2. Reykjavik: Mál og Menning.

Capelle, Torsten, and Susanne Kramarz-Bein. 2001. "Zeithorizonte der 'Egils saga.'" *Frühmittelalterliche Studien* 35:227–42.

Cederschiöld, Gustaf. 1890. *Kalfdråpet och vänpröfningnen. Ett bidrag till kritiken af de isländska sagornas trovärdighet.* Lund: Gleerup.

Clover, Carol J. 1974. "Scene in Saga Composition." *ANF* 89:57–83.

——. 1982. *The Medieval Saga.* Ithaca: Cornell University Press.

——. 1986a. "Hildigunnr's Lament." In *Structure and Meaning in Old Norse Literature: New Approaches to Textual Analysis and Literary Criticism,* ed. John Lindow, Lars Lönnroth, and Gerd Wolfgang Weber, 141–83. Odense: Odense University Press.

——. 1986b. "The Long Prose Form." *ANF* 101:10–39.

Clunies Ross, Margaret. 1978. "The Art of Poetry and the Figure of the Poet in *Egils saga.*" *Parergon* 22:3–12; rpt. in *Sagas* 1989:126–45.

——. 2001. "The Skald Sagas as a Genre: Definitions and Typical Features." In Poole, 2001:25–49.

Conroy, Patricia, and T. C. S. Langen. 1988. "*Laxdæla saga:* Theme and Structure." *ANF* 103:118–41.

Cook, Robert. 1992. "Women and Men in Laxdæla saga." *Skáldskaparmál* 2:34–59.

Danielsson, Tommy. 1986. *Om den isländska släktsagans uppbyggnad.* Skrifter utgivna av Litteraturvetenskapliga institutionen vid Uppsala universitet 22. Stockholm: Almqvist & Wiksell.

——. 2002a. *Hrafnkels saga eller Fallet med den undflyende traditionen.* Hedemora, Sweden: Gidlunds Förlag.

——. 2002b. *Sagorna om Norges kungar. Från Magnús góði till Magnús Erlingsson.* Hedemora: Gidlunds Förlag.

Davíð Erlingsson. 1988. "'Höfðingsskapar spegill og skilnings stýri.' Um tvær frásagnir í Laxdælasögu og hlutverk þeirra." *Tímarit Háskóla Íslands* 3:19–25.

Drever, James. 1937–45. "The Psychology of Laxdœlasaga." *SBVS* 12:107–18.

Dronke, Ursula. 1979. "Narrative Insight in *Laxdæla Saga.*" In *J. R. R. Tolkien, Scholar and Storyteller: Essays in Memoriam,* ed. Mary Salu and Robert T. Farrell, 120–37. Ithaca: Cornell University Press.

——. 1981. *The Role of Sexual Themes in Njáls saga.* London: Viking Society for Northern Research.

Durrenberger, E. Paul. 1992. *The Dynamics of Medieval Iceland: Political Economy and Literature.* Iowa City: University of Iowa Press.

Durrenberger, Paul, Dorothy Durrenberger, and Ástráður Eysteinsson. 1987–88. "Economic Representation and Narrative Structure in *Hœnsa-Þóris saga.*" *SBVS* 22: 143–64.

Durrenberger, E. Paul, and Jonathan Wilcox. 1992. "Humor as a Guide to Social Change: *Bandamanna saga* and Heroic Values." In *From Sagas to Society: Comparative Approaches to Early Iceland*, ed. Gísli Pálsson, 111–23. Enfield Lock, England: Hisarlik Press.

Ebel, Uwe. 1982. "Zum Erzählverfahren der mittelalterlichen isländischen Prosaerzählung—Das Beispiel der 'Hønsna-Þóris saga.'" In Uwe Ebel, *Beiträge zur nordischen Philologie*, 26–55. Frankfurt am Main: Haag und Herchen.

———. 1989. *Der Untergang des isländischen Freistaats als historischer Kontext der Verschriftlichung der Isländersaga. Zugleich ein Beitrag zum Verständnis der "Hœnsa-Þóris saga."* Metelen: Dagmar Ebel.

Einar Ólafur Sveinsson. 1933. *Um Njálu.* Vol. 1. Reykjavik: Bókadeild Menningarsjóðs.

———. 1950. "Njáls saga." *SI* 1:5–30.

———. 1958. *Dating the Icelandic Sagas.* London: Viking Society for Northern Research.

———. 1971. *Njáls saga: A Literary Masterpiece.* Trans. Paul Schach. Lincoln: University of Nebraska Press.

Erichsen, Adolfine. 1919. "Untersuchungen zur Liósvetninga Saga." Diss., Univesity of Berlin.

Eysteinn Þorvaldsson. 1968. "Hugleiðingar um ástarsögu Egils." *Mímir* 13:20–24.

Fidjestøl, Bjarne. 1982. *Det norrøne fyrstediktet.* Universitetet i Bergen Nordisk institutts skriftserie 11. Øvre Ervik, Norway: Alvheim & Eide.

Finlay, Alison. 1992. "*Egils saga* and Other Poets' Sagas." In *Introductory Essays*, 33–48.

———. 2001. "Skald Sagas in Their Literary Context 2: Possible European Contexts." In Poole, 2001, 232–71.

Finnur Jónsson. 1904. "Om Njála." *ÅNOH*, 89–166.

———. 1920–24. *Den oldnorske og oldislandske litteraturs historie.* 2 vols. 1894–1901; 2nd ed., 3 vols., Copenhagen: Gad, 1920–24.

Foote, Peter. 1979. "Review Article: New Dimensions in *Njáls saga.*" *Scandinavica* 18:49–58.

Frank, Roberta. 1985. "Skaldic Poetry." In *ONIL*, 157–96.

Fries, Ingegerd. 1981. "Njals saga 700 år senare." *SI* 32:30–54.

Fulk, R. D. 1986. "The Moral System of *Hrafnkels saga freysgoða.*" *SBVS* 22:1–32.

Gísli Sigurðsson. 2002. *Túlkun Íslendingasagna í ljósi munnlegrar hefðar. Tilgáta um aðferð.* Reykjavik: Stofnun Árna Magnússonar á Íslandi. Eng. trans. Nicholas Jones, *The Medieval Icelandic Saga and Oral Tradition: A Discourse on Method.* Publications of the Milman Parry Collection of Oral Literature 2. Cambridge, Mass.: The Milman Parry Collection of Oral Literature, Harvard University; distr. Harvard University Press, 2004.

Gottzmann, Carola L. 1982. *Njáls saga. Rechtsproblematik im Dienste sozio-kultureller Deutung.* Frankfurt am Main: Peter Lang.

Grimstad, Kaaren. 1976. "The Giant as a Heroic Model: The Case of Egill and Starkaðr." *SS* 48:284–98.

Guðbrandur Vigfússon. 1922. "Rök um aldr Njálu." *Skírnir* 96:147–53.

Hagland, Jan Ragnar. 1987. "Njáls saga i 1970- og 1980-åra: Eit oversyn over nyare forskning." *SI* 38:36–50.

Hallberg, Peter. 1962. *Snorri Sturluson och Egils saga Skallagrímssonar. Ett försök till språklig författarbestämning.* Studia Islandica 20. Reykjavik: Prentsmiðjan Leiftur.

——. 1963. *Ólafr Þórðarson hvítaskáld, Knýtlinga saga och Laxdæla saga.* Studia Islandica 22. Reykjavik: Prentsmiðjan Leiftur.

——. 1966. "Några anteckningar om replik och dialog i Njals saga." In *Festschrift Walter Baetke dargebracht zu seinem 80. Geburtstag am 28. März 1964,* ed. Kurt Rudolph, Rolf Heller, and Ernst Walter, 130–50. Weimar: Hermann Böhlaus Nachfolger.

——. 1973. "Njála miðalda helgisaga?" *Andvari* 98:60–69.

——. 1975a. "Hrafnkell Freysgoði the 'New Man'—A Phantom Problem." *SS* 47:442–47.

——. 1975b. "Hunting for the Heart of Hrafnkels saga." *SS* 47:463–66.

——. 1976. "Två mordbränder i det medeltida Island." *Gardar* 7:25–45.

——. 1984. "Der Dialog in der Laxdœla Saga. Strukturelle und künstlerische Funktion." In *Linguistica et Philologica. Gedenkschrift für Björn Collinder (1894–1983),* ed. Otto Gschwantler, Károly Rédei, and Hermann Reichert, 191–211. Vienna: Wilhelm Braumüller.

Ham, Johannes van. 1932. *Beschouwingen over de literaire betekenis der Laxdœla saga.* Amsterdam: Uitgevers-Maatschappij.

Hamer, Andrew. 1992. "It seemed to me that the sweetest light of my eyes had been extinguished." In *Introductory Essays,* 93–101.

Harris, Joseph. 1994. "Sacrifice and Guilt in *Sonatorrek.*" In *Studien zum Altgermanischen,* 173–96.

Hauch, C. [Carsten]. 1855. "Indledning til forelæsninger over Njalssaga og flere med den beslægtede Sagaer." In *Afhandlinger og æsthetiske Betragtninger,* 411–67. Copenhagen: Reitzel.

Heimir Pálsson. 1967. "Rittengsl Laxdælu og Njálu." *Mímir* 6:5–16.

Heinemann, Fredrik. 1975a. "*Hrafnkels saga Freysgoða:* The Old Problem with the New Man." *SS* 47:448–52.

——. 1975b. "The Heart of *Hrafnkatla* Again." *SS* 47:453–62.

Heinrichs, Anne. 1989. *Der Óláfs þáttr Geirstaðaálfs. Eine Variantenstudie.* Heidelberg: Winter.

——. 1994. "Hallgerðs Saga in der Njála: Der doppelte Blick." In *Studien zum Altgermanischen,* 327–53.

——. 1996. "Gunnhild konungamóðir: Porträt einer Königin." In *Herrscher, Helden, Heilige,* ed. Ulrich Müller and Werner Wunderlich, 213–29. St. Gallen: UVK Fachverlag für Wissenschaft und Studium.

———. 2000. "Gunnhild Ǫzurardóttir und Egil Skalla-Grímsson im Kampf um Leben und Tod." In *Studien zur Isländersaga,* 72–108.

Heinrichs, Heinrich Matthias. 1975. "Die Geschichte vom sagakundigen Isländer (Íslendings þáttr sǫgufróða). Ein Beitrag zur Sagaforschung." In *Literaturwissenschaft und Geschichtsphilosophie. Festschrift für Wilhelm Emrich,* ed. Helmut Arntzen, Bernd Balzer, Karl Pestalozzi, and Rainer Wagner, 225–31. Berlin: de Gruyter.

———. 1976. "Mündlichkeit und Schriftlichkeit. Ein Problem der Sagaforschung." *Jahrbuch für internationale Germanistik,* ser. A, 2:114–33.

Helga Kress. 1977. "Ekki hǫfu vér kvennaskap. Nokkrar laustengdar athuganir um karlmennsku og kvenhatur í Njálu." In *Sjötíu ritgerðir,* 1:293–313.

———. 1979. "Manndom og misogyni. Noen refleksjoner omkring kvinnesynet i Njáls saga." *Gardar* 10:35–51.

———. 1980. "'Mjǫk mun þér samstaft þykkja'—Um sagnahefð og kvenlega reynslu í Laxdæla sögu." In *Konur skrifa til heiðurs Önnu Sigurðardóttur,* ed. Valborg Bentsdóttir, Guðrún Gísladóttir, and Svanlaug Baldursdóttir, 97–109. Reykjavik: Prentsmiðjan Oddi hf.

———. 1992. "'Gægur er þér í augum.' Konur í sjónmáli Íslendingasagna." In *Yfir Íslandsála. Afmælisrit til heiðurs Magnúsi Stefánssyni sextugum 25. desember 1991.* Reykjavik: N.p.

Helgi Þorláksson. 1992. "Social Ideals and the Concept of Profit in Thirteenth-Century Iceland." In *From Sagas to Society: Comparative Approaches to Early Iceland,* ed. Gísli Pálsson, 231–44. Enfield Lock, England: Hisarlik Press.

Heller, Rolf. 1974. "Laxdœla saga und Landnámabók." *ANF* 89:84–145.

———. 1976. *Die Laxdœla saga. Die literarische Schöpfung eines Isländers des 13. Jahrhunderts.* In Abhandlungen der Sächsischen Akademie der Wissenschaften zu Leipzig, philol.-hist. Kl., vol. 65, no. 1. Berlin: Akademie-Verlag.

———. 1977. "Zur Entstehung der Grönlandsszenen der Fóstbrœðra saga." In *Sjötíu ritgerðir* 1:326–34.

Hermann Pálsson. 1984. *Uppruni Njálu og hugmyndir.* Reykjavik: Bókaútgáfa Menningarsjóðs.

———. 1986. *Leyndarmál Laxdælu.* Reykjavik: Bókaútgáfa Menningarsjóðs.

Heusler, Andreas. 1922. "Einleitung." In *Die Geschichte vom weisen Njal,* 1–20. Jena: Eugen Diederichs.

———. 1941. *Die altgermanische Dichtung.* 2nd ed. Potsdam: Akademische Verlagsgesellschaft Athenaion.

Hines, John. 1992. "Kingship in *Egils saga.*" In *Introductory Essays,* 15–32.

Hofmann, Dietrich. 1972. "Reykdœla saga und mündliche Überlieferung." *Skandinavistik* 2:1–26; rpt. in Hofmann, *Studien zur Nordischen und Germanischen Philologie,* ed. Gert Kreutzer, Alastair Walker, and Ommo Wilts, 1:142–67. Hamburg: Helmut Buske, 1988.

Holtsmark, Anne. 1971. "Skallagrims heimamenn." *MM,* 97–105.

Indrebø, Gustav. 1917. *Fagrskinna*. Christiania: Grøndahl.

Jakobsen, Alfred. 1984. "Njåls saga og Selsbane-tåtten." *ANF* 99:126–30.

——. 1985. "Om parallellepisoder i Egils saga." *Edda* 85:315–18.

Jesch, Judith. 1992. "'Good Men' and Peace in *Njáls saga*." In *Introductory Essays*, 64–82.

Johnsen, Oscar Albert. 1916. "Friðgerðar-saga. En kildekritisk undersøkelse." (Norsk) *Historisk tidsskrift*, ser. 5, 3:513–39.

Jón Helgason. 1957. "Ek bar sauð." *Acta Philologica Scandinavica* 23:94–96.

Jón Jóhannesson. 1974. *A History of the Old Icelandic Commonwealth*. N.p.: University of Manitoba Press.

Jónas Kristjánsson. 1972. *Um Fóstbrœðrasögu*. Reykjavik: Stofnun Árna Magnússonar.

——. 1976. "The Legendary Saga." In *Minjar og menntir. Afmælisrit helgað Kristjáni Eldjárn 6. desember 1976*, 281–93. Reykjavík: Bókaútgáfa Menningarsjóðs.

——. 1977. "Egils saga og konungasögur." In *Sjötíu ritgerðir*. 2:449–72.

——. 1988. *Eddas and Sagas: Iceland's Medieval Literature*. Trans. Peter Foote. Reykjavik: Hið Íslenska Bókmenntafélag.

Ker, W. P. [William Paton]. 1897. *Epic and Romance*. London: Macmillan; rpt. New York: Dover, 1957.

Kersbergen, Anna Cornelia. 1927. *Litteraire motieven in de Njála*. Rotterdam: Nijgh & Dietmar's Uitgevers-Maatschappij.

——. 1933. "Frásagnir in de Laxdæla." *Neophilologus* 19:53–67.

Kinck, Hans E. 1916. "Et par ting om ættesagaen. Skikkelser den ikke forstod." In *Samlede essays* (1916; rpt. 1921, 1951), 1:171–96. Oslo: H. Aschehoug, 1982.

Kolbrún Bergþórsdóttir. 1989. "Hver var Guðrún?" *Mímir* 37:18–22.

Kramarz-Bein, Susanne. 1994. "'Modernität' der *Laxdœla saga*." In *Studien zum Altgermanischen*, 421–42.

Kristján Albertsson. 1976. "Egill Skallagrímsson í Jórvik." *Skírnir* 150:88–98.

Larrington, Carolyne. 1992. "Egill's Longer Poems: *Arinbjarnarkviða* and *Sonatorrek*." In *Introductory Essays*, 49–63.

Lárus H. Blöndal. 1982. *Um uppruna Sverrissögu*. Reykjavik: Stofnun Árna Magnússonar.

Lehmann, Karl. 1905. "Jurisprudensen i Njála." *Tidsskrift for retsvidenskab* 18:183–99.

Lehmann, Karl, and Hans Schnorr von Carolsfeld. 1883. *Die Njálsage, insbesondere in ihren juristischen Bestandtheilen. Ein kritischer Beitrag zur altnordischen Rechts- und Literaturgeschichte*. Berlin: R. L. Prager.

Lie, Hallvard. 1937. *Studier i Heimskringlas stil. Dialogene og talene*. In NVAOS II, hist.-filos. kl., no. 5. Oslo: Jacob Dybwad.

——. 1946. "Jorvikferden. Et vendepunkt i Egil Skallagrimsson's liv." *Edda* 33:145–248: rpt. in Lie, *Om sagakunst og skaldskap. Utvalgte avhandlinger*, 5–108. Øvre Ervik, Norway: Alvheim & Eide, 1982.

——. 1989. "Egil Skallagrimsson's livsaften. Et semifilologisk kåseri." In *Festskrift til Finn Hødnebø 29. desember 1989*, ed. Bjørn Eithun, Eyvind Fjeld Halvorsen, Magnus Rindal, and Erik Simensen, 180–92. Oslo: Novus.

Liestøl, Knut. 1930. *The Origin of the Icelandic Family Sagas.* Trans. A. G. Jayne. Oslo: Aschehoug.

Lönnroth, Lars. 1963. "Studier i Olaf Tryggvasons saga." *Samlaren* 84:54–94.

——. 1975. "Charlemagne, Hrolf Kraki, Olaf Tryggvason: Parallels in the Heroic Tradition." In *Les relations littéraires franco-scandinaves au moyen âge. Actes du colloque de Liège (avril 1972),* Bibliothèque de la Faculté de Philosophie et Lettres de l'Université de Liège 208, 20–52. Paris: Société d'Edition "Les Belles Lettres."

——. 1976. *Njáls saga: A Critical Introduction.* Berkeley: University of California Press.

——. 1980. "New Dimensions and Old Directions in Saga Research." *Scandinavica* 19:57–61.

——. 1996. *Skaldemjödet i berget. Essayer om fornisländsk ordkonst och dess återvändning i nutiden.* Stockholm: Atlantis.

——. 2000. "The Baptist and the Saint: Odd Snorrason's View of the Two King Olavs." In *International Scandinavian and Medieval Studies in Memory of Gerd Wolfgang Weber,* ed. Michael Dallapiazza, Olaf Hansen, Preben Meulengracht Sørensen, and Yvonne S. Bonnetain, 257–64. Trieste: Edizioni Parnaso.

Looze, Laurence de. 1989. "Poet, Poem, and Poetic Process in *Egils saga Skalla-Grímssonar.*" *ANF* 104:123–42.

Lotspeich, Claude. 1903. *Zur Víga-Glúms- und Reykdœlasaga.* Leipzig: Hesse & Becker.

Louis-Jensen, Jonna. 1977. *Kongesagastudier. Kompilationen Hulda-Hrokkinskinna.* Bibliotheca Arnamagnaeana 32. Copenhagen: Reitzel.

Magerøy, Hallvard. 1956. *Sertekstproblemet i Ljósvetninga saga.* Avhandlinger utgitt av Det Norske Videnskaps-Akademi i Olso II, hist.-philos. kl, no. 2. Oslo: Aschehoug.

——. 1957. *Studiar i Bandamanna saga.* Bibliotheca Arnamagnaeana 18. Copenhagen: Munksgaard.

——. 1959. "Guðmundr góði og Guðmundr ríki." *MM,* 22–34.

——. 1971. "Har Sturla Þórðarson skrivi Laxdœla saga? Marina Mundt: Sturla Þórðarson und die Laxdæla saga." *MM,* 4–33.

——. 1998. "Vergil-påverknad på norrøn litteratur." *Gripla* 10:75–136.

Martínez Pizarro, Joaquín. 1985. "Conversion Narratives: Form and Utility." In "The Sixth International Saga Conference 28.7–2.8, Workshop Papers," 2:813–32.

Maurer, Konrad. 1895. *Zwei Rechtsfälle in der Eigla.* In Sitzungsberichte der philos.-philol. und der histor. Cl. der Königlichen Bayerischen Akademie der Wissenschaften, 65–124. Munich. N.p.

Maxwell, I. R. 1957–59. "Pattern in *Njáls saga.*" *SBVS* 15:17–47.

McTurk, Rory. 1990. "The Supernatural in *Njáls saga:* A Narratological Approach." *SBVS* 23:28–45.

Meulengracht Sørensen, Preben. 1977. "Starkaðr, Loki, and Egill Skallagrímsson." In *Sjötíu ritgerðir,* 2:759–68, rpt. and trans. in *Sagas,* 146–59.

———. 1993. *Fortælling og ære. Studier i islændingesagaerne.* Aarhus: Aarhus Universitetsforlag.

———. 1994. "Græder du nu, Skarpheðinn?" In *Studien zum Atlgermanischen,* 480–89.

———. 2001. "Norge og Island i *Laxdæla saga.*" In *At fortælle Historien; Telling History; Studier i den gamle nordiske litteratur; Studies in Norse Literature.* Ed. in collaboration with Sofie Meulengracht Sørensen, 71–80. Trieste: Edizioni Parnaso.

Miller, William Ian. 1983. "Justifying Skarpheðinn: Of Pretext and Politics in the Icelandic Bloodfeud." *SS* 55:316–44.

———. 1985. Review of *Njáls saga. Rechtsproblematik im Dienste sozio-kultureller Deutung* by Carola Gottzmann. *SS* 57:84–85.

———. 1990. *Bloodtaking and Peacemaking: Feud, Law, and Society in Saga Iceland.* Chicago: University of Chicago Press.

Möbius, Theodor. 1852. *Über die ältere isländische Saga.* Leipzig: Giesecke & Devrient.

Monclair, Hanne. 2004. *Lederskapsideologi på Island i det trettende århundret. En analyse av gavegivning og lederfremtoning i islandsk sagamateriale.* Oslo: Unipub AS.

Müller, Harald. 2000. ". . . und gut ist keines von beiden'. Gedanken zur Akzeptierung der Brenna in der *Njáls Saga.*" In *Studien zur Isländersaga,* 198–207.

Müller, Harald (in Zusammenarbeit mit John W. Daly, Christopher Graz, Vera Johanterwage, Thomas Küper, Bert Röbekamp, Marcel Schmutzler, Jessica Wessels). 2005. "Ethische Konzepte und transtemporales Bewusstsein in der *Hrafnkels saga Freysgoða.*" In *Neue Ansätze in der Mittelalterphilologie—Nye veier i middelalderfilologien. Akten der skandinavistischen Arbeitstagung in Münster vom 24. bis 26. Oktober 2002,* ed. Susanne Kramarz-Bein., 161–95. Frankfurt am Main: Peter Lang.

Mundal, Else. 1977. *Sagadebatt.* Oslo: Universitetsforlaget.

———. 1990. "Den norrøne episke tradisjonen" in *Hellas og Norge. Kontakt, komparasjon, kontrast,* ed. Øivind Andersen and Thomas Hägg, 65–80. Bergen: Klassisk institutt i Bergen.

Mundt, Marina. 1969. *Sturla Thordarson und die Laxdæla saga.* Bergen: Universitetsforlaget.

———. 1976. "Kvinnens forhold til ekteskapet i Njáls saga." *Edda* 63:17–25.

———. 2000. "Skiftende syn på *Njáls saga.*" In *Studien zur Isländersaga,* 208–22.

Nanna Ólafsdóttir. 1977. "Nokkur menningar-söguleg dæmi úr Njálu." *Skírnir* 151:59–72.

Netter, Irmgard. 1935. *Die direkte Rede in den Isländersagas.* Leipzig: Hermann Eichblatt.

Njörður P. Njarðvík. 1971. "Laxdœla saga—en tidskritik?" *ANF* 86:72–81.

Nordal, Sigurður. See Sigurður Nordal.

Nordland, Odd. 1956. *Hǫfuðlausn i Egils saga. Ein tradisjonskritisk studie.* Oslo: Det Norske Samlaget.

Norseng, Per G. 2000. "Hønse-Tore en gang til: Synet på profitt-motivert handel i de islandske sagaene." In *Holmgang. Om førmoderne samfunn. Festskrift til Kåre Lunden,* 166–87. Oslo: Historisk institutt, Universitetet i Oslo.

O'Donoghue, Heather. 1992. "Women in Njáls saga." In *Introductory Essays,* 83–92.

Óláfía Einarsdóttir. 1990. "Sigurd hjort og hans børn i islandske kilder. En sagnhistorisk undersøgelse." *Gripla* 7:267–301.

Ólafur Halldórsson. 1991. "Nema skyld nauðsyn banni." In *Lygisögur sagðar Sverri Tómassyni fimmtugum 5. apríl 1991,* ed. Gísli Sigurðsson and Örnólfur Thorsson, 73–77. Reykjavik: N.p.

Ólsen, Björn Magnússon. 1904. "Landnáma og Egils saga." *ÅNOH,* ser. 2, 19:167–247.

———. 1905a. "Landnáma og Hœnsa-Þóris Saga." *ÅNOH,* ser. 2, 20:63–80.

———. 1905b. "Landnáma og Eyrbyggja Saga." *ÅNOH,* ser. 2, 20:81–117.

———. 1908. "Landnáma og Laxdœla Saga." *ÅNOH,* ser. 2, 23:151–232.

———. 1910. "Landnáma og Gull-Þóris (Þorskfirðinga) saga." *ÅNOH,* ser. 2, 25:35–61.

———. 1920. "Landnáma og Eiríks saga rauða." *ÅNOH,* ser. 3, 10:301–7.

Ordower, Henry. 1991. "Exploring the Literary Function of Law and Litigation in *Njáls saga.*" *Cardozo Studies in Law and Literature* 3:41–61.

Óskar Halldórsson. 1976. *Uppruni og þema Hrafnkels sögu.* Reykjavik: Hið Íslenzka Bókmenntafélag.

Poole, Russell. 1991. *Viking Poems on War and Peace.* Toronto: University of Toronto Press.

———, ed. 2001. *Skaldsagas: Text, Vocation, and Desire in the Icelandic Sagas of Poets.* Berlin: de Gruyter.

Ralph, Bo. 1976. "Om tillkomsten av *Sonatorrek.*" *ANF* 91:153–65.

Reichardt, Konstantin. 1929. "Die Entstehungsgeschichte von Egils Hǫfuðlausn." *ZDA* 66:267–72.

Reichborn-Kjennerud, I. [Ingvald]. 1932. "Hǫrundfall." *ANF,* 48:99–120.

Reuschel, Helga. 1938. "Melkorka." *ZDA* 75:297–304.

Sand Sørensen, Jan. 1980. "Komposition og værdiunivers i Egils saga." *Gripla* 4:260–72.

Sävborg, Daniel. 2002. "Kjartan och Guðrún—en kärlekssaga?" *Tidskrift för litteraturvetenskap* 2:41–68.

Sayers, William. 1988. "Kjartan's Choice: The Irish Disconnection in the Sagas of the Icelanders." *Scandinavian-Canadian Studies* 3:89–114.

——. 1991. "Clontarf and the Irish Destinies of Earl Sigurðr of Orkney and Þorsteinn Síðu-Hallsson." *SS* 63:164–86.

——. 1994. "Njáll's Beard, Hallgerðr's Hair, and Gunnarr's Hay: Homological Patterning in *Njáls saga.*" *Tijdschrift voor Skandinavistiek* 15:5–31.

——. 1997. "Gunnarr, His Irish Wolfhound Sámr, and the Passing of the Old Heroic Order in *Njáls saga.*" *ANF* 112:43–66.

Schildknecht-Burri, Margrit. 1945. *Die altertümlichen und jüngern Merkmale der Laxdœla Saga.* Luzern: Unionsdruckerei.

Schottmann, Hans. 1994. "Friðgerðarsaga." In *Studien zum Altgermanischen,* 539–53.

Scovazzi, Marco. 1960. *La saga di Hrafnkell e il problema delle saghe islandesi.* N.p.: Paideia.

See, Klaus von. 1976. "Die Überlieferung der Fóstbrœðra saga." *Skandinavistik* 6:1–18; rpt. in von See 1981a, 443–60.

——. 1979. "Die Hrafnkels saga als Kunstdichtung." *Skandinavistik* 9:47–56; rpt. in von See 1981a, 486–95.

——. 1981a. *Edda, Saga, Skaldendichtung. Aufsätze zur skandinavischen Literatur des Mittelalters.* Heidelberg: Winter.

——. 1981b. "Altnordische Literaturgeschichte als Textgeschichte." In von See 1981a, 527–39.

Sigfús Blöndal. 1978. *The Varangians of Byzantium.* Trans. and rev. Benedikt A. Benedikz. Cambridge: Cambridge University Press.

Sigurður Guðmundsson. 1918. "Gunnar á Hlíðarenda." *Skírnir* 92:63–88, 221–51.

Sigurður Nordal. 1914. *Om Olaf den helliges saga.* Copenhagen: Gad.

——. 1919. "Björn úr Mörk." *Skírnir* 93:141–52.

——. 1924. "Átrúnaður Egils Skallagrímssonar." *Skírnir* 98:145–65.

——. 1940 and 1958. *Hrafnkatla.* Studia Islandica 7. Reykjavik: Ísafoldarprentsmiðja H. F. Trans. R. George Thomas as *Hrafnkels saga freysgoða.* Cardiff: University of Wales Press, 1958.

——. 1953. *Litteraturhistorie B. Norge og Island.* In Nordisk kultur. Vol. VIIIB. Stockholm: Albert Bonniers Förlag.

——. 1941 and 1965. "Gunnhildur konungamóðir." *Samtíð og saga* 1:135–55. Rpt. as "Gunnhild kongemor" in Sigurður Nordal, *Islandske streiflys,* trans. Magnús Stefánsson, 31–49. Bergen: Universitetsforlaget, 1965.

Stefán Karlsson. 1979. "Islandsk bogeksport til Norge i middelalderen." *MM,* 1–17. Rpt. in Stefán Karlsson, *Stafkrókar,* 188–205. Reykjavik: Stofnun Árna Magnússonar, 2000.

Sveinn Bergsveinsson. 1983. "Tveir höfundar Egils sögu." *Skírnir* 157:99–116.

Sverrir Tómasson. 1988. *Formálar íslenskra sagnaritara á miðöldum. Rannsókn bókmenntahefðar.* Reykjavik: Stofnun Árna Magnússonar.

Taylor, Marvin. 1997. "Rúmr inngangs, en þrǫngr brottfarar." *ANF* 112:67–95.

Torfi Tulinius. 1994. "'Mun konungi eg þykja orðsnjallur': Um margræðni, textatengsl og dulda merkingu í *Egils sögu.*" *Skírnir* 168:109–33.

———. 2004. *Skáldið í skriftinni. Snorri Sturluson og Egils saga.* Reykjavik: Hið Íslenska Bókmenntafélag; ReykjavíkurAkademían.

Tucker, John, ed. 1989. *Sagas of the Icelanders: A Book of Essays.* New York: Garland.

Úlfar Bragason. 1986. "On the Poetics of Sturlunga." Ph.D. diss., University of California–Berkeley.

Vésteinn Ólason. 1968. "Er Snorri höfundur Egils sögu?" *Skírnir* 142:48–67.

———. 1978. "Frásagnarlist í fornum sögum." *Skírnir* 152:166–202.

———. 1985. "Íslendingaþættir." *Tímarit máls og menningar* 46:60–73.

———. 1990. "Jorvik Revisited—with Egil Skalla-Grímsson." *Northern Studies* 27:64–76.

———. 1994. "Emosjon og aksjon i *Njáls saga.*" *Nordica Bergensia* 3:157–72.

———. 1998. *Dialogues with the Viking Age: Narration and Representation in the Sagas of the Icelanders.* Reykjavik: Heimskringla.

———. 1999. "Gísli Súrsson—A Flawless or Flawed Hero?" In *Die Aktualität der Saga. Festschrift für Hans Schottmann,* ed. Stig Toftgaard Andersen, 163–75. Berlin: de Gruyter.

Vries, Jan de. 1930. "Normannisches Lehngut in den isländischen Königssagas," *ANF* 47:51–79.

Whaley, Diana. 1998. *The Poetry of Arnórr jarlaskáld: An Edition and Study.* Westfield Publications in Medieval Studies 8. Turnhout, Belgium: Brepols.

Wieselgren, Per. 1927. *Författarskapet till Eigla.* Lund: Carl Bloms boktryckeri.

Wolf, Alois. 1982. "Zur Stellung der Njála in der isländischen Sagaliteratur." In *Tradition und Entwicklung. Festschrift Eugen Thurnher zum 60. Geburtstag,* ed. Werner M. Bauer, Achim Masser, and Guntram A. Plangg, 61–85. Innsbruck: N.p.

———. 1994. "Aspekte des Beitrags der Laxdœlasaga zur literarischen Erschliessung der 'Sagazeit'." In *Studien zum Altgermanischen* 722–50.

Würth, Stefanie. 1998. *Der "Antikenroman" in der isländischen Literatur des Mittelalters. Eine Untersuchung zur Übersetzung und Rezeption lateinischer Literatur im Norden.* Beiträge zur nordischen Philologie 26. Basel: Helbing & Lichtenhahn.

———. 1999. "*New Historicism* und altnordische Literaturwissenschaft." In *Verhandlungen mit dem New Historicism. Das Text-Kontext-Problem in der Literaturwissenschaft,* ed. Jürg Glauser and Annegret Heitmann, with Christiane Küster, 193–208. Würzburg: Königshausen & Neumann. Pp. 193–208.

———. 2001. "Die Temporalität der *Laxdœla saga.*" In *Sagnaheimur: Studies in Honour of Hermann Pálsson on His 80th Birthday, 26th May 2001,* ed. Ásdís Egilsdóttir and Rudolf Simek, 295–308. Vienna: Fassbaender.

Zimmermann, Günter. 1982. *Isländersaga und Heldensage. Untersuchungen zur Struktur der Gísla saga und Laxdœla saga.* Vienna: Karl M. Halosar.

———. 1984. "Die Vorausdeutungen in der Njáls saga unter strukturellem Aspekt." In *Linguistica et Philologica. Gedenkschrift für Björn Collinder (1894–1983)*, ed. Otto Gschwantler, Károly Rédei, and Hermann Reichert, 597–607. Vienna: W. Braumüller.

Ziolkowski, Theodore. 1997. "The Ambivalence toward Pagan Law." In Ziolkowski, *The Mirror of Justice: Literary Reflections of Legal Crises*, 42–62. Princeton: Princeton University Press.

INDEX

Note: The special Icelandic characters þ and ǫ are alphabetized at the end of the Index. The umlauted vowels ä, ö, and ü are treated as if they were a, o, and u.

Thórir Ingimundarson (in *Vatnsdæla saga*), 156, 159, 161

Thórir sel, 49

Thorkel (antagonist of Víga-Glúm's mother), 62

Thorkel Blund-Ketilsson, 23–24

Thorkel dydrill, 32

Thorkel Geitisson (in *Ljósvetninga saga*), 124–25

Thorkel Gellisson (uncle and informant of Ari Thorgilsson), 21, 44

Thorkel hák Thorgeirsson (in *Ljósvetninga saga*), 121, 126–28, 131

Thorkel krafla Thorgrímsson (in *Vatnsdæla saga*), 156, 160

Thorkel Súrsson, 79–82

Thorkel the Tall (strategist in the employ of Eirík jarl Hákonarson), 39

Thorkel Thjóstarsson (West Fjord ally of Sám Bjarnason in *Hrafnkels saga*), 178

Thorkel trefil Rauda-Bjarnarson (in *Hænsa-Þóris saga*), 166–68

Thórlaug Atladóttir (wife of Gudmund the Powerful), 126

Thorleik Bollason, 144–45

Thormód (missionary), 21

Thormód Bersason, 9, 12, 47, 50, 56, 70–73, 77, 83, 85, 119, 152–53, 205–6

Thórodd Snorrason (son of Snorri the Chieftain), 48

Thórodd Tungu-Oddsson, 163

Thórólf (quarrels with Hall in *Laxdæla saga*), 142

Thórólf bægifótr Bjarnarson (in *Eyrbyggja saga*), 151

Thórólf Eysteinsson (follower of Thórd gellir), 24

Thórólf heljarskinn (evildoer in *Vatnsdæla saga*), 159

Thórólf Kveld-Úlfsson, 15, 104–7, 111

Thórólf Skallagrímsson, 111

Thórólf sleggja (thief in *Vatnsdæla saga*), 159

Thórsnesingar, 151

Thorstein Egilsson, 19, 114, 146

Thorstein Gíslason (in *Heiðarvíga saga*), 75

Thorstein Ingimundarson (in *Vatnsdæla saga*), 155–60

Thorstein knarrarsmid (participant in the killing of Olaf Haraldsson), 57

Thorstein raud Óláfsson (son of Unn the Deepminded), 132–33

Thórunn Gunnarsdóttir (niece of Thórd gellir), 24

Thorvald Gizurarson (chieftain in southern Iceland), 109

Thorvald Halldórsson (first husband of Gudrún Ósvífrsdóttir), 143

Thorvald Oddsson (son of Tungu-Odd), 23, 163, 165–68, 174, 177

Thorvald Ósvífrsson (first husband of Hallgerd Hǫskuldsdóttir), 189

Thorvard Hǫskuldsson, 129–131, 137

Thorvard Thorgeirsson (chieftain in Eyjafjord, died 1207), 120

Thráin Sigfússon, 195–97, 201–2

Thrándheim (Trondheim), 29, 33, 109, 144

Thrœndalǫg, 31, 86, 89, 96–97, 124

Thuríd Barkardóttir (half sister of Snorri the Chieftain), 153

Thuríd Óláfssdóttir (mother of Bardi Gudmundarson), 75

Thuríd Snorradóttir (informant of Ari Thorgilsson), 21–23, 44, 99

Thverá (Víga-Glúm's farm), 62

Thyri (sister of Svend Forkbeard), 30–31, 33, 36

Torfi Tulinius, 103, 105, 113

Tostig (brother of Harold Godwinson), 97–98

Traninn (the Crane), 30

Turville-Petre, Gabriel, 63, 68

Tvídœgra (heath in *Heiðarvíga saga*), 76

Úlf the Red (Olaf Tryggvason's lieutenant), 38

Úlfar Bragason, 12–13

Úlfhild (daughter of Olaf Haraldsson, according to Theodoricus and other sources), 45, 49, 92

Uni (in *Vatnsdæla saga*), 159

Unn the Deepminded, 132–35, 158, 186–87

Unn Mardardóttir (in *Njáls saga*), 190, 193

Upplǫnd (Norwegian province), 45–46

Valgard (a Gautlander in the *Legendary Saga*), 50

Valgard Jǫrundarson (the Gray; in *Njáls saga*), 193, 198

Valgerd Óttarsdóttir (in *Vatnsdæla saga*), 160

Váli (kinsman of Odd Ófeigsson), 170–72